Educator's Sourcebook *of* AFRICAN AMERICAN HERITAGE

Johnnie H. Miles ♦ Juanita J. Davis
Sharon E. Ferguson-Roberts ♦ Rita G. Giles

PRENTICE HALL
Paramus, NJ 07652

Library of Congress Cataloging-in-Publication Data

Educator's sourcebook of African American heritage / Johnnie H. Miles…[et al.].
       p. cm.
     Includes Bibliographical references.
     ISBN 0-13-084364-4
     1. Afro-Americans—Miscellanea. I. Miles, Johnnie H.

E185 .A2535 2000
973.04'96073—dc21   00-037305

Acquisitions Editor: Connie Kallback
Production Editor: Mariann Hutlak
Interior Design: Robyn Beckerman
Cover & Interior Art: Ed Kirkland
Composition: Oakland Publishing Services, Inc.

Printed in the United States of America
10 9 8 7 6 5 4 3 2 1

ISBN 0-13-084364-4

ATTENTION: CORPORATIONS AND SCHOOLS

Prentice Hall books are available at quantity discounts with bulk purchase for educational, business, or sales promotional use. For information, please write to: Prentice Hall Direct; Special Sales; 240 Frisch Court; Paramus, NJ 07652. Please supply: title of book, ISBN, quantity, how the book will be used, date needed.

Prentice Hall
Paramus, NJ 07652

Visit us at http://www.phdirect.com

DEDICATION

This book is dedicated to the courageous Africans who, with extraordinary resolve, survived the Middle Passage and still contributed their knowledge and talents to the building of a New World.

ACKNOWLEDGMENTS

This book was a labor of love. There are a number of people who participated lovingly and made the completion of this book possible. To them we want to say thank you and share with you what their contributions meant to us.

To our editor Connie Kallback, who had the vision and the courage to take on this project, even though it was a unique departure from the traditional line in the Book of Lists series.

Many thanks to Jason N. Davis and Sharrone Steele for the many hours devoted to researching elusive facts and features for this book.

The production of this book would not have been possible without the expert talent, processing skills, and gracious nudging of Vanessa M. Robinson. Thank you Vanessa.

To the library staff of the Sojourner Truth Room, Oxon Hill Library, Oxon Hill, Maryland, for their patience in retrieving and reshelving resource materials day after day, week after week and always with a smile. The staff at the Johnston Library, Virginia State University, Petersburg—particularly Mary Ann Bailey, James Holmes, and Anthony Lewis—spent many hours providing directions and suggestions during our research efforts.

To Reverend Peter E. Hogan, S.S.J., Archivist, Josephite Archives, who gave generously of his time and resources in responding to our request for information.

To Lillian Holloman and Robert T. Holbrook, respected friends and colleagues, whose ideas and resources so freely shared helped us to add breadth and depth to our perspective.

To Nelson Kief for his expert counsel.

To Suzanne Flandreau at the Center for Black Music Research in Chicago for her help with classical music dates.

To Sheree Crute, editor with, *Heart & Soul,* for her suggestions and review of the manuscript.

To Helen Hume, author of *The Art Teacher's Book of Lists,* Prentice Hall, for her time and research in compiling lists 8–2 through 8–9.

To Ed Wallace, author of *Track and Field Coach's Survival Guide,* Parker Publishing Company, for the lists of Olympic champions and body builders.

Appreciation is extended to our many colleagues in the Advanced Level Program of Educational Leadership at Virginia State University, who listened, supported, and encouraged us; and to our friends who cheered from the sidelines and kept reminding us of the importance of this work.

Special thanks to Leroy Miles, Perry E. Roberts, George K. Davis, and Samuel L. Giles, our husbands, for their loving support, sacrificial spirits, and unwillingness to let us lose focus. Finally, to family members, parents, children, siblings, and friends, we say thanks for your patience and understanding. Moreover, we thank you for the lessons you taught by allowing us the space and the time to complete this project.

ABOUT THE AUTHORS

Johnnie H. Miles, Ed.D., is President and owner of JH Miles and Associates, a consulting and training firm in Fairfax, Virginia. She recently retired as an associate professor of Counselor Education from Virginia Polytechnic Institute and State University. She has experience as a secondary teacher, university counselor, and as professor of counselor education. She currently serves as a consultant to educational institutions, and to public and private corporations. She is a licensed professional counselor in Virginia, a skilled facilitator, and is certified as a mediator by the Virginia Supreme Court. Dr. Miles has a strong record of professional involvement and has conducted research on career development of women and minorities, authored several book chapters, two edited textbooks, numerous refereed journal articles, research reports, and conference proceedings. She has made presentations at national and state conventions and served as editor of two professional journals.

Juanita J. Davis, Ed.D., has over 20 years' experience as a licensed counselor, trainer, college instructor, administrator, and consultant. Currently, she is serving as adjunct professor for Trinity College and Bowie State University and as an administrator in the Washington, D.C. public schools. She also maintains a small private counseling and career development practice. Active in her professional associations, Dr. Davis has held elected and appointed offices, served on numerous committees and commissions, and was involved in the development and coordination of an intact counselor training program. She has made presentations at regional and national conferences and is a recognized resource in her field. Dr. Davis is committed to providing the highest possible quality of service to clients, assisting in developing individual initiative, and in helping people fulfill their potential.

Sharon E. Ferguson-Roberts, Ed.D., is an assistant professor of guidance and counseling at Virginia State University in Petersburg. She has had over 20 years' experience in the public school system, serving as a director of Student Services, coordinator of pupil services, school psychologist, and elementary counselor. She has held offices in national, state, and local organizations and was a Fellow in two nationally recognized programs: the Institute for Educational Leadership, Inc. and the Institute for the Development of Educational Activities, Inc. Dr. Ferguson-Roberts holds certifications as a Virginia Supreme Court mediator, school psychologist, NBCC counselor, and Myers-Briggs trainer. She is a proficient presenter and is the president and owner of Consulting & Training Associates, LLC, in Emporia, Virginia.

Rita G. Giles, Ed.D., is currently the director of the Transition Support Resource Center, a state-funded program designed for youth with special needs in the Fairfax County (Virginia) Public Schools. She has 15 years of experience working with diverse populations within the public schools. Dr. Giles is an adjunct professor at George Washington University. She is the author of *In Your Face: Words of Conversation to Encourage Our Youth...The ABC of It.* Dr. Giles is certified by the Virginia Supreme Court as a mediator. She is also a Board Member of the National Capitol Chapter of the American Red Cross.

ABOUT THIS BOOK

The United States is a pluralistic society. Pluralism or diversity was evident prior to its early exploration and settlement. The arrival of immigrants, free or enslaved—along with the Indians—created an unparalleled mix of peoples and talents who worked in varying ways to forge a country that is among the leading nations of the world. The United States has benefited from its diversity. The characteristics taken for granted as symbolic of the United States reflect unique dimensions contributed from the cultures of each of its constituent groups.

The focus of this sourcebook is on one of those constituent groups, African Americans. African Americans are descendents of people from Africa, who were enslaved and brought to America to work in bondage. African Americans are a people with unprecedented experiences in the history of this country. With persistence and fortitude, they withstood the brutality of slavery and emerged as a people full of hope for the future. The country was not waiting with open arms for African Americans after emancipation. Instead, a carefully crafted system of segregation or institutional racism was put in place, preserving privileges for some citizens and creating a new form of bondage for others. African Americans challenged that system on every front. They sought education, developed commerce, and created organizations to restore the sense of community disrupted by enslavement. With undaunted zeal they used established legal channels to combat racism and gain freedom and equality.

African Americans have a remarkable history, though not readily known by the general population. This book presents facts and features about African American experiences in the United States beginning with the Middle Passage (voyage across the Atlantic to America), through slavery and reconstruction, to the beginning of the twenty-first century. By describing typical conditions under which the enslaved lived and their constant struggle to break the bonds of enslavement, we hope to explode the myth of the happy, contented slave. A review of the legislation that created and maintained slavery will reveal the brutal and dehumanizing nature of bondage and the remnants of that system that remain in our society today. Listing the achievements and contributions of African Americans will show their involvement in the establishment of American Culture.

Vestiges of racism remain in America. The 1990s were marred by a resurgence of hate crimes against minority groups, an ugly reminder of a history we have tried to forget. The ultimate challenge for each of us is to do our part in creating an environment where differences are valued and people can live, learn, work, and play together.

Terminology. African American is only one of the many terms used to describe the largest ethnic minority group in the United States. Other terms include black, Afro-American, Negro, enslaved Africans, and people of color. For purposes of this book African American, enslaved African, and black will be used interchangeably as terms of choice.

How to Use This Book

This book is designed for educators who are committed to establishing positive, creative environments for learning and work. Its purpose is to respond to the needs of educators—teachers, administrators, counsellors, and librarians—for a resource to increase awareness, knowledge, and understanding about diverse populations in general and African Americans specifically.

Teachers and Counselors. Teachers are committed to designing and implementing effective programs for all students. To accomplish this goal, they must first learn about and understand the diverse populations they seek to educate. As diversity increases in the classroom, traditional instructional methods are challenged. Teachers need more information about diverse cultures, values, and languages to enhance their ability to design and deliver effective educational programs. This reference book provides information for analyzing and understanding the cultural and historical experience of African Americans. These experiences contribute to beliefs and behaviors students bring to the classroom. Teachers may use information from this book to integrate African American history and culture into the curriculum.

This book can be used in general as a reference to jog the memory, serve as a reminder about leaders or events in specific areas, or simply as a resource that can intrigue and stimulate. In the classroom, the lists may be reproduced and given to students as information sheets, which have added value as springboards for discussion or topics for research reports.

The list format offers many advantages:

- A great deal of information can be gleaned at a glance,

- one list can demonstrate the scope of accomplishments in a way that many text pages cannot,

- students can more easily draw conclusions from the concise presentation of facts, and

- a single list may provide a chronology that imprints on the mind as well as a time line.

Educators who are looking for past and present heroes and role models for their students need only to open the pages of this book. Each section is replete with names of people who were pioneers or have subsequently excelled, most in the face of obstacles that would have defeated less determined individuals. "Spotlights" that focus on one person and list the accomplishments of his or her life are sprinkled throughout the book. Teachers may want to use one spotlight as a model and assign students to create their own by choosing a name from the many lists of people in a favorite area of their interest such as science, music, literature, government, or the military.

Counselors and teachers may use the information to understand behaviors of African American students in a broader context, especially if the behaviors are not typical reactions to typical situations. Counselors will find the information on predominantly African American colleges and universities a useful resource.

Students and Parents. Students in junior high and high school and their parents will find this book an intriguing resource. They may find the historical data and the information on cultural traditions useful supplements to school assignments. The experiences chronicled in this book will increase understanding and perhaps intercultural sensitivity. It may serve as a reference for parents in teaching children about the similarities and differences that exist in a pluralistic environment.

We hope you find the *Educator's Sourcebook of African American Heritage* informative and useful as we learn to increase our understanding of diverse populations.

Johnnie Miles, Juanita Davis,
Sharon Ferguson-Roberts, and *Rita Giles*

CONTENTS

SECTION 2

CULTURAL TRADITIONS **49**

SECTION 3

EDUCATION 85

SECTION 7

LAW AND GOVERNMENT **211**

SECTION 8

ARTS, LETTERS, AND MEDIA **245**

SECTION 9

SPORTS 303

SECTION 10

SECTION 11

Section 1

HISTORY OF AFRICAN AMERICANS IN THE UNITED STATES

AFRICAN AMERICANS IN THE UNITED STATES
1-1   Coming to the Shores of the Americas (1400-1700)
1-2   Resistance and Servitude: Two Worlds Clash (1700-1800)
1-3   War, Freedom, and Institutional Oppression (1800-1900)
1-4   African American Leaders in the Forefront (1900-1950)
1-5   Nonviolence to Activism (1950-2000)

ECONOMICS OF SLAVERY
1-6   The Middle Passage
1-7   Slave Ships
1-8   Names of Selected Slave Ships
1-9   Economics of the Slave Trade

SLAVERY IN THE UNITED STATES
1-10   Recognition and Abolition of Slavery in Original Colonies
1-11   States in Rebellion Against the United States in 1863

PLANTATION LIFE
1-12   Life on the Plantation
1-13   Work
1-14   Housing
1-15   Food
1-16   Day-to-Day Life on the Plantation
1-17   Punishment
1-18   The Slave Market

RESISTANCE TO SLAVERY
1-19   Slave Resistance and Revolts
1-20   Escape to Freedoms—The Underground Railroad (1780s-1860s)
1-21   Routes
1-22   Selected Underground Conductors
1-23   Abolitionists

THE COURTS AND SLAVERY
1-24   Legislation and Slavery (1600-1863)
1-25   Legislation and the Reconstruction Era (1865-1877)
1-26   Legislation and Segregation of African Americans (1877-1953)

VIOLENCE AGAINST AFRICAN AMERICANS
1-27   Recorded Lynchings (1882-1969)

FIGHT FOR FREEDOM
1-28   The Civil Rights Movement in Review (1600s-1999)
1-29   Nonviolent Resistance to Segregation
1-30   Civil Rights Organizations
1-31   Civil Rights Leaders
1-32   Spotlight: MARTIN LUTHER KING JR.
1-33   Spotlight: DOROTHY IRENE HEIGHT

AFRICAN AMERICAN DEMOGRAPHICS
1-34   African Americans in U.S. Population (1870-1990)
1-35   States with Largest African American Populations

SECTION 1

HISTORY OF AFRICAN AMERICANS
IN THE UNITED STATES

People of African descent are an integral part of the fabric of the United States of America. They were among the explorers who first visited this country serving as navigators, scouts, and servants. There were twenty Africans, believed to be indentured servants, among the first group of permanent colonists who settled on the shores of Jamestown, Virginia in 1619. The majority of Africans in the colonies, however, were brought to America against their will, enslaved, and exploited in the development of the new country. The practice of slavery was instituted in North America in the 1600s. It increased in scope and continued until the late 1800s because it was a profitable enterprise for everyone, except the enslaved.

Slavery was a brutal system. Africans were captured or sold by their countrymen; transported across the ocean under inhumane conditions; arrived in a strange, inhospitable land; and were forced to work a lifetime in service to others. These conditions were intolerable and the Africans vigorously resisted enslavement. Africans revolted from the beginning and their captors and owners responded with severe and punitive measures. For the enslaved to have survived at all was a testament to the capacity of humans to overcome adversity. Despite repeated attempts to stamp out the culture of the Africans, their knowledge, skills and traditions in many fields endured and have contributed to the enrichment of the culture of America we know today.

Section 1 highlights selected aspects of the unique history of Africans and their descendants in the United States. The history will cover 250 years of slavery or involuntary servitude, a decade of reconstruction, 75 years of Jim Crow, and some 48 years of constructive action against segregation. Some of the experiences reflected here include details about the voyage to America, how slaves rebelled, life during and after slavery, and the ongoing struggle for freedom. This section also chronicles significant historical events, identifies critical legal and social actions designed to control African Americans, and captures the experiences of free and enslaved African Americans.

AFRICAN AMERICANS IN THE UNITED STATES

List 1-1. Coming to the Shores of the Americas (1400-1700)

1492   Blacks are part of crew on Christopher Columbus's voyages to the Americas.

1493   Columbus transports slaves to Jamaica on his second voyage.

1501   Queen Isabella authorizes transport of Africans to New World colonies.

1502   Portugal transports the first Africans to Hispaniola.

1510   Spain ships 250 Africans to Hispaniola as slaves.

1513   Spain earns major profits by licensing shipping companies that transport slaves.

1513   Thirty blacks are on the voyage with Vasco de Balboa in discovery of the Pacific Ocean.

1514   Spain restricts the number of slaves (ratio of 3:1) for security purposes.

1517   Spanish Bishop encourages Charles V to allow Spanish settlers to import slaves.

1519   Blacks accompany Hernando Cortez on his march into Mexico.

1526   Africans are brought to the Carolinas to erect a Spanish settlement; they flee and live with Indians.

1538   Black explorer, Estevanico, leads an expedition into the territory known as Arizona and New Mexico.

1562   Britain permits the sale of Africans to Spanish planters.

1619   Twenty African indentured servants arrive in Jamestown, Virginia as permanent settlers.

1629   Slaves are transported to Connecticut (1629), Maryland and Massachusetts (1634), and New Amsterdam (1637).

1641   Massachusetts is first to make slavery a legal institution.

1650   By 1700, six other colonies have legalized slavery: Connecticut (1650), Virginia (1661), Maryland (1663), New York (1665), and South Carolina (1682).

1662   Virginia is first to pass laws to restrict slaves; for example, status of mother determines status of a black child; prohibits free blacks from voting.

1663   First documented slave rebellion occurs in Gloucester County, Virginia.

1688   Mennonites sign the first antislavery resolution.

List 1-2. Resistance and Servitude: Two Worlds Clash (1700-1800)

1700	Approximately 28,000 enslaved Africans are in the colonies in early 1700s; about 23,000 of those are in the South.
1700	Boston operates a slave port and sells slaves to other colonies.
1707	Massachusetts permits free blacks to serve in the militia.
1712	Slave revolts in New York leave 9 whites dead; 21 slaves are killed in retaliation.
1723	Virginia prohibits free blacks from voting or carrying weapons.
1739	New York slave revolts leave 51 whites dead and an unreported number of slaves killed.
1741	Rumor of slave conspiracies lead a white mob in New York City to kill 31 slaves and execute 5 white sympathizers.
1750	The number of slaves in the population reaches 20 percent.
1770	Crispus Attucks, an escaped slave, is killed in the Boston Massacre.
1770	Quakers establish a school for African Americans in Philadelphia.
1773	Former slaves, George Leile and Andrew Bryan, establish the first African American Baptist church in Silver Bluff, South Carolina.
1773	The first Society for the Abolition of Slavery is founded in Pennsylvania.
1775	The Continental Congress bars African Americans from serving in the Army and adopts the Declaration of Independence in same year.
1776	Vermont becomes the first state to abolish slavery.
1787	Constitution of the U.S. is adopted, containing the three-fifths compromise.
1787	Jean Baptiste Point Du Sable establishes a trading post now known as Chicago.
1790	Benjamin Banneker is appointed to survey the District of Columbia.
1790	Virginia law prohibits free African Americans from entering the state.
1793	Congress passes the Fugitive Slave Act.
1794	Tennessee is admitted to the Union as a slave state.

List 1-3. War, Freedom, and Institutional Oppression (1800-1900)

1800	According to the U.S. Census, over one million African Americans are in the United States; make up 18.9 percent of the population.
1800	Gabriel Prosser plans a slave insurrection in Richmond, Virginia.
1804	Ohio, Illinois, Indiana, and Oregon pass anti-immigration laws.
1807	Congress legalizes the importation of new slaves until 1908.
1811	Louisiana joins the Union as a slave state; troops suppress two slave uprisings.
1817	Mississippi joins the Union as a slave state; prohibits teaching blacks to read.
1819	Alabama joins the Union as a slave state.
1820	Congress passes the Missouri Compromise that bans slavery in the Plains states and admits Missouri as a slave state.
1822	The infamous revolt to seize Charleston, South Carolina is betrayed. Denmark Vesey and 47 others are executed.
1831	Nat Turner leads an uprising that leads to the killing of approximately 50 whites. He is later captured and hanged.
1836	Congress adopts a "gag rule" to avoid actions on antislavery petitions.
1839	Revolts occur on the high seas aboard the *Amistad* (1839) and the *Creole* (1841) slave ships.
1842	Blacks are granted the right to vote in Rhode Island.
1843	Texas is admitted to the Union as a slave state.
1847	Frederick Douglass publishes the *North Star* in Rochester, New York.
1850	The 1850 Compromise toughens the 1793 Fugitive Slave Act.
1857	The Supreme Court denies citizenship rights to blacks in the *Dred Scott* case.
1859	John Brown, a white abolitionist, raids the U.S. Arsenal at Harpers Ferry.
1861	The Civil War begins; blacks are denied service in the army.
1862	Slavery is abolished in the District of Columbia; blacks' enlistment in the Union Army is legalized.
1863	President Lincoln frees slaves from ten states in signing the Emancipation Proclamation.
1865	The Confederacy surrenders at Appomattox, Virginia.
1865	Ku Klux Klan is formed to restore white supremacy.

1865   Congress passes the Thirteenth (1865), Fourteenth (1866), and Fifteenth (1868) Amendments.

1871   Congressional Investigating Committee reports severe acts of violence by Ku Klux Klan. Ku Klux Klan Act is adopted.

1875   The U.S. Congress passes the second Civil Rights Act recognizing the right to public accommodations for all men.

1881   Southern states pass a variety of "Jim Crow" laws over a nine-year period.

1883   The Supreme Court declares the 1875 Civil Rights Act unconstitutional.

1895   Booker T. Washington makes his historic Atlanta Exposition speech.

1896   The Supreme Court upholds the "separate but equal" doctrine in *Plessy* v. *Ferguson* that leads to the return of segregation across the South.

1897   Missions in foreign lands receive a boost as the Lott Carey Baptist Mission begins operation in Liberia.

1898   The North Carolina Mutual Life Insurance Company, the largest black-owned insurance company, is founded by John Merrick and six associates.

1898   Louisiana adds a "grandfather clause" to the state constitution exempting anyone from meeting voting requirements whose grandfather voted on January 1, 1867. The clause effectively prevents African Americans from voting.

List 1-4. African American Leaders in the Forefront (1900-1950)

1900   At 8.8 million in 1900, African Americans make up 11.9 percent of the population. Ninety percent live in the South.

1901   Booker T. Washington dines with President Theodore Roosevelt at the White House.

1902   Virginia adopts a "grandfather clause" to deny blacks the right to vote.

1904   George C. Poage becomes the first African American Olympic Medal winner when he places third in the 400-meter hurdles in St. Louis, Missouri.

1904   Booker T. Washington (moderate) and W.E.B. Du Bois (activist) debate ideological differences at an Atlanta meeting to promote interests of African Americans.

1905   African American leaders begin the Niagara Movement at a conference called by civil rights activists William Trotter and W.E.B. Du Bois.

1909   The National Association for the Advancement of Colored People (NAACP) is founded in New York City.

1910   The National Urban League (NUL) is founded in New York City.

1913	President Woodrow Wilson rejects a proposal for a National Race Commission and begins segregating blacks and whites in government offices.
1916	The first issue of the *Journal of Negro History* is published.
1917	Forty to 200 African Americans are killed in an East St. Louis, Illinois riot.
1917	African American leaders vow to work for equal education, voting rights, and an end to lynching at a silent march down Fifth Avenue in New York City.
1921	Approximately 30 people are killed in a race riot in Tulsa, Oklahoma.
1924	The U.S. Congress restricts blacks of African descent from entry into the United States.
1925	A. Philip Randolph organizes the Brotherhood of Sleeping Car Porters.
1926	The Negro Society for Historical Research is founded by E. Bruce and A. Schomburg.
1926	Carter G. Woodson first introduces Negro History Week to study African American heritage.
1931	The "Scottsboro Boys" are arrested for allegedly raping two white women.
1933	President Franklin D. Roosevelt creates an advisory group of prominent African Americans, including Mary McLeod Bethune.
1939	The Supreme Court rules against discrimination in wages, unions, and housing and mandates equal educational facilities be provided African Americans within state boundaries.
1941	Executive Order 8802 prohibits racial and religious discrimination.
1944	The United Negro College Fund is chartered.
1946	The Supreme Court finds segregation on interstate buses unconstitutional in defense industries and government training.
1947	Tuskegee Institute begins gathering statistics on lynching in the U.S. About 3,426 African Americans were lynched from 1882 to 1947.
1948	Executive Order 9981 provides equality of treatment in the armed forces.
1949	New Jersey is first state to end discrimination in public accommodations.

List 1-5. Nonviolence to Activism (1950-2000)

1950   Ralph Bunche is awarded the Nobel Peace Prize.

1951   The last all-black unit, the 24th Infantry Regiment, is deactivated.

1952   For the first time in 71 years, Tuskegee Institute finds no reported incident of an African American being lynched.

1954   The "Separate but Equal" clause is found unconstitutional in *Brown* v. *Board of Education*.

1956   Autherine Lucy is admitted to the University of Alabama and expelled one month later for making "false statements" about the university.

1956   One hundred Southern Senators sign the *Southern Manifesto* protesting the 1954 *Brown* v. *Board of Education* Supreme Court decision.

1957   Prince Edward County, Virginia closes its public schools to avoid integration.

1957   U.S. Congress passes the Voting Rights Act of 1957, Civil Rights Acts of 1960 and 1964, and ratifies the Twenty-fourth Amendment. President Lyndon Johnson signs the 1965 Voting Rights Act.

1957   President Dwight D. Eisenhower sends federal troops to escort nine African American children past a white mob to attend Central High School in Little Rock, Arkansas.

1960   Civil rights movement takes on a nonviolent, passive resistance theme with staged freedom rides, sit-ins, and marches.

1960   The Student Nonviolent Coordinating Committee (SNCC) is organized.

1963   Violence accompanies desegregation efforts: Mack C. Parker is lynched in Poplarville, Mississippi; Medgar Evers is assassinated; and Birmingham, Alabama police use dogs and fire hoses against civil rights marchers.

1963   Over 250,000 participate in the August 28 March on Washington.

1963   A bomb at the Sixteenth Street Baptist Church in Birmingham kills four young girls in attendance at Sunday school; three civil rights workers are murdered in Philadelphia, Mississippi.

1965   Watts area of Los Angeles is the site of a massive 6-day riot.

1965   Malcolm X is assassinated on February 21 at a Muslim rally in New York City.

1966   SNCC and CORE call for an activist, Black Power approach to racial liberation. Huey Newton and Bobby Seale found the Black Panther Party.

1966   Edward Brooke is elected to the U.S. Senate from Massachusetts, the first black since reconstruction.

1967	Forty cities explode in riots during summer 1967, including Newark, New York City, Atlanta, Buffalo, Detroit, Milwaukee, and New Haven.
1967	Thurgood Marshall is appointed to the U.S. Supreme Court, a post he holds until 1991.
1968	The National Advisory Commission on Civil Disorders concludes that the primary cause of the 1967 civil unrest is white racism.
1968	Martin Luther King, Jr. is assassinated on April 4 during a trip to support striking sanitation workers in Memphis, Tennessee.
1968	Congress passes the 1968 Civil Rights Bill.
1969	Police raid the headquarters of the Black Panther Party in Chicago, Illinois, killing two people.
1969	The U.S. Department of Justice sues the state of Georgia to end all public school segregation. Governor Lester Maddox vows to fight the suit.
1970	Governors in Alabama, Florida, Georgia, and Louisiana vow to fight school busing to achieve integration.
1974	Desegregation plans for higher education are approved for Arkansas, Florida, Georgia, Maryland, North Carolina, Oklahoma, Pennsylvania, and Virginia.
1978	The Supreme Court, in *University of California* v. *Bakke*, rules special admission program at University of California at Davis unconstitutional.
1981	Departments of Labor and Justice relax antidiscrimination rules and actions to achieve President Ronald Reagan's "economic emancipation" for all Americans.
1985	Senate designates the third Monday of January a federal holiday to celebrate Martin Luther King, Jr.'s birthday.
1988	Jesse Jackson campaigns for the Democratic Party's nomination for president.
1989	The Supreme Court strikes a blow against affirmative action in *City of Richmond* v. *J.A. Croson Co.*; *Milliken* v. *Michigan Road Builders Association*; and *Wards Cove Packing Co.* v. *Antonio*.
1989	President George Bush nominates General Colin Powell as Chairman of the Joint Chiefs of Staff.
1989	L. Douglas Wilder is elected governor of Virginia.
1989	Ron H. Brown is selected as Chair of the Democratic National Committee.
1990	President George Bush vetoes the 1990 Civil Rights Bill but signs the 1991 Civil Rights Act.
1991	Clarence Thomas is appointed to the Supreme Court following an investigation of sexual harassment charges.

1991   Los Angeles police are captured on videotape beating a black motorist, Rodney King; four white policemen are charged and acquitted; riots break out in Los Angeles; the four are later tried and convicted.

1992   The Supreme Court strikes down a "hate crime" law in St. Paul, Minnesota.

1993   African Americans are appointed to key positions in President Bill Clinton's Cabinet: Secretaries of Energy, Agriculture, Commerce, and Veterans Affairs, and as Surgeon General.

1995   University of California votes to end affirmative action in hiring and admissions.

1996   California approves Proposition 209, ending affirmative action in all aspects of government business.

1997   A formal apology is offered by President Bill Clinton for involving blacks, without their knowledge, in the Tuskegee syphilis experiment (1932-1972).

1997   Seven African Americans are awarded Medals of Honor for actions performed during World War II. All, except one, are awarded posthumously.

1998   Texaco settles a class action suit with African American employees.

1998   The FBI reports racial prejudice was primary motivation in 4,710 incidents of hate crime during the year, down from 5,396 incidents in 1996.

1999   USDA settles multimillion-dollar class action suit with African American farmers.

ECONOMICS OF SLAVERY

List 1-6. The Middle Passage

- Africans were forcibly removed from their lands, families, and culture.

- The enslaved included royalty, artisans, warriors, mothers, and children.

- Some Africans colluded with the slave traders by capturing and selling their brethren.

- Tribes were mixed—for example, Mandingo, Yoruba, Ibos, Ashantis—creating language and cultural conflicts.

- Africans were taken to forts or factories (holding pens) built on the shores of Africa.

- Before sale, Africans were inspected (head to toe) and branded.

- They were chained together, leg to leg or yoked, and rowed to slave ships.

- Enslaved Africans were transported from their homelands across the Atlantic Ocean to the Americas.

- The trip took from 35 to 90 days or more.

- Packed tightly into holds of ships in cramped spaces about 18 by 24 inches, the Africans were unable to turn or shift.

- Ships were often packed beyond expected capacity.

- Men, women, and children were packed, often naked, side by side, with poor ventilation, little or no light, and no toilet facilities in the hold.

- Chained in the hold for up to 16 hours per day, the Africans were forced to lie in filth.

- The food was poorly prepared and of small quantity.

- Untold numbers succumbed to sea sickness, dysentery, malaria, and other diseases.

- The people suffered severe sores and blisters from the chains.

- The death rate was often as high as 50 percent.

- Some women were abused during the voyage.

- The Africans resisted continually through armed revolts, starvation, suicide, or infanticide.

- Many Africans jumped overboard, preferring death to slavery.

- The Africans were taken on deck periodically for exercise and to use tubs (toilet facility).

- They were forced to eat and exercise or dance to stay healthy.

- Compliance was enforced by flogging.

- The crew had to keep constant vigil to avoid being attacked.

- There were reported incidents of Africans being thrown overboard to collect insurance and avoid being stopped or boarded by British and U.S. naval vessels.

- The Africans endured cruel and dehumanizing treatment on the journey, which was just the beginning of their woeful experience.

- Details of the Middle Passage were described in ship logs, Captains' journals, and slave narratives.

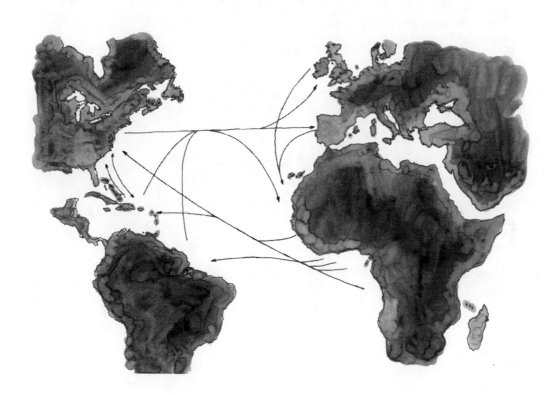

List 1-7. Slave Ships

- Slave trading was an international enterprise.

- Countries established trading relationships with African leaders, whereby they traded goods for African slaves.

- The countries set up forts or factories for holding Africans until transported.

- Primary among those countries were France, the Netherlands, Spain, Portugal, and Great Britain.

- They also built and provided the vessels for transporting the enslaved.

- Liverpool, England supplied almost half the ships.

- Hundreds of ships were involved in transporting Africans to new colonies.

- Some ships traversed the course only once, while others made repeated voyages.

- Research to identify those involved and the extent of that involvement continues to this day.

- The practice of transporting slaves continued for over 300 years.

List 1-8. Names of Selected Slave Ships

Aguia	Creole	Louisa
Albion-Frigate	Deligencia	Maria da Gloria
Amalia	Don Carlos	Maria Segundo
Amistad	Eagle	Prince of Orange
Antelope	Elizabeth	Regulo Vinca
Arthur	Elize	St. Jan
Brilhante	Esperanza	Undine
Brookes*	Hannibal	Veloz Pasajera
Butterfly	Josefina	Vigilante
Carolina	Le Rodeur	Wildfire
Clara	Little Betzy	Wyoming
Clothilde	Little George	Zong

---

* Diagram of the Brookes revealed spaces for transporting 451 slaves; ordered by the Law of 1788 to carry 454; reported to have carried as many as 609 on one voyage.

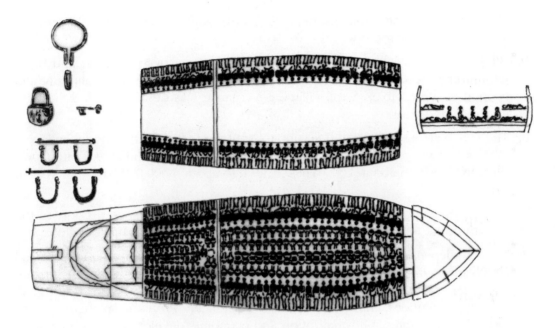

The Brookes: Middle Passage Ship

List 1-9. Economics of the Slave Trade

1. The slave trade contributed to the development of economies in European countries, African tribal leaders, and the Americas. Primary motivation for all involved in the slave trade was financial profit.

2. Spain, Portugal, the Netherlands, France, Great Britain, and the Americas (North, South, and Central) were direct beneficiaries of the sale of human beings.

3. Some countries thrived by building ships for the slave trade. Ship owners, shipping companies, and sailors profited from the trading of human flesh.

4. Britain, Spain, and Portugal and other countries gained from the taxes paid by those transporting or receiving slaves.

5. Enslaved Africans were sent to colonies in the Americas to either replace Native Americans dying from diseases or to be a ready source of manpower for agriculture.

6. Spain created a contract called the Asiento that gave traders a 30-year monopoly on transporting enslaved Africans to the colonies. The Asiento was sold to the highest bidder.

7. African slave labor was central to development of agriculture in the colonies; enslaved Africans brought expertise in growing crops in tropical climates—for example, rice.

8. Slave owners counted the number of slaves as part of their net worth; presumably, more slaves, more wealth.

9. While some African tribal leaders received bribes, tobacco, textiles, and other gifts for the capture and sale of Africans, African nations became politically and economically unstable. Small village governance was destablized and the family structure disrupted.

10. The U.S. benefited from the free, unpaid source of labor. After the invention of the cotton gin, cotton production in the South became profitable (cotton production rose from about 3,000 bales in 1790 to about 4,000,000 bales per year in 1860).

11. Cotton was exported to the North and to Britain, giving a special boost to the growth of the textile industry and the industrial revolution in those regions.

12. The interdependence of cotton production and growth of the textile industry led to advancement in other areas, such as development of steam power; lumber, concrete, and steel needed for building factories; demands for iron and coal; banking institutions; transportation; and insurance. Profits from these growth industries catapulted industrialization and economic development on both sides of the Atlantic Ocean.

13. As each industry grew, it led to an increase in the demand for workers. In a manner of speaking, the slave system led to creation of jobs in a variety of industries.

14. The real losers in this enterprise were the enslaved Africans and the continent from which they were stolen.

SLAVERY IN THE UNITED STATES

List 1-10. Recognition and Abolition of Slavery in Original Colonies

State	Legalized Slavery	Abolished Slavery
Massachusetts	1641	1783
Connecticut	1650	1784
Virginia	1661	*
Maryland	1663	†
New York	1665	1827
South Carolina	1682	*
Pennsylvania	1700	1780
New Jersey	1702	1804
Rhode Island	1703	1784
New Hampshire	1714	1783
North Carolina	1715	*
Delaware	1721	†
Georgia	1755	*

* Emancipation Proclamation in 1863 declared freedom for all slaves in states in rebellion.

† Delaware and Maryland did not secede from the Union; African Americans in those states remained enslaved until the end of the Civil War in 1865.

List 1-11. States in Rebellion Against the United States in 1863

State	Secession
Alabama	January 11, 1861
Arkansas	May 6, 1861
Florida	January 10, 1861
Georgia	January 19, 1861
Louisiana	January 26, 1861
Mississippi	January 9, 1861
North Carolina	May 20, 1861
South Carolina	December 20, 1860
Tennessee	June 8, 1861
Texas	February 1, 1861
Virginia	April 17, 1861

PLANTATION LIFE

List 1-12. Life on the Plantation

1. Over the years, enslaved Africans in the colonies made up 10 to 20 percent of the population; most (up to 90 percent) lived in the South; in some states, the population of slaves was up to 60 percent.

2. Regardless of status or rank in Africa, new arrivals were reduced to nonpersons.

3. African languages, cultural values, and traditions were suppressed.

4. Extreme punishment was meted out to those found speaking their own language.

5. Africans were forced to learn European values and customs.

6. African names were changed to European names.

7. Some colonists even considered African people inhuman and inferior.

8. Depending on owners, slaves were either mistreated or provided only basic needs.

9. Africans were imported primarily for economic reasons, to perform manual labor.

10. For all their hard work, the enslaved were housed, fed, and clothed.

List 1-13. Work

- Most worked in the fields, clearing new land, planting, and harvesting crops.

- Cotton, tobacco, rice, sugar, and hemp were typical crops.

- Men, women, and older children labored under the back-breaking work.

- Younger children weeded, carried water for adults, and picked insects from plants.

- To do their work, slaves used tools such as shovels, plows, collars, sweeps, wagons, hoes, and bridal bits.

- Slaves made the tools or farm implements they used.

- Work was constant during and after the growing season, six days per week.

- All worked long hours, from dawn to dusk.

- Slaves built barns, repaired tools, dug ditches, and cared for livestock.

- Slaves with lighter skin tones were assigned to domestic work in homes of slave owners.

- Older women and men fed farm animals, cleaned the yard, and provided care for young children and the sick.
- New mothers cut weeds, hoed vegetables, and suckled babies (theirs and others).
- Some slaves spun the cloth used for clothing for slaves and owners; others would sew, tailor, or mend garments for owners.
- Slaves made their own garments; owners were only required to provide a single change of clothing, coat, and shoes.
- Some were hired out to other plantations for special skills, such as blacksmiths or carpenters or porters.
- Slaves worked under close supervision of the overseer.
- Some overseers were fair in their treatment; others were abusive.
- Slaves were called to work with a horn or bell.
- The overseer was armed with a whip, knife, and gun, often rode a horse, and generally was accompanied by a vicious dog.

List 1-14. Housing

- Archaeological research has shown diversity in early slave dwellings.
- Slave quarters, prior to the mid-1800s, were generally cabins built from rough-hewn logs.
- Cabins were often built over trenches, and had earthen floors, mud walls, thatched roofs.
- Slaves lived in one-room cabins (about 14 by 14 feet), with small windows and maybe a shutter to keep out the elements.
- Some cabins had a rough fireplace that was used for heating and cooking, more nineteenth-century European influence.
- The structures were prone to termite and insect infestation.
- Cabins were hot in summer and cold in winter.
- Some cabins were built in clusters, similar to African villages.
- Furnishings were meager: bed, board table, and benches.
- Grease lamps were used for inside light; torches were used outside.
- Cabins and furnishings were built by slaves.
- Early styles of dwellings are believed similar to dwellings in Africa.

- Personal possessions were meager; artifacts include pottery shards, buckles, lead fishing weights and hooks, gun flints, lead shots, and a few gun parts.

- Decorative possessions were uncommon; few glass beads and bits of copper wire have been found.

- Pottery resembled that made by Native Americans.

List 1-15. Food

- Cooking for the owner was done in a kitchen, built a few yards from the main house.

- Cooking for slaves was done outside in open outdoor hearths or large pits near the cabins.

- Research shows less awareness of cooking processes in the winters.

- Water was drawn and carried from a well.

- Bread was baked in old-fashioned ovens or kitchen fireplaces.

- Staples included peas, greens, cabbage, sweet potatoes, rice, molasses, and corn bread.

- Meat was rare; when available, probably was the least desired pieces of the animal.

- Dried peas and meat (fatback) were staples in winter.

- Corn meal dumplings were served frequently; stews and one-pot meals were common.

- White bread was eaten only on holidays and special occasions.

- The major meal was served during mid-day.

- Supper included two slices of bread and a small amount of meat.

- Breakfast was not provided on many plantations.

- A small part of supper was saved for a morning bite.

- A short break was taken in the fields mid-morning for that morning bite.

- Slaves were allowed to grow their own vegetables on some plantations.

- Slaves grew and preserved vegetables for the plantation.

- Meats were butchered and preserved.

- Food was generally poor and meager.

List 1-16. Day-to-Day Life on the Plantation

- Some owners kept families together, while others split and sold family members at will.

- Fathers, mothers, or children were sold to different plantations, breaking all family ties.

- Family life was important to slaves and they gathered together during off-work time.

- They maintained, when possible, close-knit ties with grandparents, cousins, etc.

- The extended family, with roots in Africa, was maintained during slavery.

- Women were sometimes used as concubines.

- The treatment of children born from slave and owner unions varied depending on the owner.

- Slaves passed on bits and pieces of African culture through their storytelling.

- They engaged in cultural practices when possible, that is, naming children, marriage ceremony if allowed to marry, and funerals.

- The slaves used free time to express their talent in dance and music and to worship.

- Folk medicine was practiced and passed down through generations.

- Slaves provided protection for each other, sometimes in the face of personal danger.

- Enslaved parents taught children strategies for survival.

- Slaves worked to earn money to purchase freedom for themselves and family members.

- Though their native religions were taken away, they readily accepted Christianity.

- Their strong faith and belief in God helped them deal with the harshness of enslavement.

- The slaves welcomed church and poured themselves into preaching and teaching, even though most did not know how to read.

- They brought their skills and talent in music and enriched the music of the church.

- When given insufficient food, the slaves would take what was needed from the storehouses.

- They resisted enslavement by revolting, work slowdowns, running away, suicide, infanticide, etc.

List 1-17. Punishment

- Slaves were regarded as valuable property, so they had no rights or recourse.
- They were closely guarded.
- Laws were written to restrict their movement and determine punishment.
- Owners could impose any penalty deemed appropriate.
- Owners could burn, cut off appendages, starve, or whip the enslaved.
- A 1723 Virginia law determined that death resulting from punishment of a slave was not a crime.
- Slaves were not allowed outside after dark, could not gather in groups of three or more, could not own weapons, and could not leave the plantation without the owner's permission.
- They were prohibited from learning to read or write.
- Free African Americans were limited in amount of contact with the enslaved.
- If any laws were broken, punishment was swift and savage.
- Whippings were common.
- Wounds would be salted after whipping, which caused even more pain.
- Heavy leg iron shackles, slave yokes, iron collars, and wrist irons with spikes were used to punish defiant or runaway slaves.
- Runaway slaves were often sold as an example to discourage others.
- Runaway slaves were tracked with hounds.
- Slave tags were worn for identification.
- Slaves would be placed in a "bull ring" and whipped by other slaves; if slaves refused to mete out punishment, they too would be whipped.
- Care was taken to avoid permanent damage to the slaves, which would lessen their value when sold.

List 1-18. The Slave Market

- Sale of human beings was not unusual in the antebellum South or other colonies.
- The slave auction was a common business practice.
- Slaves were advertised for sale much the same as any other property, sometimes on the same bill.
- Slave traders used broadsides to advertise the sale.
- The broadsides included information on sex, age, skills, condition, and price.
- Key words found on broadsides:

Mulatto	Unassuming manner
Griff*	Tractable dispositions
Yellow	Skilled
Likely	Valuable
Suitable	Available for inspection
Condition	Wenches
Capable	Sound
Disabilities	

- By the mid 1800s, a skilled artisan would bring between $1,800 and $3,000; a field worker was worth between $800 to $1,500; and a domestic or house servant could sell for $1,200.
- Slaves were readied for the auction days in advance by being washed and neatly dressed.
- Women and men were sometimes separated in different rooms or on opposite sides of the same room for review and inspection.
- They were interviewed about their skills.
- Slaves were physically inspected in the yard or while on the auction block.
- Slaves without scars or other deformities were bought quickly.
- Mulatto slaves brought in good prices.
- Slaves were sold individually or in lots.
- Slaves were purchased with cash or secured by a mortgage.

---

*A slave trade word meaning "the child of an African and a Creole slave" or "an offspring of a Negro and a Mulatto."

RESISTANCE TO SLAVERY

List 1-19. Slave Resistance and Revolts

Date	Event
1663	Insurrection by white servants and African American slaves in Gloucester County, Virginia is betrayed by one of the other servants
1712	Maiden Lane slave revolt leaves nine whites dead; 21 slaves are killed in response
1730	Slave uprisings are crushed in Princess Anne County in Virginia
1739	Sixty-five white and black people are killed in Stono, South Carolina
1741	Responding to rumor of slave conspiracy, New York City mob burns 11, hangs 18, and sells 70 African Americans into slavery in the South
1791	Slave revolt in Louisiana results in execution of 23 slaves and deportation of three white sympathizers
1795	Several slave uprisings are discovered; some 50 slaves are killed or executed
1800	Gabriel Prosser and 1,000 slaves plan to seize arsenal at Richmond; Prosser and 15 slaves hang after two slaves betray plot
1811	U.S. troops suppress slave uprisings led by Charles Deslands in two Louisiana parishes; 100 slaves are killed or executed
1815	Approximately 300 fugitive slaves and 30 Creek Indians capture Fort Blount in Florida, use it to attack slave owners, and hold it until overrun by U.S. troops
1816	Slave rebellion led by George Boxley, a white man, fails
1822	Denmark Vesey plans a revolt of slaves in Charleston, South Carolina; plot is betrayed; Vesey with 36 of his followers hang
1825	Josiah Henson escapes with his family; participate in bringing over 200 other slaves to freedom through Underground Railroad
1829	White mob attacks African American residents in Cincinnati, Ohio; loot and burn their homes; over 1,200 blacks flee to Canada
1831	Nat Turner and 70 slaves kill 55-60 white men, women, and children on plantations in Southampton County, Virginia; Turner and 18 other slaves hang
1839	Joseph Cinque leads revolt aboard *L'Amistad,* a slave vessel, which results in killing of captain and crew
1841	Slaves revolt aboard the *Creole;* overpower crew; sail ship to Bahamas and to freedom

1848	William and Ellen Craft escape by posing as slave owner and slave; write about experience in *Running a Thousand Miles for Freedom*
1849	Harriet Tubman escapes; makes 19 trips back to help over 300 others flee
1851	Fugitive slave is rescued from Boston courtroom by African American abolitionists
1859	Five African Americans participate with John Brown in attack on Harpers Ferry, West Virginia on October 16-17; Brown is captured and hanged for treason in December

List 1-20. Escape to Freedom—The Underground Railroad (1780s–1860s)

- Vast loosely connected network of committed individuals and groups
- At personal risk, they provided aid to runaway slaves
- Opportunity to attack an oppressive system
- Origin of the Underground Railroad or when it started is unclear
- Title was popularized by a nineteenth-century author, William Still
- Network relied on secrecy, using coded language
- Abolitionists made arrangements for the *stations* (personal homes, safe houses, barns, or other hiding places)
- Abolitionists provided food, clothing, and financial assistance
- Abolitionists were courageous whites and African Americans, some former slaves who were anti-slavery advocates
- *Conductors* escorted slaves along the familiar routes to freedom, or provided available resources and directions
- Churches often provided assistance as well
- Routes took passengers over roads or paths, through woods, over rivers and mountains, mostly by night, following the North Star
- Slaves using the system were called *passengers*
- Passengers traveled mainly on foot but sometimes by boat, train, or wagon

List 1-21. Routes

- Traveled from southern states to the north and midwest primarily
- Some escapees went west and others far north to Canada
- Routes followed the Mason-Dixon line
- From Louisiana across Mississippi, Tennessee, and Kentucky to free states
- From Georgia across South Carolina, North Carolina, and Virginia to free states
- From Texas into Mexico or across Oklahoma and Missouri into free states

List 1-22. Selected Underground Conductors

Levi and Catherine Coffin opened their home to thousands of runaway slaves; Levi became known as the President of the Underground Railroad for his dedicated efforts.

James Fairfield was a celebrated Underground Railroad conductor; traveled to the deep South and rescued slaves while posing as a slave trader.

Thomas Garrett was a Quaker iron merchant in Wilmington, Delaware devoted to abolitionism. His work in sheltering slaves earned him a fine so heavy he lost all his property. He continued his work and recovered financially. He was called "Our Moses" by blacks in Wilmington.

Leonard A. Grimes, a free African American, used his livery horses and carriages to rescue slaves. He was captured and spent two years in a Richmond, Virginia prison.

Josiah Henson escaped slavery after becoming a Methodist Episcopal preacher; helped nearly 200 slaves to escape through the Underground Railroad.

John Parker was an African American abolitionist from Ripley, Ohio. He traveled into Kentucky and Virginia and transported hundreds of fugitives to freedom by boat.

Robert Purvis, David Ruggles, and William Still organized vigilance committees in Northern states during the 1830s to help fugitive slaves.

Alexander Ross, a Canadian-born physician, recruited slaves from Richmond, Nashville, Selma, and New Orleans interested in escaping.

Harriet Tubman was one of the best-known conductors on the Underground Railroad. Called "Moses" by her people, she led hundreds of escaped slaves to freedom.

List 1-23. Abolitionists

1840s	Amos Beman	one of the founders of the American Foreign Anti-Slavery Society
1840s	James Birney	founded the first anti-slavery political party, the Liberty Party
1825–1921	Antoinette Blackwell	abolitionist, feminist, and first woman ordained minister (1853); preached her last sermon at age 90 and published the last of eight books at 93
1800–1859	John Brown	militant abolitionist; led the raid on the U.S. Armory at Harpers Ferry, West Virginia in 1859
1814–1884	William Wells Brown	escaped from slavery in 1834; traveled back into slave states to lead other slaves north; lectured against slavery at home and in Great Britain; studied medicine and practiced as a physician after the Civil War
1806–1899	Elizabeth Buffum Chase	influenced by William Lloyd Garrison, she and her sisters found the Fall River Anti-Slavery Society; she and husband, Samuel, sheltered runaway slaves in their home; continued her anti-slavery activities after moving to Rhode Island; lobbied for admission of women to Brown University and resigned from a Providence Woman's Club over its refusal to admit a black member
1840s	Salmon P. Chase	an attorney; defended fugitive slaves without charging fees
1798–1867	Levi Coffin	over 35 years, helped over 3,000 runaway slaves to freedom; home in Indiana was known as "Grand Central Station"
1827	Samuel Cornish	co-founder of *Freedom's Journal,* the first black newspaper in America
1840s	Alexander Crumwell	secretary of the New York State Anti-Slavery Society
1817–1895	Frederick Douglass	strong anti-slavery proponent, human rights activist, orator, author, and social reformer; founded the *North Star* newspaper
1830s	Grace Bustill Douglass	active member of the interracial Philadelphia Female Anti-Slavery Society founded in 1833; her father, Cyrus Bustill, established a school for black children in his home in 1803

ND*	Charlotte Forten	joined the Salem Female Anti-Slavery Society and fought for equality for blacks and women
1766–1842	James Forten	successful entrepreneur who fought against the colonization of blacks; advocated for temperance, women's rights, and abolition of slavery
1815–1882	Henry Highland Garnet	militant abolitionist; called for slave revolt and general strike; urged slaves to "Let your motto be resistance! resistance! resistance"
ND	Thomas Garrett	his Wilmington home was the best known "station" in the East on the underground railroad network
1805–1879	William Lloyd Garrison	white journalist; founded *The Liberator*, an abolitionist newspaper in 1831
1830s	Sarah & Angelina Grimke	led anti-slavery society from 1836–1838 and fought for rights of women and abolition of slavery
1789–1883	Josiah Henson	escaped slavery after becoming a Methodist Episcopal preacher; helped nearly 200 slaves to escape to freedom through the underground railroad
1820s	James T. Holly	Episcopalian Bishop and anti-slavery advocate; emigrated to Haiti to do missionary work
ND	Jermain W. Loguen	New Yorker; named vice president of the first convention for equal rights for women
ND	John Malvin	a Negro; moved fugitive slaves on canal boats he owned
1833	Lucretia Coffin Mott	formed the Philadelphia Female Anti-Slavery Society
1830s	James Mott	along with wife, Lucretia, was active in the underground railroad and was a delegate to the World Anti-Slavery Convention
1840s	Daniel Payne	AME Bishop; emigrated from the Carolinas to the North; outspoken advocate against slavery in his church and denomination
1840s	J.W.C. Pennington	black clergyman and abolitionist of Hartford, Connecticut
1840s	Wendell Phillips	strong orator; lectured against slavery and Jim Crow schools

---

* ND = no date

ND	Charlotta Gordon Pyles	was transported along with her entire family from Kentucky to Iowa by her owner for man-umission; raised $3,000 in six months to buy freedom for two sons-in-law; assisted run-aways passing through Iowa on the way to Canada; descendants run Piney Woods School in Mississippi, a private school for blacks
1845–1850	Charles Lenox Remond	president of the Essex Anti-Slavery Society; encouraged young Negroes to get involved with the anti-slavery crusade
ND	Grant Richie	black barber in Sandusky, Ohio; organized blacks to assist fugitive slaves on their journey through Ohio to Canada
1840s	Christopher Rush	AMEZ Bishop and outspoken abolitionist in his church and denomination
1799–1851	John Russwurm	co-founder of *Freedom's Journal* (1827), the first black newspaper in America
1847	Gerritt Smith	offered to subdivide thousands of acres of land in New York to attract black farmers; due to lack of capital and poor land quality, the project failed
1833	Elizabeth Cady Stanton	assisted Lucretia Coffin Mott in the founding of the Philadelphia Female Anti-Slavery Society
1821–1902	William Still	executive secretary of Philadelphia's Anti-Slavery Society; assisted fugitive slaves on the underground railroad
1840s	Arthur & Lewis Tappan	founded the American and Foreign Anti-Slavery Society; agitated for the emancipation of slaves
1797–1883	Sojourner Truth	spread the "truth" about the evils of slavery across the country
1826–1913	Harriet Tubman	conductor on the underground railroad; made some twenty trips into the South to free over 300 slaves
1843	Samuel Ringgold Ward	one of three blacks in the Liberty Party Convention; president (1850) of the American League of Colored Laborers
1720–1772	John Woolman	anti-slavery advocate from New Jersey; encouraged Quakers to free their slaves out-right or upon their deaths

THE COURTS AND SLAVERY

List 1-24. Legislation and Slavery (1600-1863)

Date	Legislation
1641	Massachusetts legalizes slavery
1661	In Virginia, the status of mother determines status of a black child
1664	Maryland makes it illegal for a white woman to marry a black man
1775	Continental Congress disallows black enlistment in the army
1787	Constitution of U.S. is adopted with three-fifths compromise and an agreement that slavery could continue legally until 1808
1793	Congress passes the first Fugitive Slave Law
1800-1860	Northern states pass numerous laws restricting the rights of blacks
1808	A law prohibiting the importation of African slaves goes into effect
1820	Congress passes the Missouri Compromise
1833	Georgia forbids hiring blacks in positions requiring reading or writing
1836	U.S. Congress adopts the "gag rule," no action on antislavery petitions
1842	Supreme Court rules states do not have to enforce Fugitive Slave Law of 1793
1850	Compromise outlaws slavery in D.C. but toughens fugitive slave laws
1851	Virginia rewrites constitution to return emancipated slaves to slave status if they remain in the state for more than 12 months
1854	Kansas-Nebraska Act repeals the Missouri Compromise
1857	*Dred Scott* case rules that Negroes are not citizens of the U.S.
1861	The Civil War begins; Congress passes the Confiscation Act
1862	Slavery is abolished in the District of Columbia and in federal territories
1862	Congress authorizes recruitment of African Americans for service in Union Army; black soldiers are paid almost 50% less than white soldiers
1863	President Lincoln signs the Emancipation Proclamation on January 1

List 1-25. Legislation and the Reconstruction Era (1865-1877)

Date	Legislation
1864	Congress authorizes equal pay for African American soldiers; prohibits discrimination in hiring U.S. mail carriers
1865	Thirteenth Amendment to the Constitution is passed and ratified
1865	"Black Codes" are enacted in southern states; "Black Laws" of Illinois are repealed
1866	The first Civil Rights Bill is passed by Congress
1866	Fourteenth Amendment is adopted over Presidential veto; is ratified in 1868
1867	Passage of Reconstruction Acts; passes suffrage for blacks in D.C.
1868	Fifteenth Amendment to Constitution is passed; is ratified in 1870
1871	Congress passes the Enforcement Act (Ku Klux Klan Act)
1872	Congress allows Ku Klux Klan Act to expire; passes Amnesty Act
1875	Civil Rights Act prohibits discrimination in public accommodation
1876	*United States* v. *Cruikshank* and *United States* v. *Reese*

List 1-26. Legislation and Segregation of African Americans (1877-1953)

Date	Legislation and Supreme Court Cases
1878	*Hall* v. *DeCuir*
1880	*Strauder* v. *WVA*
1881	Tennessee segregates railroad cars; other states follow with "Jim Crow" laws
1883	Civil Rights Act of 1875 is ruled unconstitutional
1890	Supreme Court finds segregation on railroad cars constitutional
1894	Congress repeals 1870 Enforcement Act
1896	*Plessey* v. *Ferguson*
1898	*Williams* v. *Mississippi;* poll tax not a violation of Fourteenth Amendment
1907	Supreme Court upholds segregation on railroad cars in interstate travel
1915	*Guinn* v. *United States*
1917	*Buchanan* v. *Warley*
1921	Immigration Act
1923	*Moore* v. *Dempsey*
1924	Immigration Act; restricts entry of blacks of African descent
1927	*Nixon* v. *Herndon*
1938	*Missouri ex rel Gaines:* Supreme Court rules that Missouri must supply equal educational facilities for blacks and whites
1940	*Hansberry* v. *Lee*
1941	Executive Order 8802; establishes Fair Employment Practices Committee
1944	*Smith* v. *Allwright;* black voters are admitted to primaries
1947	*United Public Workers* v. *Mitchell;* outlaws discrimination in federal service
1948	Executive Order 9981; ends segregation in armed forces and federal employment
	Shelley v. *Kraemer;* rules segregation clauses in housing covenants unconstitutional
1950	*Henderson* v. *United States;* dining cars cannot be segregated
1952	Immigration and Nationality Act
1953	*District of Columbia* v. *John R. Thompson;* desegregates Washington, D.C. restaurants

VIOLENCE AGAINST AFRICAN AMERICANS

List 1-27. Recorded Lynchings (1882-1969)

Year	Number of Lynchings
1882–1884	153
1885–1889	381
1890–1894	611
1895–1899	500
1900–1904	429
1905–1909	345
1910–1914	313
1915–1919	552
1920–1924	231
1925–1929	63
1930–1934	77
1935–1939	32
1940–1944	17
1945–1949	13
1950–1954*	2
1955–1959	4
1960–1964	3
1965–1969	0

*According to Tuskegee University data, there was no report of lynching in 1952, the first time in 71 years.

FIGHT FOR FREEDOM

List 1-28. The Civil Rights Movement in Review (1600s–1999)

1600s	1700s	1800–1850	1850–1900
Slavery recognized by law in the colonies	Quakers vowed not to own slaves	Antislavery societies organized with blacks and whites	Supreme Court denied citizenship to African Americans in *Dred Scott* decision, 1857
Pennsylvania Mennonites—Slavery violated Christian Principles	Richard Allen and Absalom Jones formed Free African Society	North Carolina, South Carolina, and Mississippi prohibited teaching black children, free or enslaved, to read	Abraham Lincoln elected president, 1860
Quaker Resolution—Set time of service for African slaves	Declaration of Independence—the promise of equality	Slave importation banned in 1787; went into effect in 1808	African Americans served on both sides of the Civil War
Colonies passed laws to restrict rights of free and enslaved African Americans	Slaves ran away or rebelled; major revolts in 1712 and 1741	Northern states passed laws to restrict rights of free African Americans	The Emancipation Proclamation freed slaves in Confederate states in 1863
Slaves resisted their plight daily; were punished severely	African Americans barred from military service	Harriet Tubman escaped and began Underground Railroad	Ku Klux Klan formed in 1865 to restore white supremacy
Massachusetts passed law to protect slaves from abusive owners	Congress passed Fugitive Slave Act	First black paper, *Freedom's Journal,* entered publication in 1827	Congress passed Thirteenth Amendment abolishing slavery, 1865
Connecticut forbade blacks in military	First Abolitionist Society established	Free blacks denied right to vote in Rhode Island	Congress passed 1866 Civil Rights Bill
African cultural rites prohibited by owners	Crispus Attucks shot in Boston Massacre, 1770	Denmark Vesey planned a massive slave revolt, 1822	Reconstruction Acts (1867-1869)
Slaves blocked from Quaker meetings	Quakers opened a school for Blacks	Slavery abolished in New York	Fourteenth Amendment was enacted
Unlawful for black men to marry white women in Maryland	Pennsylvania passed law to gradually free the slaves	Nat Turner led largest slave rebellion in U.S. history, 1831	Fifteenth Amendment cleared right to vote to all citizens
Virginia passed law to enslave for life any black entering the colony by sea who was not a Christian	Prince Hall led blacks in petitioning government of Massachusetts for equal school facilities	Oberlin College in Ohio was first to admit black students	1875 Civil Rights Act prohibited discrimination in public accommodations
Massachusetts trained Africans, Indians, and Scots for the colonial militia	Delegates of nine states formed American Convention of Abolition Societies	First National Negro Convention devised plan to improve blacks' social status	Supreme Court ruled 1875 Civil Rights Act unconstitutional
Virginia enacted law to pay bounty for runaway slaves called Maroons; many slaves escaped and lived with Indians	U.S. Constitution adopted three-fifths rule (five slaves the equivalent of three whites)	Frederick Douglass began work with the Massachusetts Anti-Slavery Society	Supreme Court ruled "separate but equal" accommodations were reasonable in *Plessy* v. *Ferguson*

List 1-28. (*continued*)

1900–1950	1950–1960	1960–1970	1970–1980
William Trotter and W.E.B. Du Bois called a conference in Niagara Falls that gives rise to NAACP	Supreme Court ruled segregated dining facilities in interstate travel as unconstitutional	President Eisenhower signed 1960 Civil Rights Act allowing federal agencies to act in civil rights cases	Jesse Jackson organized People United to Save Humanity (PUSH)
National Association for the Advancement of Colored People established in 1909	Law schools (University of Texas, University of Virginia, Louisiana State University) ordered to admit African American students	College students sat-in at a lunch counter in Greensboro and started a movement	Charles C. Diggs became first chair of new Congressional Black Caucus
Over 25 riots occurred during summer 1919; 40 to 200 blacks in East St. Louis, and 2 blacks and 17 whites in Houston died	Paul Robeson & William L. Patterson accused U.S. government of genocide against African Americans	Student Nonviolent Coordinating Committee (SNCC) formed in April 1960; Marion Barry was first chairman	Employment tests that discriminate ruled unconstitutional in *Griggs* v. *Duke Power*
Supreme Court upheld right of railroads to segregate passengers by race	Supreme Court found segregated schools to be inherently unequal	CORE sent freedom riders south to test compliance with federal laws	Supreme Court found school busing to achieve desegregation was constitutional
National Urban League founded in 1911	White "Citizens Council" organized in Indianola, Mississippi	Martin L. King, Jr. received Nobel Peace Prize	Equal Employment Opportunity Act passed in 1972
Powell Amendment denied federal funds to any project that discriminated based on race	*Brown* v. *Board of Education* called for "all deliberate speed" in desegregating schools	Over 250,000 attended the 1963 March on Washington for jobs and freedom	Barbara Jordan was first African American to keynote Democratic National Convention
Supreme Court legitimized picketing as legal means for protest	Rosa Parks refused her seat to a white man and started a movement	Four little girls killed at Sixteenth Street Baptist Church, Birmingham, Alabama	Black students increase attendance at black colleges and universities
Thurgood Marshall joined NAACP as Special Council	University of Alabama admitted Autherine Lucy, its first black student	Thurgood Marshall sworn in as Supreme Court Justice	Desegregation plans approved in MD, VA, NC, GA, FL, AR, PA, and OK universities
Equal educational opportunities mandated by states in *Sipuel* decision	Ministers from different denominations form Southern Christian Leadership Conference (SCLC)	President Johnson signed Civil Rights Act of 1964 and Voting Rights Act of 1965	President Carter appointed record number (6) of blacks to key positions in his administration
Fair Employment Practice Commission created by Executive Order 9980	Federal troops sent to protect black students admitted to Central High in Little Rock	Martin L. King, Jr. assassinated in April 1968 in Memphis, Tennessee	Supreme Court ruled unions have right to correct racial imbalances at work
Armed services desegregated by Executive Order 9981	Right to vote is protected in the 1957 Civil Rights Act	Executive Order 11478 mandated affirmative action programs in all federal agencies	*Bakke* decision ruled use of special admissions criteria as unconstitutional

List 1-28. *(continued)*

1980–1990	1990–1999
Tax exempt status may be denied to private universities that discriminate	President George Bush vetoed the 1990 Civil Rights Bill
In *Fullilove* v. *Klutznick,* Supreme Court validated minority set-asides to remedy past discrimination	Congress passed Civil Rights Act of 1991 and President Bush signed it
Schomburg Center for Research in Black Culture opened in Harlem	Bobby Rush, former Black Panther Party leader, elected to Congress from Illinois
St. Louis schools are peacefully de-segregated with court-ordered bus-ing	Gary Franks elected as first African American Republican Congressman in 56 years
Martin L. King, Jr. Center for Nonvio-lent Social Change established in At-lanta, Georgia	August 1993—the 30th anniversary of 1963 March on Washington
1965 Voting Act renewed for an ad-ditional 25 years	William H. Gray III left Congress to become President of United Negro College Fund
Federal agencies pulled back from busing and timetables to remedy past discrimination and sought rever-sal of affirmative action laws	Clarence Thomas confirmed for Supreme Court seat vacated due to retirement of Thurgood Marshall
Prosecutor may not strike a prospec-tive juror based on race	Carol Mosely Braun became first African American woman elected to U.S. Senate
Marion Barry elected to third term as mayor of Washington, D.C.	Supreme Court struck down a hate crime law in St. Paul
In *City of Richmond* v. *Croson* and *Wards Cove Packing* v. *Antonio,* employee must show intent to dis-criminate	Fifty people killed in Los Angeles ri-oting following acquittal of four po-lice officers for beating Rodney King
Three black men attacked by white mob in Howard Beach, New York while looking for help to repair their car; Michael Griffith struck by a car and killed trying to escape	University of California voted to end affirmative action in hiring and ad-missions in 1995; voters passed Proposition 209 ending affirmative action in government activities
General Colin Powell named chair-man of the Joint Chiefs of Staff	Benjamin Chavis and Louis Far-rakhan organized Million Man March
Ronald H. Brown elected chair of Democratic National Committee	Kweisi Mfume and Julian Bond pro-vided leadership for NAACP
L. Douglass Wilder elected governor of Virginia	Congressional Black Caucus grew to over 40 members
Jesse Jackson campaigned for Demo-cratic Party's nomination for presi-dent of the U.S.	Three white men charged with the dragging death of James Byrd, Jr. in Jasper, Texas

List 1-29. Nonviolent Resistance to Segregation

African Americans have resisted slavery since its inception. Some actions were open and violent, some were open and nonviolent, while others were quietly unobtrusive and indirect. Other lists have reported on some of the techniques African Americans applied over the centuries. The focus in List 1-29 is nonviolent civil disobedience used from the 1940s to the present to confront unjust laws and traditional practices that disfranchised African Americans. Civil rights actions were taking place in numerous localities all across the country, with many incidents not being captured and recorded. The List, therefore, presents selective incidents only. The success of these strategies is a tribute to the power of personal commitment, community action, and a shared vision.

Boycotts

1953   Blacks boycotted buses in Baton Rouge, Louisiana to protest segregation.

1955   One-year bus boycott in Montgomery, Alabama led to a U.S. Supreme Court ruling outlawing bus segregation in the city.

1956   A six-month boycott desegregated buses in Tallahassee, Florida.

1957   Tuskegee boycotted white merchants to protest gerrymandering local electoral districts to reduce black voting strength.

Desegregation of Schools

1956   Autherine J. Lucy admitted to the University of Alabama.

1957   Black students desegregated Central High School in Little Rock, Arkansas.

1962   James Meredith gained admission to University of Mississippi with aid of federal troops.

Lunch Counter Sit-Ins

1949   CORE staged sit-ins to protest segregated public accommodations in St. Louis.

1958   Oklahoma City's NAACP Youth Council began sit-ins to desegregate lunch counters.

1960   Students from Fisk University staged a sit-in to demonstrate against segregation.

1960   College students sit-in at an F. W. Woolworth lunch counter in Greensboro, North Carolina and in 15 days similar actions had spread to 15 other cities.

Kneel-Ins/Pray-Ins/Lock-Ins

1957   Martin Luther King, Jr. led over 25,000 in a "prayer pilgrimage" to the Lincoln Memorial to support voting rights.

1961   Students arrested in Rock Hill, North Carolina refused to pay fines and remained in jail leading to the call by SNCC, "Jail, No Bail."

1967   Welfare mother locked herself in a building in Roxbury to protest discrimination.

Freedom Bus Rides

1947   CORE sent the first load of black and white freedom riders south to test public accommodations.

1961   CORE began recruitment of freedom riders.

1961   CORE sent several busloads of black and white freedom riders to the South, some of whom were met with violence from white mobs.

Training Centers for Nonviolent Action Centers

College campuses in the North and South became centers for training demonstrators in nonviolent techniques. Demonstrators were trained to be orderly; not fight back in word or deed; don't talk, laugh, or block entrances; sit straight; take off hats; face the counter; walk in straight lines; hold head high; and be strong and determined.

Before and after protests, demonstrators would gather to sing and pray.

Considerable organization and leadership from a variety of sources poured into the movement in support of nonviolent resistance.

Protests and Marches

1955   Montgomery Bus Boycott

1960   Over 2,000 African Americans marched to city hall in Nashville, Tennessee in protest of the bombing of Z. Alexander Looby's home.

1963   Marches in Savannah forced desegregation of hotels, bowling alleys, and most theaters.

1963   Birmingham marchers attacked by police dogs and sprayed with fire hoses.

1963   March on Washington

1965   Selma to Montgomery march

1966   March in Chicago aimed at housing discrimination

1968   Poor Peoples March on Washington

Protests Through Music, Art, Literature, and Dance

Music, art, dance, and literature expressed the frustration and anger of the 1960s and at the same time was full of hope and promise of a better day.

Anti-War Protests

The struggle for human rights quickly broadened into saving lives by stopping the Vietnam War.

1967   Martin Luther King, Jr. led marchers past the United Nations building in New York City.

1968   Demonstrators protested across the country and at the Democratic National Convention in Chicago. Police used tear gas and clubs to beat back protesters.

Voter Education and Registration Drives

1959   Major voting drive added 15,000 African Americans as registered voters.

1960   NAACP sponsored voter registration drives in Jacksonville, Tampa, Savannah, and Memphis.

1960   Congress of Federated Organizations (SNCC, CORE, SCLC, and NAACP) recruited over 1,000 black and white volunteers to help African Americans register to vote.

1965   SCLC launched voter registration drive in Selma, Alabama with the Selma to Montgomery march. The idea caught on and escalated nationwide.

List 1-30. Civil Rights Organizations

Alabama Christian Movement for Human Rights (ACHR)

American Civil Liberties Union (ACLU)

Black Free Masonry in the United States

Black Panther Party

Congress of Racial Equality (CORE)

Inter-Civic Council (ICC)

Leadership Conference on Civil Rights

Mississippi Freedom Democratic Party (MFDP)

Montgomery Improvement Association (MIA)

National Association for the Advancement of Colored People (NAACP)

National Council of Negro Women

National Rainbow Coalition

National Urban Coalition

National Urban League (NUL)

Organization of Afro-American Unity

People United to Save Humanity (PUSH)

Southern Christian Leadership Conference (SCLC)

Southern Poverty Law Center (SPLC)

Student Nonviolent Coordinating Committee (SNCC)

TransAfrica

Universal Negro Improvement Association (UNIA)

List 1-31. Civil Rights Leaders

Ralph David Abernathy (1926-1990)—Chief deputy and associate of Martin Luther King, Jr. and co-organizer of the Montgomery Improvement Association, the forerunner of the Southern Christian Leadership Conference (SCLC).

Ella Josephine Baker (1903-1986)—Quiet "activist behind the movement." Worked with the Young Women's Christian Association, Works Progress Administration, the Urban League, was field secretary for the NAACP and the first executive secretary for the SCLC. She encouraged youth involvement in the movement and was a central figure in organizing the Student Nonviolent Coordinating Committee.

Ida B. Wells Barnett (1862-1931)—Mounted strong attacks on segregation as a journalist; organized anti-lynching campaigns across the country and was involved in the founding of the NAACP.

Daisy Lee Gatson Bates (1914-1999)—Publisher of the *Arkansas State Press* and reported racially motivated brutality against blacks; central figure in organizing and supporting the Little Rock Nine, the nine students chosen to integrate Central High School in Little Rock, Arkansas.

Julian Bond (1940-)—One of the founding members of SNCC; elected and denied his seat in the Georgia State Legislature in 1965; nominated for vice president of the U.S. in 1968 but was too young to qualify; served in the Georgia Senate from 1974 to 1986; became Chair of the NAACP in 1998.

Stokely Carmichael (Kwame Toure) (1941-1998)—Chairman of SNCC in 1966 and steered the organization from a nonviolence stance to one of self-defense and black nationalism; joined the Black Panther Party in 1967; changed his name to Kwame Toure in 1973, moved to Ghana and became a spokesperson for Pan-Africanism.

Benjamin F. Chavis, Jr. (1948-)—Former executive director of the NAACP and co-chair with Louis Farrakhan of the 1995 Million Man March in Washington, D.C.

Angela Davis (1944-)—Outspoken activist and member of the Communist Party; placed on the FBI's Most Wanted list when guns she purchased were used by the Black Panthers; she was arrested and later acquitted of all charges.

Frederick Douglass (1817-1875)—Ardent abolitionist who became an active agent in the Massachusetts Anti-Slavery Society.

W. E. B. Du Bois (1868-1963)—Early advocate for full citizenship rights for blacks; helped organize the Niagara Movement which evolved into the NAACP; editor of the NAACP's magazine, *Crisis,* for 25 years.

Marian Wright Edelman (1939-)—Civil rights advocate and one of the organizers of the 1968 Poor Peoples March on Washington; founder of the Children's Defense Fund.

Medgar Evers (1925-1963)—Gunned down in the driveway of his home for his work as field secretary for the NAACP. Byron De La Beckwith, an unrepentant member of a white supremacist group, was convicted of his death February 5, 1994, after having been twice acquitted by all-white juries.

Myrlie Evers-Williams (1933-)—Wife of slain civil rights leader Medgar Evers; was active in keeping the case alive until his killer could be brought to justice; former executive director of the NAACP.

James Leonard Farmer (1920-1999)—A tireless civil rights activist and one of the organizers of the Congress of Racial Equality (CORE).

Fannie Lou Hamer (1917-1977)—A Mississippi sharecropper fired for trying to register to vote; became a field worker for SNCC and was one of the founders of the Mississippi Freedom Democratic Party (MFDP), an organization that challenged the all-white Mississippi delegation at the 1964 Democratic National Convention. While the MFDP was not successful in 1964, the National Democratic Party pledged not to seat any delegation excluding blacks for the 1968 convention.

Dorothy I. Height (1912-)—Civil rights activist; long-term president of the National Council of Negro Women; recipient of the Medal of Freedom, America's highest civilian honor.

Benjamin L. Hooks (1925-)—Former executive director of the NAACP.

Roy Innis (1934-)—Former national director of the Congress of Racial Equality.

Jesse L. Jackson (1941-)—Close associate of Martin Luther King, Jr.; active in SCLC; founder of Operation PUSH (People United to Save Humanity); campaigned for president of the United States.

John E. Jacob (1934-)—Former president of the National Urban League.

Barbara Charline Jordan (1936-1996)—Eloquent orator and civil rights activist; first African American elected to the U.S. House of Representatives from Texas since Reconstruction and the first black woman from the South in that body.

Vernon E. Jordan, Jr. (1935-)—Former president of the National Urban League from 1972 to 1981; chair of President-elect Bill Clinton's transition team.

Coretta Scott King (1927-)—Wife of Martin Luther King, Jr. and chief executive officer of the Martin Luther King, Jr. Center for Non-violent Social Change, Atlanta, Georgia.

Martin L. King, Jr. (1929-1968)—Central civil rights leader of the 1960s; key figure in the Montgomery, Alabama bus boycott and other civil rights activities; recipient of the Nobel Peace Prize in 1964; assassinated in 1968.

John Lewis (1940-)—Civil rights activist in the Nashville student movement, freedom rides, and was the Chair of SNCC from 1963 to 1966; elected to the Atlanta City Council in 1981 and has served in the U.S. House of Representatives from Georgia since 1990.

Joseph E. Lowery (1924-)—Past president and co-founder of the Southern Negro Leaders Conference, a precursor to the SCLC.

Thurgood Marshall (1908-1993)—Attorney for the renown *Brown* v. *Board of Education* Supreme Court decision; first African American Supreme Court justice.

Floyd B. McKissick (1922-1981)—Former national director of the Congress of Racial Equality (CORE).

Kweisi Mfume (1948-)—Former congressman from Baltimore, Maryland; president and chief executive officer of the NAACP.

Rosa L. Parks (1913-)—Refused to give up her seat on a bus to a white man and spurred a successful movement, the Montgomery, Alabama Bus Boycott.

Adam Clayton Powell (1908-1972)—Activist pastor of Abyssianian Baptist Church and congressman from New York.

Asa Philip Randolph (1889-1979)—Organized an employment bureau for untrained blacks; founder of the Brotherhood of Sleeping Car Porters; spearheaded the idea of a March on Washington to protest discrimination.

Bayard Rustin (1910-1987)—Former executive director of the A. Philip Randolph Institute; founding member of CORE and active in SCLC activities.

Bobby Seale (1936-)—Co-founder with Huey P. Newton of the Black Panther Party, Oakland, California.

Al Sharpton (1954-)—Rousing civil rights and community activist in New York, New York.

Leon H. Sullivan (1922-)—Civil rights activist who fought diligently against racism in hiring practices; formed the Opportunities Industrialization Center, Philadelphia, Pennsylvania to provide job training for the underserved.

Mary Church Terrell (1863-1954)—Vocal opponent of white racism and sexism in America; played a central role in organizing the National Association of Colored Women (NACW) in 1896 and in the founding of the NAACP.

William M. Trotter (1872-1934)—Activist publisher and founder of the *Boston Guardian,* known as a militant newspaper, in 1901.

Sojourner Truth (1797-1883)—Outspoken abolitionist.

Harriet Tubman (1820-1913)—Conductor on the underground railroad helping hundreds escape to freedom.

Booker Taliaferro Washington (1856-1915)—Advocated for practical, manual training for black economic self sufficiency; president of Tuskegee Normal and Industrial Institute (now Tuskegee University).

Roy Wilkins (1901-1981)—Former editor of the *Crisis* magazine; executive director of the NAACP from 1955 to 1977.

Andrew Young (1932-)—Civil rights activist and associate of Martin Luther King, Jr.; executive director of SCLC from 1964 to 1970; elected to Congress from Georgia in 1972; appointed as Ambassador to the United Nations; later elected as mayor of Atlanta for two terms.

Whitney Moore Young, Jr. (1921-1971)—Director of the National Urban League from 1961 to 1971; played a key role in influencing President Lyndon Johnson's War on Poverty programs.

List 1-32. Spotlight: MARTIN LUTHER KING, JR.

- Born January 15, 1929, Michael Luther King, Jr.; later renamed Martin

- Graduate of Morehouse College, 1948

- Ordained minister (Baptist)

- Married Coretta Scott, 1953; within 10 years, they have four children

- Pastor of Dexter Avenue Baptist Church, Montgomery, Alabama, 1954

- Received a doctorate from Boston University

- Provided leadership in the Montgomery Bus Boycott, 1955

- First president of the Southern Christian Leadership Conference (SCLC), 1957

- Author of *Stride Toward Freedom: The Montgomery Story*, 1958 (Harper)

- Pastor of his father's church, Ebenezer Baptist Church, Atlanta, Georgia, 1960

- Rose quickly as the visible leader of the mid-1960s Civil Rights Movement

- Arrested an untold number of times for protesting segregation

- Wrote *Letter from a Birmingham Jail*, 1963

- One of the organizers of the 1963 March on Washington

- Delivered his memorable "I Have a Dream" speech at the March on Washington, 1963

- The first African American selected as *Time* magazine's "Man of the Year"

- Wrote *Why We Can't Wait*, published 1964

- Awarded the Nobel Prize for Peace in Oslo, Norway, 1964

- Organized march from Selma to Montgomery to gain federal protection for voting rights, 1965

- Planned the Poor Peoples March on Washington (carried out after his death)

- Gave support to anti-war efforts in the Vietnam struggle

- Led a march of sanitation workers in a labor protest in Memphis; delivered his last speech "I've Been to the Mountaintop," 1968

- Assassinated in Memphis at the Lorraine Motel on April 3, 1968

- King's birthday is celebrated as a national holiday (third Monday in January)

- Martin Luther King, Jr. Center for Nonviolent Social Change, Inc. was established

- Martin Luther King, Jr. Nonviolent Peace Prize issued first time in 1983

List 1-33. Spotlight: DOROTHY IRENE HEIGHT

- Born in Richmond, Virginia in 1912

- Earned Bachelor and Master's degrees at New York University in four years

- Joined National Council of Negro Women (NCNW) in 1937 and became a leader in the struggle for human rights

- Served on national staff of the Young Women's Christian Association from 1944 to 1977; active in developing leadership and human relations training and education; inaugurated the Center for Racial Justice at the YWCA

- Visiting professor at Delhi School of Social Work in New Delhi, India, 1952

- Appointed to Social Welfare Board of New York, 1958 and 1961

- President, National Council of Negro Women (NCNW), 1957

- Worked closely with other leaders in the 1950s and 1960s civil rights movement

- Worked tirelessly on issues relevant to women, minorities, and the poor

- Conceived and organized the Annual Black Family Reunion Celebration, 1986

- Services in selected organizations:

    —White House Advisory Council on Historically Black Colleges

    —National Advisory Council on Aging

    —Defense Advisory Committee on Women in the Services

    —Delta Sigma Theta Sorority, Inc., President

    —National Council of Negro Women, Vice President

    —Women in Community Services, Inc., President

- Received numerous awards for long-term service:

    —NAACP Spingarn Medal, 1993

    —National Women's Hall of Fame, 1993

    —Presidential Medal of Freedom, 1994

    —NAFEO Distinguished Leadership Award

    —Received 23 honorary doctoral degrees

- Truly a model of a "giving and caring spirit"

AFRICAN AMERICAN DEMOGRAPHICS

List 1-34. African Americans in U.S. Population (1870-1990)

Year	Population (in thousands)	Percent
1870	5,392	13.5
1880	6,581	13.1
1890	7,489	11.9
1900	8,834	11.6
1910	9,828	10.6
1920	10,463	10.0
1930	11,891	9.7
1940	12,866	9.7
1950	15,042	10.0
1960	18,860	10.6
1970	22,600	11.1
1980	26,495	11.2
1990	31,500	12.2

According to the U.S. Census Bureau (March 1998 Current Population Survey), African American demographics reveal dramatic improvements in some areas and gradual shifts in others. Some of those changes are presented below:

- In 1998 African Americans numbered 34.5 million, making up 13 percent of the U.S. population.

- African Americans have realized a steady rise in educational attainment since the 1940s. High school completion gap between whites and African Americans showed no statistical difference in 1998. In the same year, 88 percent of ages 25 to 29 had high school diplomas and 15 percent had bachelor's degree or higher.

- The median family income in 1998 was $28,602, up from $25,050 the year before. Twenty-six percent of African American families had income below the poverty level. African American median family income was 58 percent of white families.

- From 1987 to 1992, businesses owned by African Americans increased by 46 percent.

- Twenty-three percent of African American women and 17 percent of men 16 years and over worked in managerial and professional jobs in 1998, up from 10.7 percent in 1970 and 16.6 percent in 1980.

- Nearly 60 percent of African Americans lived in the South in 1998. Most African American families (59 percent) lived in central cities of metropolitan areas.

- From 1950 to the present, it is estimated that over 5 million African Americans have moved from the rural South to cities in the North and West.

- Metropolitan areas with the largest number of African American households are New York City, Chicago, Washington, D.C.-Maryland-Virginia, Los Angeles-Long Beach, and Detroit. Jackson, Mississippi had the highest percentage—37 percent—of African American households.

List 1-35. States with Largest African American Populations

State	Population (in millions)
New York	3.2
California	2.4
Texas	2.4
Florida	2.3
Georgia	2.1
Illinois	1.8
North Carolina	1.6
Louisiana	1.4
Maryland	1.4
Michigan	1.4

Source: U.S. Census 1997 Current Population Survey

Section 2

CULTURAL TRADITIONS

FAMILIES

2-1 Family Demographics
2-2 Family Structures
2-3 Family Life

SUPERSTITIONS

2-4 Bad Luck
2-5 Good Fortune

LANGUAGE

2-6 Proverbs in African American Culture
2-7 Languages of Black Races (Native and Foreign)
2-8 Styles of Languages
2-9 Slang in the 1990s

CELEBRATIONS AND HOLIDAYS

2-10 Church-Related Celebrations
2-11 African American Celebrations/Holidays
2-12 African American Festivals

FUNERAL PRACTICES

2-13 Funeral Rituals
2-14 Funeral Customs of Specific Regions (Past and Present)
2-15 Burials
2-16 Locations of Cemeteries
2-17 Selected Historic Cemeteries

MUSIC

2-18 Freedom Songs
2-19 Styles of Music
2-20 Alternative Instruments

DANCE

2-21 Popular Dances
2-22 Slave Dances
2-23 Traditional African Dances

FASHION

2-24 Fashion Status
2-25 Purpose of Dressing
2-26 Textures and Types of Materials
2-27 Styles of Dressing
2-28 Hair Fashions
2-29 Finishing Touches for the Hair
2-30 Fashions and Church
2-31 Fashion Designers
2-32 Fashion Models
2-33 Spotlight: FUBU

SOCIAL AND CIVIC ORGANIZATIONS

2-34 Sororities
2-35 Fraternities

SECTION 2

CULTURAL TRADITIONS

The cultural contributions of African Americans have been powerful, personal, and profound. Like other racial, religious, and ethnic groups, African Americans have made their presence felt in fields ranging from science and industry to literature and the arts. From African-influenced sculptures to rap and hip-hop music, from all-black cowboy movies to award-winning modern novels, nothing could be more diverse than their contributions. African traditions of storytelling and oral history endured under the yoke of enslavement. Slave carpenters and quilters, metalworkers, potters and basket weavers created objects that were beautiful as well as useful. In the unrelenting labor of the fields, African Americans sang out with hollers, work chants, and spirituals to begin a heritage of creativity that has helped define American music to this day.

In the midst of injustices of racial, social, and economic exploitation, African Americans forged and nurtured a culture of folktales, proverbs, aphorisms, verbal games, and narrative oral poems. This diverse and vibrant culture has been handed down from one generation to the next. Drawings, paintings, and patches of oral history depict the rich folklore that provided the only entertainment and means of self-expression for early generations of African Americans.

Today, African American musicians, filmmakers, poets, dancers, playwrights, novelists, and artists continue to share their talents which influence the culture, not only of the United States, but of the world. African American culture is as diverse as the people it encompasses, making it a challenge to capture its essence. In Section 2 we focus selectively on some of the traditional ways of life that African Americans express. In this section we will highlight customs related to family structures, beliefs, music, dance, fashions, and food.

FAMILIES

List 2-1. Family Demographics

- 8.5 million African American families in the U.S. in 1997
- 46 percent of families were married couples
- Family size was 3.42 persons
- 6 out of 10 families had children under age 18
- 36 percent of those children lived with both parents
- Median family income in 1998 was $28,602
- 26 percent had incomes below the poverty level

List 2-2. Family Structures

- Extended family (temporary or long-term residence)
    - Immediate relatives
    - Distant relatives
    - Unofficially adopted persons (play mother, brothers, etc.)
    - Unrelated persons (Foster Care)
    - Adopted persons
- Blended families
- Married couples (with and without children)

- Single-parent families (male and female headed)
- Common law
- Shared residence without marriage
- Single-person households

List 2-3. Family Life

- Belief in a Supreme Being
- Church and Sunday School are central
- Values and discipline based on religious tenets
- Religious leaders are held in high regard in the family
- Respect for elders and their care
- Family members eat together regularly
- Hospitality extended to visitors at all times
- Husband and wife roles vary
- Display manners and respect in public
- Remove hats while inside
- Ask to be excused from the table
- Remain quiet when elders are speaking
- Preparing children for appropriate sex, age, and social roles
- Parent-child bond centered on unconditional expression of love
- Extended family support
- Providing a sense of well-being
- Strong work ethic
- Inculcating a sense of cultural history
- Respect for the law
- Sharing resources with family
- Shared responsibility
- Generally close family relationships
- Maintain close family ties
- Teach children strategies for survival

SUPERSTITIONS

List 2-4. Bad Luck

- Spilling of salt
- Walking under a ladder
- Step on a crack, break your mother's back
- Breaking a mirror (seven years' bad luck)
- Left eye itching
- Black cat crossing your path
- Getting out of bed on the wrong (left) side
- Rooster crowing at your window
- A woman entering your house first on Monday
- A blister on your tongue means you have told a lie

List 2-5. Good Fortune

- A man being first to visit on Christmas, New Year's
- Finding a four-leaf clover
- A spider descending a web signals that company is coming
- Right palm itching (money coming your way)
- Left palm itching (letter coming your way)
- Right eye itching
- Break longer end from wishbone of chicken
- Rabbit's foot
- Spitting on your hand and rubbing it
- Being born as the seventh child
- The sun shining while it is raining (the devil is beating his wife)

LANGUAGE

List 2-6. Proverbs in African American Culture

- You can fool some of the people some of the time, but you can't fool all of the people all of the time.
- You shall reap what you sow.
- A rolling stone gathers no moss.
- Seeing is believing.
- You can run but you can't hide.
- That's like the pot calling the kettle black.
- A bird in the hand is worth two in the bush.
- You can drive a horse to water, but you can't make him drink.
- Don't put all your eggs in one basket.
- Let sleeping dogs lie.
- A leopard can't change his spots.
- A stitch in time saves nine.
- You make your bed, you have to lie in it.
- Charity begins at home.
- It's like the blind leading the blind.
- Hoe your row.
- Beauty is only skin deep, but ugly is to the bone.
- You don't miss your water 'til your well runs dry.
- Don't burn your bridges behind you.
- The grass ain't greener on the other side.
- Everything that glitters ain't gold.
- Where there's a will, there's a way.
- Wear it like a loose garment.
- One monkey don't stop no show.
- One rotten apple spoils the barrel.
- We'll cross that bridge when we get to it.
- What goes around comes around.
- The fish wouldn't have gotten caught if it had kept its mouth closed.

- A slip of the lip will sink a ship.

- Don't buy a pig in a poke.

- Every goodbye ain't gone and every shut eye ain't sleep.

- If you lie down with dogs, you get up with fleas.

- Still water runs deep.

- Sticks and stones may break your bones but words will never hurt you.

- Pretty is as pretty does.

- Actions speak louder than words.

- A hard head makes a soft behind.

- An idle mind is the devil's workshop.

List 2-7. Languages of Black Races (Native and Foreign)

Acholi	English	Kanuti	Luo	Portuguese
Afsikaan	Ewe	Khoisan	Madi	Rwanda
Akan	French	Kiswahili	Malinka	Sango
Arabic	Fulani	Kongo	Mande	Swahili
Bambara	Gambai	Krio	Mangbetu	Tswana
Bantu	Gbaya	Kwa	Masai	Twi
Bari	Gullah	Lango	Mende	Wolof
Cajun	Hausa	Lendu	Mossi	Xhosa
Dinka	Hindi	Lingala	Nandi	Yoruba
Dyula	Ibo	Lugbara	Nubian	Zulu

List 2-8. Styles of Languages

- BeBop
- Black Dialect
- Black English Vernacular (BEV)
- Black Language
- Black Semantics
- Creole
- Dozens
- Ebonics

- English
- Hip Hop
- Jive
- Numerics
- Pig Latin/Language
- Prison Slang
- Rap
- Slang

List 2-9. Slang in the 1990s

Slang	Meaning
Style'n, Flex'n	Showing off material possessions
Jock'n	Want to be like somebody else
Loot, Cheese, Doe, A Rack, Cake, Bonz, Papers	Money
Dinky Honeys	DKNY clothing
Push'n	Driving a car
That's wack	Something bad
You look'n smooth	Well dressed or groomed
You're off the hook	A person out of control
You be swell'n	Telling untruths
You tripping	Not focused, off task
Phat	Nice body, someone very attractive
Go ahead	Leave a person alone
Chill'n	Being calm, cool
You be blowing me	A way to confuse someone
What's up!	A form of greeting someone
What's up with you!	How are you
Beefing	Intimidating someone
Cranking	Loud sound
Fresh feet	New shoes
Lunch'n	Someone not paying attention; joking
Off the meter	Bad hairdo
I got your back	Protecting someone
Shaming	Being stingy
Player hate'n	Criticizing someone, especially a successful guy who is a rapper or hip-hop performer
They deep	Many people together
For real	A true or clear statement
Ace Boon Coon	Best Friend
All that	Excellent, fantastic
All that and then some	Better than "all that"
Bad	Good

Bag	Preference
Beaucoup	Lot of something
My bad	I made a mistake
Kicking it	Having a good time
Blood	Person of African descent
Break	Run or get away
Bro	African American male
Def	Great, excellent
Dis	Put someone down
Front	Pretend
Game	A story or rap
Hood	Neighborhood
Ice	Bold, super cool
In the house	Presence of someone
Miss Thang	Arrogant woman
Partner	Close friend or associate
Posse	Associates
Scared-a-you	Celebrating someone's achievement
Sistah	African American Woman

CELEBRATIONS AND HOLIDAYS

List 2-10. Church-Related Celebrations

- Children and Youth Days
- Sunday School Convention and Youth Conference
- Graduation and Promotion
- Deacon/Deaconess Day
- Groundbreaking
- Cornerstone Laying and Mortgage Burning
- Church Building Dedication
- Baptism
- Church Picnic
- Christening
- Choir Anniversary
- Black History Celebration
- Homecoming and Family Reunion
- Mother's Day
- Father's Day
- Men's Day
- Women's Day
- Pastor's Appreciation Day
- Officer's Rededication Day
- Board Auxiliary Day

List 2-11. African American Celebrations/Holidays

- Martin Luther King's Birthday (third Monday in January)
- Kuumba (January 31)
- Black History Month (February)
- Malcolm X Day (May 19)
- African Liberation Day (May 25)
- Ancestor Honor Day (Last Saturday in May)

- Juneteenth (June 19)
- Marcus Garvey Birthday (August 17)
- Umoja Karamu (fourth Sunday in November)
- Kwanzaa (December 26 - January 1)

Kwanzaa

List 2-12. African American Festivals

- Kunta Kinte Heritage Festival
- Annual Harambee Carnival
- Caribbean American Family Day Festival
- Festival Noir
- Indiana Black Expo
- Black Student Reunion
- Black Beach Week
- Greek Fest
- FreakNik
- Black Bike Week

FUNERAL PRACTICES

List 2-13. Funeral Rituals

- Body preparation
- *Slumber room:* after the body is prepared, the deceased is reposed in a casket for viewing
- *Viewing of the body:* body of the deceased displayed (at the home, funeral home, or church)
- *Wake:* period of time in which a family sits with the body to receive visitors
- *Funeral service:* a service of worship held at a church, mortuary chapel, or at the grave site
- *Cremation:* to burn a dead body
- *Repast:* meal often served after the burial services

List 2-14. Funeral Customs of Specific Regions (Past and Present)

- *New Orleans, Louisiana:* funerals are celebrations with music and dancing
- *South:* graves decorated with personal belongings of the deceased to symbolize freedom
- *Symbols at the home:* wreaths or flowers placed on the door of the home of the deceased to indicate mourning
- *Funeral procession:* the body of the deceased driven past the family home en route to the cemetery so the body can "come home one last time"

List 2-15. Burials

- Above the ground in tombs or mausoleums
- Stacked graves—two adult caskets buried in one funeral plot
- Caskets of three babies may be buried in one adult plot
- Buried in east (feet)-west (head) direction; person not buried "crossways of the world"

List 2-16. Locations of Cemeteries

- Church grounds
- Family plots: a family purchases land area for the purpose of burying family members
- City/county land areas in which grave sites are provided by the city/county
- Private land areas in which a family may buy a grave site

List 2-17. Selected Historic Cemeteries

- African-American Burial Ground, Higgs Beach, Key West, Florida
- African Burying Ground, New York, New York
- African Jackson Cemetery, Piqua, Ohio
- Beulah Cemetery, Vicksburg, Mississippi
- Colored Cemetery (Porterdale), Columbus, Georgia
- Daufuskie Island Historic District, Hilton Head, South Carolina
- Estate Nisky, Charlotte Amalie, St. Thomas, Virgin Islands
- Girard Colored Mission, Columbus, Georgia
- Golden West Cemetery, Port Gibson, Michigan
- Gower Cemetery, Edmond, Oklahoma
- Lewes Historic District, Lewes, Delaware
- Magnolia Cemetery (including Mobile National Cemetery), Mobile, Alabama
- Natchez National Cemetery, Natchez, Mississippi
- New Hope Missionary Baptist Church Cemetery, Lake Village, Arkansas
- Number One, Basin Street, New Orleans, Louisiana
- Odd Fellows Cemetery, Starkville, Michigan
- Odessa History District, Odessa, Delaware
- Rest Hill Cemetery, Lebanon, Tennessee
- Stanton Family Cemetery, Diana Mills, Virginia
- St. Louis Cemetery, Zion Cemetery, Memphis, Tennessee

MUSIC

List 2-18. Freedom Songs

- "We Shall Overcome"
- "We Are Soldiers"
- "I'm Gonna Sit at the Welcome Table"
- "How Did You Feel?"
- "Everybody Sing Freedom"
- "We Shall Not Be Moved"
- "This Little Light of Mine"
- "You'd Better Leave Segregation Alone"
- "Dogs, Dogs"
- "I Know (We'll Meet Again)"
- "Which Side Are You On?"
- "Freedom's Comin' and It Won't Be Long"
- "If You Miss Me from the Back of the Bus"
- "Buses Are A-Comin' Oh Yes"
- "Ain't Gonna Let Nobody Turn Me 'Round"
- "Sing Till the Power of the Lord Comes Down"
- "Come and Go With Me to the Land"
- "Certainly, Lord"
- "I'm on My Way to the Freedom Land"
- "I'm So Glad"
- "Oh Freedom"
- "Over My Head"
- "Walkin' for Freedom Just Like John"
- "Woke Up This Morning With My Mind on Freedom"
- "Fighting for My Rights"
- "Been Down into the South"
- "We'll Never Turn Back"
- "The Hammer Song"
- "Guide My Feet While I Run This Race"

- "Bull Connor's Jail"
- "Ballad for Bill Moore"
- "Ninety-Nine and a Half Won't Do"
- "Keep Your Eyes on the Prize"
- "Pick a Bale of Cotton"
- "Cotton-Eyed Joe"
- "Freedom Train"

List 2-19. Styles of Music

Ballads	Funk	Rhythm and Blues
Black Minstrel	Gospel	Rock
Blues	Hip Hop	Rock and Pop
Blues, Rock, Pop	Jazz	Rock and Rap
Boogie Woogie	Opera	Rock and Roll
Classical Soul	Play Songs	Soul
Disco	Ragtime	Spiritual
Folk	Rap	Work Song

Note: Additional musical contributions are in Section 8, Arts, Letters, and Media.

List 2-20. Alternative Instruments

- Patting knees
- Arm movement
- Back
- Head
- Hand clapping
- Clinking spoons
- Saw

- Playing the bones (flatsticks)
- Line singing
- Coastal drums
- Ban jar
- Fiddle
- Violin
- Washboard

DANCE

List 2-21. Popular Dances

Ballin' the Jack	Dog	Madison
Big Apple	Eagle Rock	Pony
Black Bottom	Electric Slide	Ranky Tank
Boogie Woogie	Football	Shag
Booty Call	Hand Dancing	Shim Sham
Breakdancing	Hussle	Shuffle
Bump	Jerk	Snake Hips
Continental	Jitterbug	Susie Q
Coonshine	Limbo	Turkey Trot
		Twist

List 2-22. Slave Dances

- Buck-and-wing . . . also called the pigeon wing
- Irish jig . . . contest with slaves of other masters
- Cakewalk . . . couples walked on a straight path with sharp, precise turns
- Ring dance . . . slaves danced individually in a shuffle that vibrated the entire body
- Buzzard lope . . . animal dance representing the behavior of a turkey buzzard chasing a hen
- Water dance . . . performed while carrying a bucket or glass of water on the head
- Djouba . . . secular dance with clapping, and slapping one's chest, thighs, or legs
- Figure dance
- Sixteen-figure dance

List 2-23. Traditional African Dances

- Calenda . . . performed by several couples circling one another
- Chica . . . rotation of hips while the rest of the body was immobile
- Bamboula . . . performed by a couple inside a ring
- Juba . . . female competitive dance

FASHION

List 2-24. Fashion Status

- African-American contributions were largely ignored

- Fashions revealed continuity with African roots

- From emancipation to the late 1950s, fashions mimicked white fashions

- Influences in dress, hairstyles, fabrics, and accessories were evident in the 1960s

- Casual dress was the order of the day during the 1970s

- In the 1980s, blacks' style of dressing was typical of the period; African attire was worn for special occasions

- Early black designers were not acknowledged in advertisements or on labels

- Lois Alexander opened the Harlem Institute of Fashion (HIF) in 1966

- African-American contributions emerged from the shadows with HIF

- HIF provided the avenue for young blacks to develop and market their talents

- The Black Fashion Museum was established in 1979 by the HIF and located in Harlem; the museum houses over 200 years of fashions contributed by African Americans to the fashion world

- The collection at the museum includes authentic slave dresses, replicas of garments from significant historical events, costumes, fashions, and accessories

- Sean "Puffy" Combs is first balck designer nominated to receive the Perry Ellis Award for menswear in 2000.

List 2-25. Purpose of Dressing

- Status or prestige

- An expression of personal esteem

- Reflected role or standing in group

- Styles of dress distinctly reflected the occasion (everyday, ceremonial, etc.)

- Texture and color of materials distinguished one group from another

- Patterns of dress differed among men, women, and children

- Form of self-expression

- Protection

- Attention and approval of others

- Sexual attraction

List 2-26. Textures and Types of Materials

- Dyed fabrics, tie dye, batik
- Bright colors (blue, red, gold)
- Woven patterns in fabrics
- Ornamentation of garments/applique/embroidery
- Diversity in use of fabrics (from bark cloth to silk)
- Tanning (turning animal skins into leather)
- Silversmithing (jewelry)
- Wood carving and printing (wood patterns, inked and stamped on cloth)

List 2-27. Styles of Dressing

- Body/personal adornment (body paints, makeup, tattooing, body sculpting)
- Jewelry (beads, anklets, shells reflected a special message)
- Colors expressed meaningful messages in various tribes
- Women wore red as a sign of fertility in some groups
- Blue was used as part of ceremonial dress
- Africans lured to slave ships by the promise of red cloth and jewelry
- Headdresses and headgear date back to fifteenth-century Africa
- Elaborate hair designs
- Modesty in dress designs (sleeves, longer hemlines)

List 2-28. Hair Fashions

- Bantu knots
- Braiding (microbraids)
- Afro/Natural (unrelaxed hair)
- Dreadlocs (locs, African locs, Nubian locs)
- Twists (straw curl, flat twists)
- Corkscrews
- Fades (high top, wedge, philly, gombie)
- Weaves

- Wigs
- Cornrows
- Conk (process)
- Jheri Curl
- Straightened hair (hot combed)
- Chemical relaxers
- Texturized hair
- Hair wrapping
- Designs in hair
- Fusion

List 2-29. Finishing Touches for the Hair

- Jewelry in hair
- Clips
- Decorative combs
- Hair beads
- Do rags
- Afro pick
- Barrettes
- Ribbons
- Hats/headgear
- Scarves

List 2-30. Fashions and Church

- Church is viewed as the center of religious and social activities
- Clothing shows respect for the Church and the Deity it serves
- Leaders wear distinctive clothing, often robes in varying styles
- Robes are generally in vibrant colors to distinguish leaders from others
- Designated clothing for special events
- Uniforms—ushering
- White gloves—Communion
- Gowns (usually white)—Baptism
- White garments—christening/dedications
- Robes—pastors, choir
- Coordinated clothing or colors for various auxiliary groups
- Go "dressed up" in "Sunday best" for Church; Sunday go-to-meeting clothes
- Wearing hats symbolized reverence

List 2-31. Fashion Designers

Men Designers

Frederic Jones—millinery

FUBU—full clothing line

Jeffrey Banks—men's wear

Scott Barrie—women's wear

Stephen Burrows—women's wear, furs, lingerie, McCalls patterns

Otis Caver—women's wear

James McQuay—furriery

Howard Davis—shoes

Milton Farquhar—accessory handbags

Milton Ford—metallic knit outfits

Jon Haggins—versatile apparel

Everett Hall—men's and women's wear

Bernard Johnson—Broadway costumes

Anthony Walker—fabric design

Willi Smith—Willi Wear Ltd. and Willi Wear Men

James Moore—outerwear, shoes

Albert Grey and Debra Ward—women's wear

Skaka King—men's wear

Scott Rankins—"own" shoe line

Karl Kani—urban sportswear

Tomi Smalls—shirt design

Gordon Henderson—apparel, hats

Wesley Tann—versatile apparel

Ed Austin—investment clothing

Russell Simmons—Phat Fashions, LLC

Women Designers

Sandy Baker—jewelry

Mildred Blount—millinery

Cassandra Bromfield—bridal gowns

Mary Lou Chandler—sample maker

Valerie Chisholm—children and adult apparel

Rowena Mays—millinery

Sydney DeLairre—knitwear

Myra Riguard Everett—women's wear

Therez Fleetwood—Afro-centric bridal wear

Belinda Hughes—evening wear and sportswear

Judi Jordan—sportswear

LaVetta—special occasions outerwear

Teresa Mays Jackson—millinery and gloves

Louvenia Price—dress design

Ann Lowe—women's wear

Emily Miles—millinery

Marva Louis—women's wear

Elizabeth Keckley—women's wear (for Mary Todd Lincoln)

Hazel Washington—leathercraft

Ruth West—Hollywood costumes

Lynette Williams—women's rainwear

Veronica Jones—women's contemporary

Constance Saunders—women's wear

List 2-32. Fashion Models

Karen Alexander	Grace Jones
Sheila Anderson	Magic Jordan
Tyra Banks	Kiara Kabukuru
Shari Belafonte	Khadiji
Billie Blair	Emily Miles
Naomi Campbell	Gail O'Neil
Alva Chinn	Daphne Maxwell Reid
Pat Cleveland	Rosalind
Norma Jean Darden	Ramona Saunders
Charlene Dash	Lu Sierra
Ophelia DeVore	Naomi Sims
Pat Evans	Barbara Smith
Anna Getaneh	Tony Tomba
Behann Hardison	Dorothea Towles
Sara Lou Harris	Madame C. J. Walker
Iman	Amina Warsuma
Barbara Jackson	Veronica Webb
Beverly Johnson	Alek Wek
Sheila Johnson	Helen Williams

List 2-33. Spotlight: FUBU

➢ From rags to riches, from selling hats on the street corner to running almost a half billion-dollar business is the story of FUBU.

➢ FUBU means "For Us By Us." It is a rapidly expanding global fashion empire.

➢ Four 29-year-old African American men—Damon John, J. Alexander Martin, Keith Perrin, and Carl Brown—founded FUBU.

➢ The company started in 1992 with selling tie-top hats on the street, at concerts, and sporting events.

➢ The hats were well received. To improve sales the four men created the name FUBU and imprinted it on the hats; later, additional garments were added to the line.

➢ A neighborhood friend wore their garments on a photo shoot and the line attracted a lot of attention.

➢ The group attended a Las Vegas trade show in 1993 to market the line and received their first large orders, $300,000.

➢ FUBU has diversified its clothing lines and now include: racing jackets, denim jeans, loungewear, footwear, formal wear, and eyewear. New lines are planned for perfume and NBA sports apparel.

➢ FUBU was the first African American designer with its own display window at Macy's in 1996.

➢ The corporate headquarters moved from the first floor of a personal residence to the 66th floor of the Empire State Building.

➢ The young entrepreneurs have already created a foundation to give money back to the community through grants to nonprofit organizations.

➢ FUBU clothing has wide appeal and is carried in major department stores (e.g., Bloomingdales, Dillards, Macy's) and specialty stores (e.g., Footlocker); establishing independent retail stores.

74   *Section 2   Cultural Traditions*

SOCIAL AND CIVIC ORGANIZATIONS

List 2-34. Sororities

- Alpha Kappa Alpha Sorority, 1908
- Alpha Pi Chi Sorority, 1963
- Chi Eta Phi Sorority, Inc., 1932
- Delta Sigma Theta Sorority, Inc., 1913
- Eta Phi Beta Sorority, Inc., 1943
- Iota Phi Lambda Sorority, Inc., 1929
- Lambda Kappa Mu Sorority, Inc., no date
- Sigma Gamma Rho Sorority, Inc., 1922
- Zeta Delta Phi Sorority, Inc., no date
- Zeta Phi Beta Sorority, Inc., 1920

List 2-35. Fraternities

- Alpha Phi Alpha Fraternity, Inc., 1906
- Groove Phi Groove Social Fellowship, Inc., no date
- Iota Phi Theta Fraternity, Inc., no date
- Kappa Alpha Psi Fraternity, Inc., 1911
- Omega Psi Phi Fraternity, 1914
- Phi Beta Sigma Fraternity, 1914

CHILDREN'S GAMES

List 2-36. Games

- All Hide
- Jump Rope
- Double Dutch
- Hambone
- Drop the Handkerchief
- Hide and Go Seek Rhyming
- Hopscotch
- Hula Hoops
- Skip to My Lou
- Go In and Out the Window
- Miss Lucy
- Simon Says

- London Bridge
- Punchinello
- Little Sally Walker
- Green Apple Tree
- Patty Cake
- Go to Sleep Little Baby
- This Little Piggy
- Ride, Charley, Ride
- Finger Name
- Head and Shoulder
- Way Down Yonder in the Brickyard

STORYTELLING

List 2-37. Animal Tales and Fables

- *Br'er Rabbit and the Briar Patch* by Annie Reid
- *Brer Tiger and the Big Wind* by William J. Faulkner
- *Don't Play With Your Supper* by Kwasi Asare
- *How Trouble Made the Monkey Eat Pepper* by Rita Cox
- *Rooster and Roach* by Ramona Bass
- *Uglier Than a Grinning Buzzard* by Louise Anderson

List 2-38. History Remembered Stories

- *Harriet Tubman Is in My Blood* by Mariline Wilkins
- *How We Got Over* by Jack and Rosa Maddox
- *A Pioneer's Story of Long Creek* by Gunyana-Naomi Clarke
- *Solitary Confinement* by Winnie Mandela
- *Vietnam Blues* by Haywood T. "The Kid" Kirkland
- *The Violence of Desperate Men* by Martin Luther King, Jr.

List 2-39. Tales of Ghosts and Witches

- *Big Fear and Little Fear* by Arthur H. Fouset
- *The Boogah Man* by Paul L. Dunbar
- *Daddy and the Plat-Eye Ghost* by Eleanora E. Tate
- *The Devil's Dulcimer* by Janice Harrington
- *The Two Sons* by Alice McGill
- *The Ways of a Witch* by William J. Faulkner

List 2-40. Humorous Tales and Anecdotes

- *Cindy Ellie—A Modern Fairy Tale* by Mary C. Smith
- *February* by Dick Gregory
- *Jack and de Devil* by Zora N. Hurston
- *Liberated* by J. California Cooper
- *The Lying Bee* by John H. Clarke
- *Two Kind of Women* by Tejumola F. Ologboni

List 2-41. Raps, Rhythms, and Rhymes

- *African American History Raps* by Sharon J. Holley
- *The Ballad of Joe Meek* by Sterling Brown
- *De Wedding* by Paul Keens-Douglas
- *Get Ready, Inc.* by Douglas "Jacka" Henderson
- *The Party* by Paul L. Dunbar
- *Signifyin' Monkey* by Oscar Brown, Jr.
- *Weekend Glory* by Maya Angelou

List 2-42. Sermons

- *The Creation* by James Weldon Johnson
- *Ezekiel and the Vision of Dry Bones* by Carl J. Anderson
- *The Prodigal Son* by C. L. Franklin

FOOD AND AFRICAN AMERICAN CULTURE

List 2-43. Desserts

- Sweet potato pie
- Pecan pie
- Peach skillet pie
- Apple pie
- Bread pudding
- Rice pudding
- Pound cake
- Banana pudding
- Watermelon
- Tea cakes
- Johnny cakes
- Egg custard
- Apple betty
- Fried pies
- Molasses pie
- Sweet potato pone
- Ashcake
- Cobblers

List 2-44. Meats and Main Dishes

- Hog head souse
- Scrapple
- Ham hocks
- Ribs
- Ham
- Fried catfish
- Ox tail
- Pig's feet (tomato sauce, bar-b-que, pickled)

- Neck bones
- Pot roast
- Steak and gravy
- Chicken (Southern fried, smothered)
- Smothered pork chops
- Macaroni and cheese
- Red beans and rice
- Chitterlings
- Chicken and dumplings

List 2-45. Vegetables

- Greens (collards, turnips, kale, rape, mustard, cabbage)
- Black-eyed peas
- Fried corn
- Okra
- Hominy corn

- Corn pudding
- Candied yams
- Hoppin' John
- Smothered cabbage
- Gumbo
- Succotash

List 2-46. Side Dishes

- Crackling bread
- Chow-Chow
- Spoon bread
- Hominy grits
- Hoecake
- Red-eye gravy

- Fritters
- Biscuits
- Corn bread
- Grits
- Corn bread dressing

List 2-47. Spotlight: MS. B. SMITH

➤ Television personality, fashion model, restaurateur, and author

➤ Host of "B. Smith w/Style" (half-hour nationally syndicated television series)

➤ First African American woman to grace the cover of *Mademoiselle* as well as *Essence* and *Ebony* covers

➤ Created a new lifestyle magazine titled *B. Smith Style Magazine*

➤ Recognized as one of America's "10 most outstanding nonprofessional chefs"

➤ First African American woman elected to the Board of Trustees of the prestigious Culinary Institute of America

➤ Author of *B. Smith's Entertaining and Cooking for Friends* and *B. Smith: Rituals and Celebrations*

➤ Founding partner of three B. Smith restaurants in New York City, Washington, D.C., and Long Island, New York

➤ Founding Board member of the Times Square Business Improvement District

➤ Board member of New York Women's Foundation and the Feminist Press, Metro-Manhattan Chapter of Links, the Screen Actors Guild, Equity, and AFTRA

➤ Modeling career included such clients as Revlon, Clairol, Noxzema, Hertz, Excedrin, Crest, and Oil of Olay

➤ Appeared as a product spokesperson for over 100 radio, print, and television advertisements

➤ First name is Barbara

NAMES AND TITLES USED TO DESCRIBE AFRICAN AMERICANS

List 2-48. Names and Titles*

- Slave
- Colored
- Negro
- Afro-American
- Afra-American
- Disadvantaged
- Black
- Person of Color
- African American
- Disenfranchised
- Culturally Different

* Not inclusive of derogatory references to African Americans

AFRICAN AMERICAN OR AFROCENTRIC COLLECTIBLES

Deciphering Quality of Collectibles

Select one of the systems for classifying the quality and condition of collectibles such as the one presented by P. G. Gibbs in *Black Collectibles Sold in America* (Paducah, KY: Collector Books, 1987). Gibbs devised a 5-point scale for quality that ranges from handmade or manufactured (1) to signed or unsigned (5). The higher the number, the better the quality. The better the condition of the item, the more value it contains. The 3-point scale for condition or grade ranges from excellent condition (1) to poor (3).

List 2-49. Where to Look for Collectibles

- Family home
- Grandma's house
- Dealers
- Estate sales
- Yard sales
- Flea markets
- Junk shops
- Auctions
- Collectors
- Internet
- Specialty stores
- Ethnic vendors

List 2-50. Selected Categories of Collectibles

Art and Literature

- Paintings
- Wall hangings
- Books
- Wood carvings
- Slave writings
- Posters
- Children's books
- Sculptures

Ephemera/Paper Collectibles

- Newspapers
- Political cartoons
- Stamps
- Photographs
- Post cards
- Bills of sale
- Contracts
- Wills
- Court orders
- Magazines
- Advertising labels

Kitchen Collectibles

- Pottery, Porcelain
- Glass
- Jars
- Cookbooks

- Kitchen tools
- Bar ware
- Bottle openers
- Salt and pepper shakers

Furniture

- Clocks
- Andirons
- Doorstops
- Hitching posts
- Figurines

- Wall plaques
- Tobacco humidors
- Ashtrays
- Quilts and other needlecrafts
- Basketry items

Toys

- Banks
- Board games
- Card games
- Dancing figures
- Dolls

- Mechanical games
- Pull toys
- Puppets
- Puzzles
- Tin/Cast-iron toys

Other Categories

- Blacksmith items
- Graveyard decorations
- Jewelry
- Lawn items
- Military (Buffalo Soldiers; Negro Soldiers; Cowboys)
- Motion pictures
- Music and dance memorabilia
- Musical instruments
- Sports memorabilia

MISS BLACK AMERICA (1969-1996)

List 2-51. The Winners

Year	Winner	State
1968	Sandy Williams	Pennsylvania
1969	G. O. Smith	New York
1970	Stephanie Clark	District of Columbia
1971	Joyce Warner	Florida
1972	Linda Barney	New Jersey
1973	Arnice Russell	New York
1974	Von Gretchen Sheppard	California
1975	Helen Ford	Mississippi
1976	Twanna Kilgore	District of Columbia
1977	Claire Ford	Tennessee
1978	Lydia Jackson	New Jersey
1979	Verette Shankle	Mississippi
1980	Sharon Wright	Illinois
1981	Pamela Jenks	Massachusetts
1982	Phyllis Tucker	Florida
1983	Sonia Robinson	Wisconsin
1984	Lydia Garrett	South Carolina
1985	Amina Fakir	Michigan
1986	Rachael Oliver	Massachusetts
1987	Leila McBride	Colorado
1988	No award	
1989	Paula Swynn	District of Columbia
1990	Rosie Jones	Connecticut
1991	Sharmelle Sullivan	Indiana
1992	Marilyn De Shields	Colorado
1993	Pilar Ginger Fort	not available
1994	Karen Wallace	not available
1995	Asharo Ahmed	not available
1996	Busheerah Ahmad	Oklahoma

MISS AMERICA

List 2-52. The African American Winners

1970   Cheryl Brown, Miss Iowa, first African American contestant

1984   Vanessa Williams, first African American Miss America; resigned and was succeeded by Suzette Charles, also an African American

1990   Debbye Turner

1991   Marjorie Vincent

1994   Kimberly Aiken

Section 3

EDUCATION

SECTION 3

EDUCATION

"That all and every person and persons whatsoever, who shall hereafter teach, or cause any slave or slaves to be taught or write, or shall use or employ any slave as a scribe in any manner of writing whatsoever, hereafter taught to write; every such person or persons shall, for every offense, forfeit the sum of one hundred pounds current money."

South Carolina law, 1740
(Berry & Blassingame, 1982)

This is the context from which the educational endeavors of African Americans have evolved. As the country moved toward freedom, African Americans recognized the need for education. Despite the early struggles, their determination to become educated forged a rich and proud history.

The 1998 U.S. Census update revealed that the high school completion gap between African Americans and whites had decreased, with present scores indicating no significant difference. Eighty-eight percent of African Americans, ages 25-29, were high school graduates, according to the 1998 census. The number of African Americans under age 35 enrolled in college in 1996 was nearly 40 percent higher than the number enrolled a decade earlier, and nearly 3 million African Americans age 25 or older held a bachelor's degree or higher. Of these degree holders, approximately 25 percent had advanced degrees. Predominately and historically black institutions played a major part in the educational process of African Americans.

The last twenty years brought about a resurgence of segregated K-12 schools. This resurgence occurred partially as a result of the release of court orders requiring integration and the initiation of selected educational opportunities by the African American community. Many parents and educators preferred to offer curricula that addressed the culture of the African American child. These "new segregation" efforts designed by parents and educators incorporated the educational, cultural, social, and emotional needs of the African American student into the educational process.

Section 3 highlights noted educators and pioneers; list the legal cases and policies that most influenced school desegregation efforts; identifies predominately and historically black colleges and universities (HBCUs); and presents information on scholarships, award programs, organizations, and publications.

FIRSTS IN EDUCATION

List 3-1. Firsts in Education

1787   African Free School (New York, New York)

1804   Lemuel Haynes, honorary degree

1823   Alexander L. Twilight, male graduate from college

1829   St. Francis Academy, boarding school for girls

1833   Oberlin College (Ohio), college to educate African Americans

1839   Cheyney State College (Pennsylvania), oldest black college

1847   James McCune Smith, obtained a medical degree

1849   Charles Reason, faculty member on a white campus

1850   Lucy Ann Stanton, graduate of two-year ladies course

1852   Grace Mapps, graduate of four-year college

1854   Lincoln University (Pennsylvania), incorporated as Ashmun Institute

1856   Wilberforce University (Ohio), administered by African Americans; awarded first baccalaureate degree

1858   Berea College (Kentucky), designated to educate African Americans and whites together

1863   Daniel A. Payne, president of an African American college

1867   Howard University (Washington, D.C.), first undergraduate, graduate and professional schools

1868   Howard University, law school established

1869   Fannie Jackson (Coppin), head of major educational institution, Institute for Colored Youth

1870   Snowden School (Virginia), state school

1871   Alcorn A&M College (Mississippi), land grant university

1872   James H. Conyers, appointed to Naval Academy

1874   Patrick Francis Healy, president of predominately white Catholic university

1874   Edward A. Bouchet, doctorate from an American university

1874   Alabama State University, state-supported institute for teachers

1876   Meharry Medical College (Tennessee), medical school established

1877   George Washington Henderson, elected to Phi Beta Kappa

1877   Henry O. Flipper, graduate of West Point

1879   Mary E. Mahoney, graduate nurse

1881   Spelman College (Georgia), institute of higher learning for women

1925   Xavier College (Louisiana), Catholic college

1925   North Carolina Central University, state-supported liberal arts college

1929   Atlanta University System, college consortium

1945   Tuskegee Institute (Alabama), school of veterinary medicine

1949   Wesley A. Brown, graduate of the U.S. Naval Academy

1970   Hugh S. Scott, superintendent of schools in Washington, D.C.

1976   Mary Frances Berry, chancellor of University of Colorado

1980   Mary Hatwood Futrell, president, National Educational Association

2000   The Quincy Jones Professorship at Harvard University was established by
         Time Warner Endowment. The chair is devoted to the study of African
         American Music and is first endowed professorship in African American
         studies given to any U.S. university by a corporation.

NOTED EDUCATORS

List 3-2. Noted Educators

Molefi Kete Asante	1942-	outstanding proponent of Afrocentric Education, director of the Center for Afro-American Studies at UCLA
Mary McLeod Bethune	1875-1955	founded the Daytona Normal & Industrial School (1904), which later became Bethune-Cookman College, Daytona Beach, FL
Nannie Helen Burroughs	1879-1961	founded the National Training School for Women and Girls
Jewell Plummer Cobb	1924-	president of California State University, Fullerton (1981-1990)
Johnnetta B. Cole	1936-	first woman president of Spelman College, Atlanta, GA (1987-1997)
Marva Collins	1936-	founded Westside Preparatory School, Chicago, IL (1975)

Samuel DuBois Cook   1925-   first African American to hold a profes-
                                       sorship at Duke University; president
                                       of Dillard University

James Comer   1934-   child psychiatrist who developed and
                                       implemented the Comer School
                                       Development Model, Yale Child Study
                                       Center, Yale University, New Haven,
                                       CT (1968)

Fanny Coppin   1837-1913   principal, women's department of the
                                       Institute for Colored Youth (1873);
                                       founded Women's Exchange & Girls'
                                       Home (1894)

Sarah Mapps Douglass   1806-1922   organized school for black children in
                                       Philadelphia, PA (1820s); appointed
                                       head of girls' department at the
                                       Institute for Colored Youth (1853-1877)

W.E.B. Du Bois

W.E.B. Du Bois   1868-1963   first black to receive Ph.D. from
                                       Harvard (1895); co-founded the
                                       American Negro Academy (1897);
                                       formed Niagara Movement (1905-1909)

John Hope Franklin	1915-	historian; first black president of the American Historical Association, Organization of American Historians, Southern Historian Association; recipient of the NAACP Spingarn Medal (1995); recipient of the Presidential Medal of Freedom (1995)
Mary Hatwood Futrell	1940-	first African American president of the National Education Association (1983-1989)
Henry Louis Gates, Jr.	1950-	W.E.B. Du Bois Professor of the Humanities and Chair of the Department of Afro-American Studies at Harvard (1991-present); prolific writer; co-author of *Encarta Africana* (1993) and *The Future of Our Race* (1996)
William Gray III	1941-	president and Chief Executive Officer of the United Negro College Fund (1991-present)
William Harvey	1941-	president, Hampton University; increased endowment from $29 million (1978) to $180 million (2000)
Patrick Francis Healy	1834-1910	first African American president of Georgetown University (1874-1882)
Charles Spurgeon Johnson	1893-1956	first African American president of Fisk University (1946-1956)
Alain Locke	1886-1954	first African American Rhodes Scholar (1907); wrote *The New Negro* (1925)
Samuel Proctor Massie, Jr.	1919-	first African American professor at the U.S. Naval Academy, Annapolis, MD (1966)
Benjamin E. Mays	1894-1984	president, Morehouse College (1940-1967)
Robert Russa Moton	1867-1940	second president of Tuskegee Institute (1916-1934)
Frederick Patterson	1901-1988	organized the United Negro College Fund (1994); received the Presidential Medal of Freedom (1987); recipient of the NAACP Spingarn Medal (1988)
Alvin F. Poussaint	1934-	clinical professor of Psychiatry at Harvard Medical School since 1969

Condoleeza Rice	1954-	professor and provost at Stanford University (1993-present); specialist in arms control and eastern European affairs
Arthur Schomburg	1874-1938	bibliophile and scholar after whom the Schomburg Center for Research in Black Culture was named (1972), world's leading research library on African Americans, established in 1925
Ruth Simmons	1946-	first African American to lead a Seven Sisters school, Smith College, Lawrenceville, NY (1995-present)
Mary Church Terrell	1863-1954	appointed to District of Columbia School Board (1895 and 1906); president, Bethel Literacy & Historical Association (1892-1893); member, Association for the Study of Negro Life & History (organized, 1915); charter member, NAACP (1901)
Booker T. Washington	1856-1915	established Tuskegee Institute, Tuskegee, AL (1881)
Robert Wedgeworth, Jr.	1937-	first African American to become executive director of the American Library Association (1972)
Cornel West	1953-	prolific writer and philosopher; author of *Race Matters* (1993) and *The Future of Our Race* (1996 with Henry Louis Gates, Jr.); professor of Afro-American Studies and Philosophy of Religion at Harvard University
Clifton R. Wharton, Jr.	1926-	first African American president of a predominantly white university, Michigan State University (1970-1978)
Carter G. Woodson	1875-1950	historian; "Father of Black History"; began Negro History Week (February 1926) and African-American Historical Association

List 3-3. Spotlight: BOOKER T. WASHINGTON

➤ Born a slave in Virginia in 1856; family moved to West Virginia in 1865

➤ Walked from West Virginia to Hampton, Virginia to attend Hampton Normal & Agricultural Institute (now Hampton University) in 1872

➤ Graduated from Hampton Normal & Agricultural Institute in 1876

➤ Taught in West Virginia for three years

➤ Attended Wayland Seminary

➤ Taught at Hampton Institute from 1879-1881

➤ Founded and became principal of Tuskegee Normal & Industrial Institute in Alabama (now Tuskegee University) in 1881

➤ Established National Negro Business League in 1892

➤ Spoke at the Cotton States Exposition in 1895 and made his famous "Compromise" speech, which encouraged blacks to secure their constitutional rights through vocational training and economic self-reliance rather than legal and political means

➤ Conciliatory position angered some blacks, notably W.E.B. Du Bois, who challenged Washington's leadership

➤ Movement set up to name Washington to a cabinet post; he declined and withdrew his name from consideration in 1896

➤ Served as an advisor to Presidents Theodore Roosevelt and William Taft

➤ First black to receive an honorary degree from Harvard University

➤ First black to dine at the White House; 1901

➤ Author of several books; among them are:

   The Future of the Negro (1899)

   Up From Slavery (1901, autobiography)

   Life of Frederick Douglass (1907)

   The Story of the Negro (1909)

➤ Died in Tuskegee, Alabama in 1915

CIVIL RIGHTS AND DESEGREGATION DEVELOPMENTS

List 3-4. Chronology of Major Desegregation Developments

1938   Supreme Court rules that Missouri cannot compel Lloyd L. Gaines to attend an out-of-state school

1939   NAACP initiates nine court cases claiming the right of African Americans to attend tax-supported colleges and universities in their home states

1948   Supreme Court (*Sipuel* v. *Oklahoma State Board of Education*) rules that states must provide equal access for "qualified students"

1948   The University of Arkansas opens its professional schools to black students

1950   Supreme Court rules that the University of Kentucky must allow students into graduate school

1950   Supreme Court rules that the University of Oklahoma cannot segregate a student within the school

1951   NAACP files suits to integrate elementary and secondary schools in Delaware, Kansas, South Carolina, Virginia, and Washington, D.C.

1952   Supreme Court agrees to hear cases initiated by the NAACP in 1951

1954   Supreme Court rules that segregation in public schools is unconstitutional

1954   Supreme Court rules that the University of Florida must admit black students

1954   Public school integration begins in Washington, D.C.

1955   Supreme Court orders all U.S. school boards to initiate desegregation plans

1975   NAACP files suit in federal court to force the U.S. government to impose the same desegregation measures in northern and western public schools that it does in southern public schools

1976   Supreme Court rules that private schools cannot deny admission solely on the basis of race

1978   Supreme Court finds that federal government is not liable for any costs associated with court-ordered busing to achieve public school desegregation

1978   Supreme Court states that the special admissions program favoring minority students at the University of California is unconstitutional (*Bakke* decision)

1982   Supreme Court rules to prohibit busing in Washington to achieve desegregation as unconstitutional

1983   Supreme Court determines that private schools practicing racial segregation or discrimination cannot be given tax exemptions

1993   Harvard study shows that 66% of African American students attend predominately minority schools

List 3-5. Key Dates in African American Education

1770	School established in Philadelphia, Pennsylvania by Anthony Benezet
1777	New Jersey begins an educational program

1787	African Free School opens, New York, New York
1788	New Jersey law mandates that slave owners teach slaves to read
1790	Special committee is appointed in Philadelphia to assure education of free slaves
1813	School building is erected in Philadelphia
1816	School is established for blacks taught by an African American teacher
1852	Georgia state legislature introduces bill to allow slaves to be educated
1855	Massachusetts abolishes segregated schools
1859	Ohio Supreme Court rules that children who are 3/8 African American cannot attend school with whites
1890	Blair Bill—legislation to reduce illiteracy by providing federal funds is defeated in Senate
1890	Morrill Act is amended to provide land grant funds for education where there are segregated schools
1915	Association for the Study of Negro Life and History is established
1940	Federal court in Virginia rules that black and white teachers must receive equal pay
1944	United Negro College Fund is founded
1954	Landmark education court case (*Brown* v. *Board of Education of Topeka*)
1964	Economic Opportunity Act is signed

1969   School districts must end racial segregation

1970   IRS cannot grant tax-exempt status to any new segregated private schools
         in Mississippi

1971   Ford Foundation creates a $100-million, six-year program of scholarships
         for black private colleges

1972   Moratorium on all court-imposed busing until July 1973

1976   Televised program "Parade of Stars," fundraiser for United Negro College
         Fund (UNCF) initiated

1980   March on Washington by students

1990   Walter Annenberg pledges $50 million to UNCF

1992   Spelman College (Georgia) receives a single gift of $37 million

List 3-6. Civil Rights and Desegregation Policies

1954   *Brown* v. *Board of Education*

1957   Civil Rights Act of 1957

1960   Civil Rights Act of 1960

1961   Executive Order 10925—Committee on Equal Employment Opportunity
         (EEO)

1962   Executive Order 11083—Committee on Equal Opportunity and Housing

1963   Equal Pay Act of 1963—prohibits discrimination in pay

1964   Title VI of the Civil Rights Act of 1964—prohibits discrimination under any
         program or activity receiving federal financial assistance

1965   Voting Rights Act

1965   Executive Order 11246—nondiscrimination clause in federal contracts

1968   Kerner Commission on Civil Disorders

1969   Executive Order 11458—desegregation to occur with "all deliberate speed"

1972   Equal Employment Opportunity Act of 1972—extends Title VII's clause to
         cover educational institutions

1972   Title IX of the Education Amendments of 1972—no person shall be
         excluded from participation in, denied benefits of, or be subjected to dis-
         crimination under any educational program or agency receiving federal
         funds

1974   Equal Education Opportunity Act

1982   Supreme Court let stand interdistrict transition of students

List 3-7. Prominent U.S. Supreme Court Cases

1896   *Plessy* v. *Ferguson*

1948   *Sipuel* v. *Board of Regents*

1950   *Sweatt* v. *Painter*

1954   *Brown* v. *Board of Education of Topeka I*

1955   *Brown* v. *Board of Education of Topeka II*

1963   *Goss et al.* v. *Board of Education of Knoxville, TN et al.*

1964   *Griffin et al.* v. *County School Board of Prince Edward County et al.*

1968   *Green* v. *County School Board of New Kent County*

1971   *North Carolina State Board of Education* v. *Swann, Moore* v. *Charlotte-Mecklenburg Board of Education,* and *Swann* v. *Charlotte-Mecklenburg Board of Education*

1972   *United States* v. *Scotland Neck Board of Education et al.*

1973   *Keyes* v. *School Board No. 1 of Denver, Colorado*

1974   *Milliken* v. *Bradley I*

1974   *DeFunis* v. *Odegaard*

1977   *Dayton Board of Education* v. *Brinkman*

1978   *Regents of the University of California* v. *Bakke*

1979   *Columbus Board of Education* v. *Penick*

1990   *Missouri* v. *Jenkins*

1991   *Board of Education of Oklahoma City Public Schools* v. *Dowel*

List 3-8. Resistance Efforts to Desegregation

1955   Georgia state board of education threatens to revoke the license of any teacher who teaches an integrated class

1955   Mississippi establishes a government agency to maintain segregation

1956   White protestors block enrollment of African American students at Mansfield (Texas) High School

1957   Protestors harass 18 students planning to attend Central High School in Little Rock (Arkansas)

1958   Government closes public schools in Little Rock and reopens them as private schools

1959   Prince Edward County (Virginia) closes the public school system to avoid compliance of an integration order

1960   Mississippi legislation makes school system "permissive" rather than "mandatory"; federal government cannot order reopening of public schools closed to avoid integration

1960   New Orleans (Louisiana) enforces integration after legislation closes schools; most white students boycott for the rest of the term

1961   Federal judge orders New Rochelle (New York) to integrate its school system

1967   Federal court in Alabama orders governor and state board of education to integrate all public schools; first case of an entire state placed under single federal desegregation injunction

SPECIAL EMPHASIS PROGRAMS

List 3-9. Special Emphasis Programs

The following programs are Afrocentric-based or incorporate Afrocentricity into their curriculums.

- Marcus Garvey Academy (Detroit, Michigan and Washington, D.C.)
- Paul Robeson Academy (Detroit, Michigan)
- Malcolm X Academy (Detroit, Michigan)
- Mae C. Jemison Academy (Detroit, Michigan)
- Matthew Henson Elementary (Baltimore, Maryland)
- West Side Preparatory School (Chicago, Illinois)
- Helping Hands (Raleigh, North Carolina)
- Monnier Elementary School (Detroit, Michigan)
- HAWK Project—Grant Union High School (Sacramento, California)
- Children of the Sun (Tampa, Florida)
- Inroads/Wisconsin Youth Leadership Academy (Milwaukee, Wisconsin)

YOUTH ORGANIZATIONS

List 3-10. Youth Organizations

- A Better Chance, Inc.
- Kappa League
- Young African American Achievers
- International Black Student Alliance
- ACT-SO (Academic, Cultural, Technological and Scientific Olympics)
- Back to School—Stay in School
- BLACK EXCEL

RHODES SCHOLARS

List 3-11. Rhodes Scholars (1997-1999)

1997	Benjamin Todd Jealous
1998	Gretchen Rohr
1999	Antonio Delgado
1999	Carla Peterman
1999	Antwaun L. Smith

EDUCATION WEBSITES

List 3-12. Websites

- New Intelligence Inc.: *www.newintel.com*
- Computers for Learning: *www.computers.fed.gov*
- Study Lounge: *www.studylounge.com*
- Cover-to-Cover Time Travel Adventures: *www.perfectionlearning.com*
- Cover-to-Cover Time Information Books: *www.perfectionlearning.com*
- Cover-to-Cover Time Novels: *www.perfectionlearning.com*

TEACHER EDUCATION PROGRAMS

List 3-13. Teacher Education Programs

- 21st Century Teachers: *www.21ct.org*
- Teach for America: *www.teachforamerica.com*
- George Lucas Educational Foundation: *www.glef.org*
- Urban Education League: *www.eric-web.tc.columbia.edu*

FIRST DOCTORAL DEGREES CONFERRED

List 3-14. First Recipients

Doctor of Education (Ed.D.)

1933	Howard Long	Harvard University, Cambridge, Massachusetts
1933	Edgerton Hall	Rutgers University, New Brunswick, New Jersey
1939	Rose Butler Browne	Harvard University (first black woman to receive a doctorate from Harvard)

Education

1925	Charles H. Thompson	University of Chicago, Illinois
1928	Althea Washington	Ohio State University, Columbus
1928	Jennie Porter	University of Cincinnati, Ohio
1931	Ambrose Caliver	Columbia University, New York

Psychology and Philosophy

1903	T. Nelson Baker, Sr.	Yale University, New Haven, Connecticut
1920	Francis Cecil Sumner	Clark College, Atlanta, Georgia
1934	Ruth Howard Beckham	University of Minnesota

Languages and Literature

1893	William L. Bulkley	Syracuse University, New York
1896	Lewis B. Moore	University of Pennsylvania, Philadelphia
1920	Harry S. Blackiston	University of Pennsylvania, Philadelphia
1921	Georgianna Rose Simpson	University of Chicago, Illinois
1921	Eva Beatrice Dykes	Radcliffe College, Cambridge, Massachusetts
1925	Anna Haywood Cooper	University of Paris, France
1931	Valaurez B. Spratlin	Middlebury College, Vermont

Social Sciences

1895	W.E.B. Du Bois	Harvard University, Cambridge, Massachusetts
1906	R.L. Diggs	Illinois Wesleyan, Bloomington
1911	Richard Robert Wright, Jr.	University of Pennsylvania, Philadelphia
1921	Sadie T. Mossell Alexander	University of Pennsylvania, Philadelphia
1925	Charles H. Wesley	Harvard University, Cambridge, Massachusetts
1931	Laurence Foster	University of Pennsylvania, Philadelphia
1934	Ralph J. Bunche	Harvard University, Cambridge, Massachusetts
1937	Anna Johnson Julian	University of Pennsylvania, Philadelphia
1941	Merle Johnson	State University of Iowa, Ames
1941	Merze Tate	Radcliffe College, Cambridge, Massachusetts

Biological Sciences

1889	Alfred Coffin	Illinois Wesleyan University, Bloomington
1916	Ernest E. Just	University of Chicago, Illinois
1940	Roger Arliner Young	University of Pennsylvania, Philadelphia

Professional and Vocational

1887	John Wesley Bowen	Boston University, Massachusetts
1915	Julian H. Lewis	University of Chicago, Illinois
1923	Charles Hamilton Houston	Harvard University, Cambridge, Massachusetts
1932	Frederick D. Patterson	Cornell University, Ithaca, New York
1934	George M. Jones	University of Michigan, Ann Arbor
1936	Flemmie P. Kitrell	Cornell University, Ithaca, New York
1939	Maurice W. Lee	University of Chicago, Illinois
1940	Eliza Atkins Gleason	University of Chicago, Illinois
1941	Alfred B. Turner	Pennsylvania State University, University Park
1942	Oscar A. Fuller	University of Iowa, Ames

Political Science

1916	Saint Elmo Brady	University of Illinois, Urbana
1925	Elbert Cox	Cornell University, Ithaca, New York
1942	Marguerite T. Wilson	Catholic University of America, Washington, D.C.

COLLEGES AND UNIVERSITIES

List 3-15. Historically Black Colleges and Universities

Alabama

Alabama A&M University	1875
Alabama State	1874
Bishop State Community	1927
Concordia College	1922
J.F. Drake State Technical College	1961
Lawson State Community College	1965
Miles College	1905
Oakwood College	1896
Selma University	1878
Shelton State Community	1965
Stillman College	1876
Talladega College	1867
Trenholm State Technical College	1966
Tuskegee University	1881

Arkansas

Arkansas Baptist College	1901
Philander Smith College	1877
Shorter College	1886
University of Arkansas-Pine Bluff	1873

Delaware

Delaware State University	1891

District of Columbia

Howard University	1867
University of the District of Columbia*	1976

---

* In 1976, D.C. Teachers College, Federal City College, and Washington Technical Institute merged to form UDC.

Florida

Bethune Cookman College	1904
Edward Waters College	1866
Florida A&M University	1877
Florida Memorial College	1879

Georgia

Albany State College	1903
Clark-Atlanta University**	1989
Fort Valley State College	1869
Interdenominational Theological Center	1958
Morehouse College	1867
Morehouse School of Medicine	1978
Morris Brown College	1881
Paine College	1882
Savannah State College	1890
Spelman College	1881

Illinois

Chicago State University	1867

Kentucky

Kennedy-King College	no date
Kentucky State University	1886

Louisiana

Dillard University	1869
Grambling State University	1901
Southern University and A&M College	1880
Southern University (New Orleans)	1959
Southern University (Shreveport)	1964
Xavier University	1925

** In 1989, Atlanta University and Clark College merged to form Clark-Atlanta University.

Maryland

Bowie State University	1865
Coppin State University	1900
Morgan State University	1867
University of Maryland-Eastern Shore	1886

Massachusetts

Roxbury Community College	1914

Michigan

Highland Park Community College	1918
Lewis College of Business	1874
Wayne State Community College	1967

Mississippi

Alcorn State University	1871
Coahoma Junior College	1949
Hinds Community College	1954
Jackson State University	1877
Mary Holmes College	1892
Mississippi Valley State University	1946
Rust College	1866
Tougaloo College	1869

Missouri

Harris-Store State College	1857
Lincoln University	1866

New York

LaGuardia Community College (CUNY)	1971
Medgar Evers College (CUNY)	1969
NYC Technical College (CUNY)	1946

North Carolina

Barber-Scotia College	1867
Bennett College	1889
Elizabeth City State University	1891
Fayetteville State University	1867
Johnson C. Smith University	1867
Livingstone College	1879
North Carolina A&T State University	1891
North Carolina Central University	1910
St. Augustine's College	1867
Shaw University	1865
Winston-Salem State University	1892

Ohio

Central State University	1887
Cuyahonga Community College	1963
Wilberforce University	1856

Oklahoma

Langston University	1897

Pennsylvania

Cheyney University of Pennsylvania	1837
Lincoln University of Pennsylvania***	1854

South Carolina

Allen University	1870
Benedict College	1870
Claflin College	1869
Clinton Junior College	1894
Denmark Technical College	1948
Morris College	1891
South Carolina State University	1896
Voorhees College	1897

*** Lincoln University of Pennsylvania was originally called Ashmun Institute.

Tennessee

Fisk University	1867
Knoxville College	1875
Lane College	1882
LeMoyne-Owen College	1862
Meharry Medical College	1876
Morristown College	1881
Tennessee State University	1912

Texas

Huston-Tillotson College	1876
Jarvis Christian College	1912
Paul Quinn College	1872
Prairie View A&M University	1876
St. Philip's College	1927
Southwestern Christian College	1949
Texas College	1894
Texas Southern University	1947
Wiley College	1873

Virginia

Hampton University	1868
Norfolk State University	1935
St. Paul's College	1888
Virginia State University	1882
Virginia Union University	1865

West Virginia

Bluefield State University	1895
West Virginia State College	1891

Virgin Islands

University of the Virgin Islands	1962

List 3-16. First Presidents of Colleges and Universities

1863	Daniel Payne	Wilberforce University
1871	Hiram Rhodes Revels	Alcorn College
1874	Patrick Francis Healy	Georgetown University
1882	John Mercer Langston	Virginia State University
1926	Mordecai W. Johnson	Howard University
1937	Dwight O. W. Holmes	Morgan State College (University)
1945	Horace Mann Bond	Lincoln University
1946	Charles S. Johnson	Fisk University
1946	Harold L. Trigg	St. Augustine's College
1949	Alonzo G. Moron	Hampton Institute (University)
1952	Arthur D. Gray	Talladega College
1953	Albert E. Manley	Spelman College
1955*	Samuel M. Nabrit	Texas Southern University
1960*	James M. Nabrit	Howard University
1966	James Colston	Bronx Community College
1970	Clifton R. Wharton	American University
1974	Charles S. Rooks	Chicago Theological Seminary
1981	Jewell Plummer Cobb	University of California at Fullerton
1981	Yvonne Kennedy	Bishop State Community College
1984	Yvonne Walker-Taylor	Wilberforce University
1986	Niara Sudarkasa	Lincoln University
1987	Johnetta B. Cole	Spelman College
1990	Marguerite R. Barnett	University of Houston
1991	David T. Shannon	Andover Newton Theological School
1992	Blenda J. Wilson	University of Michigan

* Samuel M. Nabrit and James M. Nabrit were the first African American brothers to simultaneously hold the presidencies of two large African American universities.

List 3-17. Top Fifty Colleges for African Americans*

The top fifty colleges/universities were selected by the Black Enterprise/Day Star Research conducted by Dr. Thomas LaVeist. More than 3,000 colleges and universities were chosen based on the following characteristics: (1) accredited four-year institutions with an African American student enrollment of at least 1.5% and (2) well-known colleges that would be of significant interest to African American students. The result was a pool of 987 colleges and universities. These schools were grouped by a modified version of the classification developed by the Carnegie Foundation. The classifications were based upon the size of the student body, national reputation, and whether the majority of the students are drawn from across the nation or from a particular region.

In addition, Day Star selected a list of 1,077 African American professionals in higher education to rate each school using the above classification. Five hundred six (506) of the questionnaires (46.9%) were returned. In computing the scores, the results from the HBCUs (Historically Black Colleges and Universities) were individually weighted to compensate for the large enrollment of African American students.

Alabama A&M University (Normal, Alabama)

Amherst College (Amherst, Massachusetts)

Bethune-Cookman College (Daytona Beach, Florida)

Bryn Mawr College (Bryn Mawr, Pennsylvania)

Clark Atlanta University (Atlanta, Georgia)

Columbia University (New York, New York)

Cornell University (Ithaca, New York)

Dillard University (New Orleans, Lousiana)

Duke University (Durham, North Carolina)

Emory University (Atlanta, Georgia)

Fisk University (Nashville, Tennessee)

Florida A&M University (Tallahassee, Florida)

Florida State University (Tallahassee, Florida)

Georgetown University (Washington, D.C.)

George Washington University (Washington, D.C.)

Grambling State University (Grambling, Louisiana)

Phi Beta Sigma

Delta Sigma Theta

---

* Schools are listed in alphabetical order.

Hampton University (Hampton, Virginia)

Harvard University (Cambridge, Massachusetts)

Howard University (Washington, D.C.)

Jackson State University (Jackson, Mississippi)

Johns Hopkins University (Baltimore, Maryland)

Johnson C. Smith University (Charlotte, North Carolina)

Lincoln University (Lincoln University, Pennsylvania)

Massachusetts Institute of Technology (Cambridge, Massachusetts)

Morehouse College (Atlanta, Georgia)

Morgan State University (Baltimore, Maryland)

Morris Brown College (Atlanta, Georgia)

Mount Holyoke College (South Hadley, Massachusetts)

New York University (New York, New York)

North Carolina A&T University (Greensboro, North Carolina)

North Carolina Central University (Durham, North Carolina)

Oberlin College (Oberlin, Ohio)

Smith College (Northampton, Massachusetts)

South Carolina State University (Orangeburg, South Carolina)

Southern University (New Orleans, Louisiana)

Spelman College (Atlanta, Georgia)

Stanford University (Palo Alto, California)

Swarthmore College (Swarthmore, Pennsylvania)

Tennessee State University (Nashville, Tennessee)

Tuskegee University (Tuskegee, Alabama)

University of California, Los Angeles (Los Angeles, California)

University of North Carolina (Chapel Hill, North Carolina)

University of Pennsylvania (Philadelphia, Pennsylvania)

University of Southern California (Los Angeles, California)

Vassar College (Poughkeepsie, New York)

Wellesley College (Wellesley, Massachusetts)

Wesleyan University (Middletown, Connecticut)

Williams College (Williamtown, Massachusetts)

Xavier University (New Orleans, Louisiana)

Yale University (New Haven, Connecticut)

List 3-18. Ten Richest African American Institutions*

Bethune-Cookman College	Morehouse College
Dillard University	St. Augustine's College
Hampton University	Spelman College
Howard University	Stillman College
Johnson C. Smith University	Tuskegee University

List 3-19. Scholarships

ALA Spectum Initiative	Coca-Cola Scholarship
APS Minorities Scholarship	Cooperative Research Fellowship
APSA Graduate Fellowships	Duracell/National Urban League
ASANTEWAA	Ethnic Minority Fellowships
ASM Foundation for Education and Research	Gates Millenium Scholars Program
American Chemical Society Scholars	Agnes Jones Jackson Scholarship
American Dental Hygienists' Association	Stanley E. Jackson Scholarship
American Geological Institute	LITA/LSSI Minority Scholarship
American Society of Naval Engineers	Thurgood Marshall Scholarship
American Symphony Orchestra	Music Assistance Fund
Ed Bradley Scholarship	NAACP Willems Scholarships
George M. Booker Collegiate Scholarship	NABA National Scholarship
Hallie Q. Brown Scholarship Fund	NABJ National Scholarship
Selana Brown Book Scholarships	National Association of Colored Women's Clubs, Inc.
Business Reporting Item Program	National Black MBA Association, Inc.
Carl Rowen's Project Excellence Scholarship	National Black Nurses
M. Elizabeth Carnegie Scholarship	Need Based Scholarship Programs
Chevrolet Excellence in Education Award	Jackie Robinson Scholarship
Civilian Shrosphire Scholarship	Carole Simpson Scholarship
	Sutton Education Scholarships
	Roy Wilkins Scholarship

---

* Largest endowment funds

PUBLICATIONS
(A Selected List)

List 3-20. Associations, Professional, and Collegiate

Afro-American Journal

Afro-Americans in New York Life and History

Atlanta University Bulletin

Black American Literature Forum

Black Perspective in Music

Black Scholar (Journal of Black Studies and Research)

Black Writers News

Campus Digest

Core

Crisis

Culture

Everybody

Gold Torch

The Ink Pen

Ivy Leaf

Journal of the National Black Association

Journal of the National Medical Association

Journal of Negro Education

Journal of Negro History

Maroon Tiger

Morehouse College Bulletin—The Alumnus

Negro History Bulletin

Southern Digest

Urban League Review

List 3-21. Magazines
(with a circulation of more than 100,000)

American Visions: The Magazine of Afro American Culture

Black Careers

The Black Collegian

Black Employment and Education Magazine

Black Enterprise

Black Family

Career Focus

Class

The Crisis

Dollars and Sense

Ebony

EM: Ebony Man

Emerge

Essence

Feelin' Good

Heart & Soul

Jet

Nightmovers

O (The Oprah Magazine)

Players

Right On!

Vibe

ORGANIZATIONS THAT PROMOTE
AFRICAN AMERICAN EDUCATION

List 3-22. Organizations

A Better Chance

American Council of Education, Office of Minority Concerns

Association of Black Women in Higher Education

Association for the Study of Afro-American Life and History

Bethune-Du Bois Fund

Carter G. Woodson Foundation, Inc.

Concerned Educators of Black Students

Institute for Independent Education

Moorland-Spingarn Research Center

NAACP Legal Defense and Educational Fund

National Alliance of Black School Educators

National Association for Equal Opportunity in Higher Education

National Association of University Women

National Black Child Development Institute

National Citizens Committee for African American Education

Office for the Advancement of Public Black Colleges

Schomburg Center for Research in Black Culture

Southern Regional Council

Thurgood Marshall Scholarship Fund

United Negro College Fund

Section 4

RELIGION

SECTION 4

RELIGION

Religion and the black church are significant dimensions to the African American experience in the United States, both past and present. The church historically was significant to the survival and liberation of the African American community.

The black church was a constant force and catalyst for social change in America. The emergence of black denominations was a protest against unequal and restrictive treatment by white churches. The early Negro Conventions were organized to combine efforts of black church leaders to confront slavery. Ministerial personnel across denominational lines have been central to the fight for freedom and equality. Richard Allen (Methodist), Henry H. Garnet (Presbyterian), Thomas Paul (Baptist), and Amos Beman (Congregationalist) were only a few of the early church leaders devoted to the abolition of slavery. Martin Luther King and Fred Shuttlesworth are representative of the preachers who used their pulpits during the 1960s to tear down the walls of segregation throughout the country. African American preachers also turned to politics as an avenue for social change. These efforts are compatible with one of the principles of Black Theology, which is that the liberation of the poor and oppressed is a central aspect and responsibility of the Christian faith.

The importance of religion and the teachings of the Bible remain a force in the African American community and culture. African Americans' belief in God and the teachings of the scripture have contributed to establishment of long-held family morals. Many churches sponsor activities and services to help improve the quality of life in the black community, such as day-care centers, Head Start programs, senior citizen programs, parochial schools, credit unions, counseling services, employment offices, tutorial programs, drug-abuse centers, homeless shelters, housing assistance, and food and clothing banks. The church has become a safety and support network for its members and the surrounding community.

Section 4 chronicles selected dimensions of religion in the African American community. It begins with a concept map presenting a chronological history of the organized church. The map has three columns that describe early actions, major contributions, and outcome(s) of those actions. There are four charts identifying distinct periods in the development of the organized church. They are followed by a list of African American firsts, women in religion, denominational traditions, and national conferences and conventions. Ministerial titles and degrees, styles in preaching, musical traditions, African American colleges, seminaries, and unconventional religions are typical topics in the remainder of the section.

THE ORGANIZED AFRICAN AMERICAN CHURCH

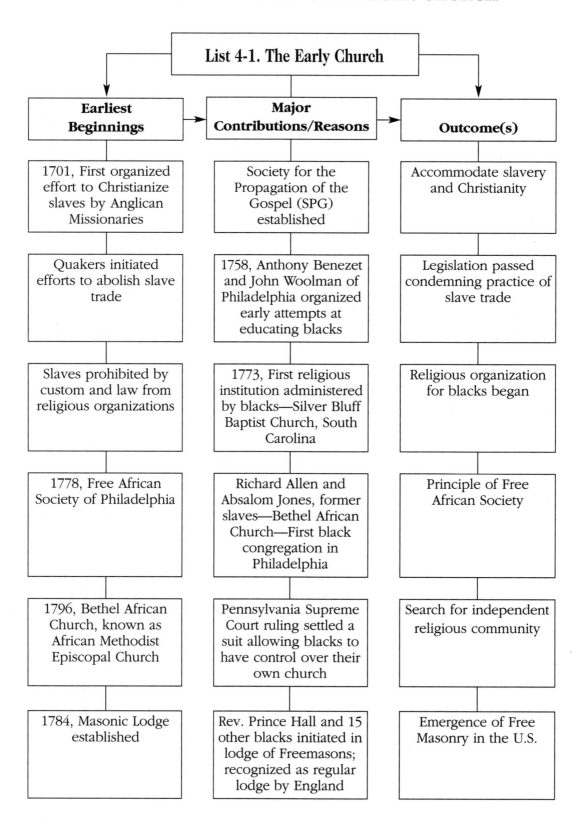

List 4-1. The Early Church		
Earliest Beginnings	**Major Contributions/Reasons**	**Outcome(s)**
1701, First organized effort to Christianize slaves by Anglican Missionaries	Society for the Propagation of the Gospel (SPG) established	Accommodate slavery and Christianity
Quakers initiated efforts to abolish slave trade	1758, Anthony Benezet and John Woolman of Philadelphia organized early attempts at educating blacks	Legislation passed condemning practice of slave trade
Slaves prohibited by custom and law from religious organizations	1773, First religious institution administered by blacks—Silver Bluff Baptist Church, South Carolina	Religious organization for blacks began
1778, Free African Society of Philadelphia	Richard Allen and Absalom Jones, former slaves—Bethel African Church—First black congregation in Philadelphia	Principle of Free African Society
1796, Bethel African Church, known as African Methodist Episcopal Church	Pennsylvania Supreme Court ruling settled a suit allowing blacks to have control over their own church	Search for independent religious community
1784, Masonic Lodge established	Rev. Prince Hall and 15 other blacks initiated in lodge of Freemasons; recognized as regular lodge by England	Emergence of Free Masonry in the U.S.

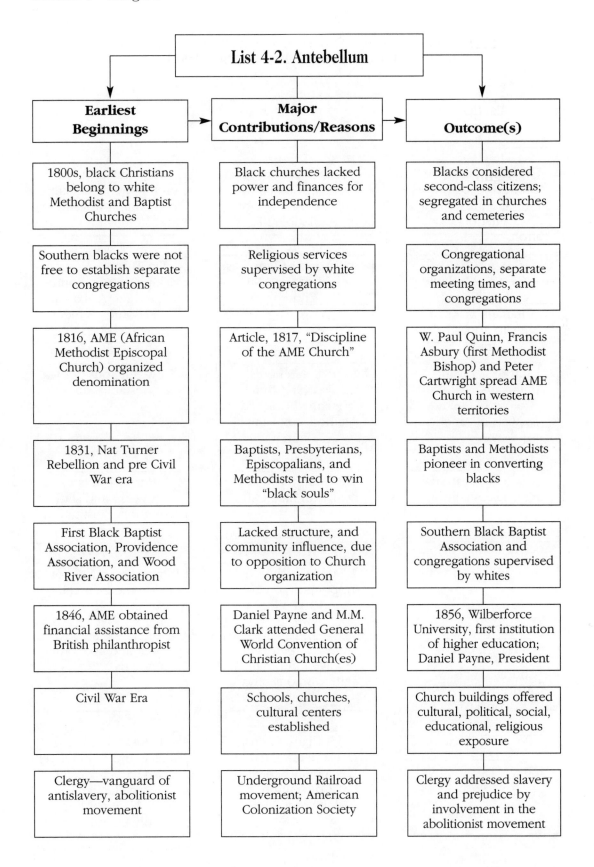

List 4-2. Antebellum

Earliest Beginnings	Major Contributions/Reasons	Outcome(s)
1800s, black Christians belong to white Methodist and Baptist Churches	Black churches lacked power and finances for independence	Blacks considered second-class citizens; segregated in churches and cemeteries
Southern blacks were not free to establish separate congregations	Religious services supervised by white congregations	Congregational organizations, separate meeting times, and congregations
1816, AME (African Methodist Episcopal Church) organized denomination	Article, 1817, "Discipline of the AME Church"	W. Paul Quinn, Francis Asbury (first Methodist Bishop) and Peter Cartwright spread AME Church in western territories
1831, Nat Turner Rebellion and pre Civil War era	Baptists, Presbyterians, Episcopalians, and Methodists tried to win "black souls"	Baptists and Methodists pioneer in converting blacks
First Black Baptist Association, Providence Association, and Wood River Association	Lacked structure, and community influence, due to opposition to Church organization	Southern Black Baptist Association and congregations supervised by whites
1846, AME obtained financial assistance from British philanthropist	Daniel Payne and M.M. Clark attended General World Convention of Christian Church(es)	1856, Wilberforce University, first institution of higher education; Daniel Payne, President
Civil War Era	Schools, churches, cultural centers established	Church buildings offered cultural, political, social, educational, religious exposure
Clergy—vanguard of antislavery, abolitionist movement	Underground Railroad movement; American Colonization Society	Clergy addressed slavery and prejudice by involvement in the abolitionist movement

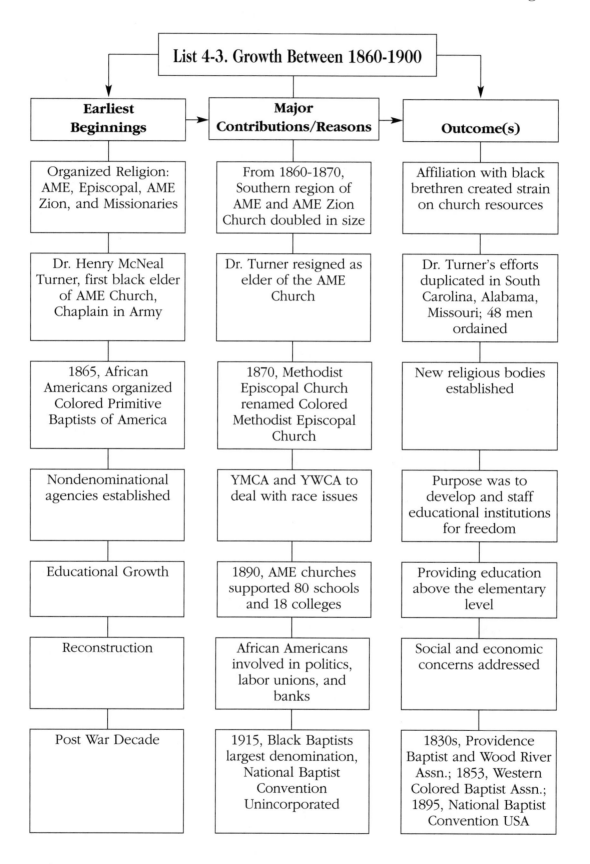

List 4-3. Growth Between 1860-1900

Earliest Beginnings	Major Contributions/Reasons	Outcome(s)
Organized Religion: AME, Episcopal, AME Zion, and Missionaries	From 1860-1870, Southern region of AME and AME Zion Church doubled in size	Affiliation with black brethren created strain on church resources
Dr. Henry McNeal Turner, first black elder of AME Church, Chaplain in Army	Dr. Turner resigned as elder of the AME Church	Dr. Turner's efforts duplicated in South Carolina, Alabama, Missouri; 48 men ordained
1865, African Americans organized Colored Primitive Baptists of America	1870, Methodist Episcopal Church renamed Colored Methodist Episcopal Church	New religious bodies established
Nondenominational agencies established	YMCA and YWCA to deal with race issues	Purpose was to develop and staff educational institutions for freedom
Educational Growth	1890, AME churches supported 80 schools and 18 colleges	Providing education above the elementary level
Reconstruction	African Americans involved in politics, labor unions, and banks	Social and economic concerns addressed
Post War Decade	1915, Black Baptists largest denomination, National Baptist Convention Unincorporated	1830s, Providence Baptist and Wood River Assn.; 1853, Western Colored Baptist Assn.; 1895, National Baptist Convention USA

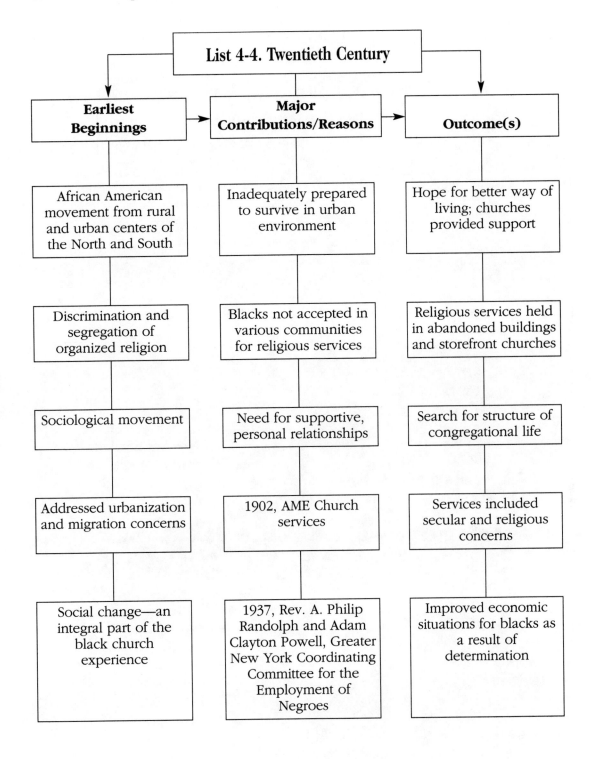

List 4-4. Twentieth Century

Earliest Beginnings	Major Contributions/Reasons	Outcome(s)
African American movement from rural and urban centers of the North and South	Inadequately prepared to survive in urban environment	Hope for better way of living; churches provided support
Discrimination and segregation of organized religion	Blacks not accepted in various communities for religious services	Religious services held in abandoned buildings and storefront churches
Sociological movement	Need for supportive, personal relationships	Search for structure of congregational life
Addressed urbanization and migration concerns	1902, AME Church services	Services included secular and religious concerns
Social change—an integral part of the black church experience	1937, Rev. A. Philip Randolph and Adam Clayton Powell, Greater New York Coordinating Committee for the Employment of Negroes	Improved economic situations for blacks as a result of determination

PIONEERS IN RELIGION

List 4-5. African American Firsts in Religion

Name	Date	Contribution
Lemuel Haynes	1780	Ordained as Congregational Minister; first to lead a white congregation
John Morront	1785	Missionary Minister; worked with Native Americans
Absalom Jones	1794	Priest; St. Thomas African Methodist Episcopal Church
Richard Allen	1794	Founded the first African Methodist Episcopal Church (with Absalom Jones)

Muslims praying toward Mecca

Richard Allen

James T. Holly	1855	Priest consecrated as Bishop in the Episcopal Church as a service to the independent Eglise Orthodoxe Apostolique in Haitienne; not assigned a number in the succession of bishops
Francis Burns	1858	Missionary Bishop of the Methodist Episcopal Church, North; first African American Missionary to work abroad
Henry McNeal Turner	1863	First African American U.S. Army Chaplain; President of Morris Brown College
Patrick F. Healy	1864	Jesuit Priest; President of Georgetown University, 1874-1882
Elizabeth Healy	1867	Convent Superior
James A. Healy	1875	Priest in 1854; first Bishop of Roman Catholic Church
Samuel D. Ferguson	1885	Second Bishop consecrated by the Episcopal Church but occupies the honor as the first due to situation with J.T. Holly in 1855
Charles M. Kinney	1889	Ordained in the ministry of the Seventh-Day Adventist Church
James R. Brown	1944	Navy Chaplain; General Secretary of the African Methodist Episcopal Church
John M. Burgess	1962	Minister in a white American diocese of the Episcopal Church; first black Episcopal Bishop
Hollis F. Price	1965	Moderator of the United Church of Christ
O. Thomas Kilgore, Jr.	1969	President of American Baptist Churches in the U.S.
William S. Cary	1972	President of National Council of Churches
Eugene A. Marino	1988	First African American Roman Catholic Archbishop, Atlanta Archdiocese
George Stallings	1989	Founder of African American Catholic Congregation, Imani Temple
Vashti Murphy McKenzie	2000	First female bishop of African Methodist Episcopal Church in its 213-year history

List 4-6. African American Women in Religion

Name	Date	Contribution
Jarena Lee	1819	Preacher; first woman licensed to preach in AME Church
Zilpha Elaw	1827	Preacher; started itinerant ministry
Elizabeth Lange	1829	Superior; founder of first Black Roman Catholic Order in U.S.
Mary Ann Prant	1830	Founder of the order from which the Independent Order of St. Luke (AME) emerged
Henriette Delille	1842	Founder of Sisters of the Holy Family
Sojourner Truth	1843	Preacher, antislave lecturer; changed name to Sojourner Truth (meaning "itinerant preacher")
Rebecca Cox Jackson	1857	Founder of first African American community of the United Society Believers in Christ's Second Appearing (Shakers)
Amanda Berry Smith	1870	Holiness evangelist; began itinerant ministry
Julia Foote	1884	Deacon Elder; first woman ordained a deacon in AME Zion Church
Harriet Baker	1889	Pastor; appointed to St. Paul's Church
Mathilda Beasley	1894	Nun in the Roman Catholic Church
Florence Randolph	1897	Elder; licensed to preach in 1897 (AME Zion); first AME Zion woman to receive honorary degree
Mary J. Small	1898	Elder; first woman to be ordered as elder in AME Zion Church
Nannie Helen Burroughs	1900	Founder of Women's Convention, an auxiliary of the National Baptist Convention, USA, Inc.
Magdalena Lewis	1903	Founder of Trinitarian Pentecostal movement; organized first demonstration to recognize ordained women
Mary Evans	1904	Preacher; preached first sermon at age 12; received license at age 14 (AME)
Mary McLeod Bethune	1904	Methodist educator; founded Bethune-Cookman College

Rosa Horn	1926	Bishop; founder of Mt. Calvary Pentecostal Faith Church
Shirley Caesar	1966	Minister; noted gospel singer
Pauli Murray	1977	Priest; first black woman ordained as Episcopal priest
Leontine T.C. Kelly	1984	Bishop; first black woman bishop of United Methodist Church
Barbara C. Harris	1989	Bishop; first black woman elected Bishop in the Episcopal Church
Cora Billings	1990	Pastor; first black nun in the U.S. to head a Catholic parish
Rose Vernell	1991	Priest; first female priest of the Imani Temple Afro-American Catholic Congregation
Vashti Murphy McKenzie	2000	First female bishop of African Methodist Episcopal Church in its 213-year history

DENOMINATIONAL TRADITIONS AND RITUALS

List 4-7. Baptist

Some beliefs and characteristics:

- Emerged during the Protestant Reformation
- Desired to purify the church of Roman Catholic influence
- First permanent Baptist congregations were in England
- First Baptist church established in Providence, Rhode Island, 1620
- Slaves were allowed to participate mid 1700s; broke with white churches in 1770s over segregation and slavery
- God is the Supreme Being
- Holy Bible is spiritual literary guide; Church Covenent is guiding principle
- Belief in the virgin birth, death, and resurrection of Jesus Christ
- Belief in Jesus and the Holy Trinity (Father, Son, and the Holy Spirit)
- Salvation (being saved) results from confession of faith in Jesus Christ

- Belief in heaven and hell, but not purgatory
- Belief in the resurrection and life everlasting
- Church is supported with tithes (10%) and offerings by members
- Familiar speech used in services (no glossolalia)
- Baptism by water immersion is the method of accepting people into the body of the church; babies are blessed by the pastor
- One method of confessing faith is through testifying, extolling God's goodness
- Intercessory prayer
- Altar call is offered to members who wish special prayer
- Liturgical dancing is accepted in many Baptist churches
- Foot washing and the laying on of hands are practiced in many Baptist churches
- Ministers are hired by the church members
- Ministers can be married
- Women may serve as ministers and officers in the church
- Polygamy and abortion not accepted
- Divorced persons are accepted as members
- Provides social services to the needy

List 4-8. Catholic

Some beliefs and characteristics:

- Bishops established a plan to evangelize the freed slaves after their emancipation in 1866
- Early Catholic slaves had owners who were Catholic
- By 1829, Catholics began to establish an African American order and develop schools for Negroes
- God is the Supreme Being
- Holy Bible is the spiritual literary guide
- Apostle's Creed is a guiding principle
- Belief in the virgin birth, death, and resurrection of Jesus Christ
- Belief in the Holy Trinity

- Heaven is the abode of the elect; hell is the abode of the damned; purgatory is a place of temporary expiation of sin
- Belief in the resurrection and life everlasting
- Belief in intercessory prayer
- Church is supported by tithes and offerings by members
- Familiar speech is used in services (no glossolalia)
- Baptism is the method of sprinkling or pouring water over the head; full body immersion may be used
- Priests are available to members for confession of sins
- Confessions are an expectation of members
- Priests may not marry
- Nuns may not marry and cannot become priests
- Women hold specific offices in the church; individual parish may make the decision
- Members may be expelled from the church (ex-communicated)
- Polygamy and abortion not accepted
- Divorce is not encouraged; a marriage may be annulled through dispensation
- Fasting is encouraged during specific religious periods

List 4-9. Episcopal

Some beliefs and characteristics:

- Attracted a small proportion of upper-class African Americans
- African American Episcopalians sought equal and full involvement throughout the church rather than separate
- God is the Supreme Being
- Holy Bible is the spiritual literary guide
- Apostle's Creed is a guiding principle
- Tenets of the church are worship, education, and service
- Belief in the Holy Trinity
- Belief in life after death

- Belief in heaven and hell, but not considered strong concepts
- Familiar speech in services (no glossolalia)
- Baptism is performed by sprinkling or pouring water over the head; or full body immersion
- Intercessory prayer
- Altar call is offered to members who wish special prayer
- Healing services, through prayer, are held; laying on of hands is a healing/prayer method
- Ministers are interviewed by the church and recommended for hire; the bishop makes the final decision
- Ministers may be married
- Women may serve as priests and hold offices in the church
- Polygamy is not accepted
- Abortion and divorce are not forbidden

List 4-10. Holiness/Pentecostal

Some beliefs and characteristics:

- Emerged in the late 1800s
- Began as an interracial movement; whites withdrew; currently interracial
- Members sought intensity in their spiritual life
- Some Holiness reject the speaking in tongues' practice of Pentecostals
- Some Pentecostals reject the Holiness doctrine of sanctification
- Both groups share similar origins and basic beliefs
- God is the Supreme Being for both groups
- Holy Bible is the literary guide
- Belief in Jesus and the Holy Trinity
- Key testimony or confessional is characteristic
- Baptism by full body immersion is the method of proclaiming faith
- Nine special gifts of the Spirit:
    —glossolalia
    —prophecy

—new interpretation of passages from the Bible

—faith, wisdom, and knowledge

—power of healing

—recognition of spirits

—performance of miracles

—"Holy Dance"

—ritual of the shout is the climatic expression of individual and collective spirit possession

- Altar call may include laying on of hand

- Ministers are appointed

- Women may serve as ministers and hold offices in the church

- Polygamy and abortion not accepted

- Some churches disallow movies, wearing makeup, and dancing

List 4-11. Jehovah's Witness

Some beliefs and characteristics:

- Began in early 1870s as a Bible Study group in Allegheny, Pennsylvania

- Legally known as the Watchtower Bible and Track Society of Pennsylvania, Inc.

- Membership exceeded 4 million by 1992 representing many races and cultures

- Ministries in 229 countries worldwide

- Jehovah (God) is the Supreme Being

- The Holy Bible is the spiritual literary guide (the New World Translation of the Holy Scriptures)

- Belief that Jehovah, God, and Jesus Christ are distinct and not combined with a "Holy Ghost" in the Trinity; the "Holy Spirit" is not a person, but God's active force

- Heaven is the habitation of spirit creatures, the place of God's throne

- Hell is the grave, the resting place in hope of restoration

- Do not believe in purgatory

- Baptism is complete submersion for person of responsible age; infants are not baptized

- Any Witness can become an ordained minister; titles like "Reverend" and "Father" belong to God and are not used for leaders of the ministry

- Women may share in congregational Bible studies and meetings, but do not serve as ministers

- Divorce can be obtained on the ground of marital unfaithfulness; if a Witness obtains a divorce for other reasons and remarries, he/she must be expelled

- Witnesses do not believe in blood transfusion; blood substitutes are acceptable

- Believe in preaching the good news (gospel) of God's Kingdom

- Witnesses visit the homes of people to convert them, as Christ went into homes

- Witnesses believe that Jehovah's Witness is the only true faith

- There is no specific organizational unit concentrated on African Americans even though they represent a significant portion of the membership

List 4-12. Methodist

Some beliefs and characteristics:

- Introduced to America from England in 1766 by Charles and John Wesley
- African Americans affiliated with Methodists from beginning
- Broke with the white Methodist church over racial segregation and slavery
- African Methodist Episcopal (AME), African Methodist Episcopal Zion (AMEZ), and Colored Methodist Episcopal (CME) were established
- God is Supreme Being
- The Holy Bible is the spiritual literary guide
- Belief in the virgin birth, death, and resurrection of Jesus Christ
- Apostle's Creed is a guiding principle
- Belief in Jesus and the Holy Trinity (Father, Son, and Holy Ghost)
- Intercessory prayer
- Salvation (being saved) results from confession of faith in Jesus Christ
- Belief in heaven and hell, but not purgatory
- Belief in the resurrection and life everlasting
- Familiar speech is used in services (no glossolalia)
- Baptism by water immersion or sprinkling is the method of admittance to the church
- Holy Communion administered to members and visitors
- Church is financially supported by tithes (10%) and offerings by members
- Ministers are assigned to the church by the council
- Ministers can be married
- Women may serve as ministers and officers in the church
- Members can be expelled from the church
- Polygamy and abortion not accepted
- Provides social services to those in need

List 4-13. Nation of Islam and Black Muslims

Some beliefs and characteristics:

- Considered one of the great religions of the world

- Monotheistic—God transcends the universe

- Requires strict discipline and adherence to the precepts of the faith

- Supreme Being is Allah, which means one who is not limited by time and space

- Literary guides: Holy Koran, Revelation of Allah revealed to Prophet Mohammed

- Members are admitted who take the Declaration of Faith—"There is no God but God, and Muhammad is the messenger of God"

- Muslims pray five times a day—dawn, noon, late afternoon, sunset, and night—facing toward Mecca

- Five pillars of Islam (worship ordinances)

  —Profession of Faith (shahadah)

  —Ritual Prayer (salah)

  —Ramadan Fast (all members fast—ninth month of the Islamic lunar calendar)

  —Almsgiving (zakah)

  —Pilgrimage to Mecca (Hajj)

- Believe Allah will judge humanity for good and bad; reward those who do good with heaven and punish those who do wrong with hell

- Fasting during Ramadan for 29 or 30 days

- Persons apply for membership by copying a designated letter on each of three blank sheets of paper; the letters must be copied perfectly

- Muslims do not believe in the Trinity

- Jesus is accepted as the son of the Virgin Mary, but not as the "Son of God"

- Muslims accept the Holy Bible but do not see the scriptures as complete; the Koran is the yardstick of God's message

- Women are seen as equal with the only distinction being that men have more "strength" and the "ability to accumulate wealth"

- Polygamy is allowed; however, most Muslims adhere to American law, which forbids polygamy

The Black Muslims

- The Black Muslims emerged in the African American Community in early 1930s

- Founded by the Honorable Prophet Elijah Muhammad (born in 1897 as Elijah Poole)

- Poole was introduced to Islam by W.D. Fard, a salesman. He changed his name to Muhammad as a sign of his conversion and began to proclaim he was the messenger of Allah.

- His teachings were radical but drew a large following

- Only black people can join the sect; the white race was the enemy

- Malcolm X was a charismatic leader who broke away from the Black Muslims; converted to Orthodox Islam and formed the Organization of Afro-American Unity; he was assassinated in 1965

- The Nation of Islam split in 1975 after the death of Elijah Muhammad

- His son Wallace D. Muhammad sought to align the teachings of the organization with Orthodox Islam and opened membership to whites

- A large group split in 1978 to follow Louis Farrakhan, who realigned teachings with the original principles of racial, economic, and geographical (separate homeland) separation; his organization is called the Nation of Islam

- Traditional Islam is practiced by a small but growing number of African Americans

- Nation of Islam groups continue to promote self sufficiency and black nationalism

List 4-14. Unconventional Religious Organizations

Selected Characteristics

- Views and beliefs inconsistent with major American religions
- Charismatic leader
- Messiah incarnate or Son of a Living God
- Extreme idealism
- Crusading spirit
- The Holy Bible is used as basis of Christian doctrine
- Abandoned concept of life after death
- Adopted practice of fulfilling life abundantly on Earth
- Merged, to a greater or lesser degree, some African-inspired rites
- Integrated visions and dreams into practices
- Code of behavior outside traditional practices
- Repatriation

Selected Groups	Central Leader
United House of Prayer for All People	Charles Manuel Grace (Sweet Daddy Grace); found church in the mid-1920s in Washington, D.C.
Peace Mission Movement	Father Divine (Father Major Jealous Divine); established in 1919 in Brooklyn, New York and moved to Philadelphia in 1941
United Church Science of Living Institute, Inc.	Reverend Frederick J. Eikerenkoetter II (Reverend Ike); church founded in 1966, headquartered in New York
Rastafarians	Marcus Garvey; Haile Selassie I (considered the incarnation of God); sect found in Jamaica and brought to the U.S. in the 1960s; Ethiopia is heaven
Vodou (Voodoo)	Priests (oungan) and Priestesses (manbos); practices and number of followers unknown; the movement is primarily underground

RELIGIOUS CONFERENCES AND CONVENTIONS

List 4-15. Denomination: Baptist

The Consolidated American Baptist Convention	1867
United American Free Will Baptist Convention	1874
National Baptist Convention of America	1880
Foreign Mission Baptist Convention of the USA	1880
American National Educational Baptist Convention	1893
National Baptist Convention of the USA	1895
Lott Carey Baptist Foreign Mission Convention	1897
National Primitive Baptist Convention, USA	1907
National Baptist Evangelical Life and Soul Saving Assembly of the USA	1920
Progressive National Baptist Convention, Inc.	1961
National Missionary Baptist Convention of America	1988
National Black Ministers Conference	no date

List 4-16. Denomination: Catholic

National Black Sisters Conference	1968
National Office for Black Catholics	1970
National Black Catholic Congress, Inc.	1986

List 4-17. Denomination: Methodist

Union American Methodist Episcopal Church, Inc. (UAME)	1813
African Methodist Episcopal Church (AME)	1816
African Methodist Episcopal Zion (AMEZ)	1821
Christian Methodist Episcopal, formerly Colored Methodist Episcopal Church (CME)	1870
United Methodists	no date

EDUCATIONAL INSTITUTIONS

List 4-18. Church-Affiliated Colleges and Universities

College/University	Founded	City, State	Affiliation
Albany State University	1903	Albany, Georgia	AMA
Allen University	1870	Columbia, South Carolina	AME
Atlanta University	1867	Atlanta, Georgia	AMA
Barber-Scotia College	1867	Concord, North Carolina	Presbyterian
Benedict College	1870	Columbia, South Carolina	Baptist
Bennett College	1873	Greensboro, North Carolina	United Methodist
Bethune-Cookman College	1904	Daytona Beach, Florida	United Methodist
Cheyney State College	1837	Cheyney, Pennsylvania	Quaker
Claflin College	1869	Orangeburg, South Carolina	United Methodist
Clark College (now Clark Atlanta University)	1869	Atlanta, Georgia	United Methodist
Daniel Payne College	1877	Birmingham, Alabama	AME
Dillard University	1869	New Orleans, Louisiana	AMA
Edward Waters College	1866	Jacksonville, Florida	AME
Fisk University	1866	Nashville, Tennessee	AMA
Hampton University	1868	Hampton, Virginia	AMA
Howard University	1869	Washington, D.C.	UCC
Huston-Tillotson College	1876	Austin, Texas	United Methodist
Jarvis Christian College	1912	Hawkins, Texas	Disciples of Christ
Johnson C. Smith University	1867	Charlotte, North Carolina	Presbyterian
Knoxville College	1875	Knoxville, Tennessee	Presbyterian
Lane College	1882	Jackson, Tennessee	CME
Lincoln University	1854	Lincoln, Pennsylvania	Presbyterian
Livingtone College	1879	Salisbury, North Carolina	AMEZ
Mary Holmes Junior College	1892	West Point, Mississippi	Presbyterian
Meharry Medical College	1876	Nashville, Tennessee	United Methodist

College/University	Founded	City, State	Affiliation
Miles College	1905	Birmingham, Alabama	CME
Morehouse College	1867	Atlanta, Georgia	Baptist
Morgan State University	1876	Baltimore, Maryland	United Methodist
Morris Brown College	1881	Atlanta, Georgia	AME
Morris College	1908	Sumter, South Carolina	Baptist
Morristown College	1881	Morristown, Tennessee	United Methodist
Norfolk State University	1935	Norfolk, Virginia	Baptist
Oakwood College	1896	Huntsville, Alabama	Adventist
Paine College	1882	Augusta, Georgia	CME
Paul Quinn College	1872	Waco, Texas	AME
Rust College	1866	Holly Springs, Mississippi	United Methodist
Selma University	1878	Selma, Alabama	Baptist
Shaw University	1865	Raleigh, North Carolina	Baptist
Shorter College	1886	North Little Rock, Arkansas	AME
Spelman College	1881	Atlanta, Georgia	Baptist
Stillman College	1876	Tuscaloosa, Alabama	Presbyterian
St. Augustine's College	1867	Raleigh, North Carolina	Episcopal
St. Paul's College	1888	Lawrenceville, Virginia	Episcopal
Talladega College	1867	Talladega, Alabama	AMA
Texas College	1894	Tyler, Texas	CME
Tougaloo College	1869	Tougaloo, Mississippi	AMA
Virginia Union University	1865	Richmond, Virginia	Baptist
Voorhees College	1897	Denmark, South Carolina	Episcopal
University of Maryland, Eastern Shore	1886	Princess Anne, Maryland	United Methodist
Wilberforce University	1856	Wilberforce, Ohio	AME
Wiley College	1873	Marshall, Texas	United Methodist
Xavier University	1915	New Orleans, Louisiana	Roman Catholic

List 4-19. African American Seminaries

College/University	Founded	City, State	Affiliation
Bay Ridge Christian College	no date	Kendleton, Texas	Church of God
Endich Theological Seminary	1922	New York, New York	African Orthodox
Hood Theological Seminary	1879	Salisbury, North Carolina	AMEZ
Howard University School of Divinity	1870	Washington, D.C.	Ecumenical
Interdenominational Theological Center	1958	Atlanta, Georgia	Ecumenical
Payne Theological Seminary	1844	Wilberforce, Ohio	AME
Richmond Virginia Seminary	1981	Richmond, Virginia	Ecumenical
Shaw Divinity School	1933	Raleigh, North Carolina	Baptist
Southern California School of Ministry	no date	Los Angeles, California	Church of God
Virginia Union University School of Theology	1865	Richmond, Virginia	Baptist

List 4-20. Bible Colleges

College/University	Founded	City, State	Affiliation
American Baptist College	1924	Nashville, Tennessee	Baptist
American Bible College	1942	Pineland, Florida	Ecumenical
Apostolic Overcoming Holy Church of God Theological Seminary	no date	Birmingham, Alabama	Apostolic Church of God
Central Baptist Theological Seminary	1942	Indianapolis, Indiana	Baptist
Crenshaw Christian Center School of Ministry	1985	Los Angeles, California	Ecumenical
Crenshaw Christian Center School of the Bible	1988	Los Angeles, California	Ecumenical

College/University	Founded	City, State	Affiliation
Jackson Theological Seminary	no date	North Little Rock, Arkansas	Ecumenical
Mt. Carmel School of Religion	no date	Houston, Texas	Ecumenical
Saint Paul's Bible Institute	no date	New York, New York	Ecumenical
Simmons Bible College	1879	Louisville, Kentucky	Baptist
Virginia Seminary and College	1886	Lynchburg, Virginia	Baptist
Washington Baptist Seminary	1926	Washington, D.C.	Baptist

List 4-21. Ministerial Titles

Allah . . . . Muslim

Archbishop. . . . . Catholic

Bishop . . . . AME, AMEZ, Church of God in Christ, Episcopal, Catholic

Chief Overseer . . Church of the Lord Jesus Christ of the Apostolic Faith, Church of the living God

Deacon. . . . . . . Episcopal, Catholic, Primitive Baptist, AMEZ

Elder . . . . AME, Church of God in Christ, United Methodist, Primitive Baptist, AMEZ

Evangelist . . . . . Pentecostal

Father . . . . . . Catholic, Episcopal

Holiness . . . . . . Catholic

Lay Minister . . . Baptist, Methodist

Messiah. . . . . . . Holiness/Pentecostal

Minister. . . . . . Baptist, Muslim, AMEZ, AME

Missionary . . . . All faiths

Pastor. . . . . . . Baptist, AME, Catholic

Preacher . . . . . Baptist

Priest . . . . Catholic, Episcopal, Presbyterian

Rector . . . . . . Catholic

Reverend. . . . . Baptist, Catholic

Vicar . . . . Catholic

List 4-22. Ministerial Degrees

B.A./A.B.	Bachelor of Arts
B.D.	Bachelor of Divinity
B.S.	Bachelor of Science
B.Th.	Bachelor of Theology
D.D.	Doctor of Divinity
D.Min.	Doctor of Ministry
D.S.T./S.T.D	Doctor of Sacred Theology
Ed.D.	Doctor of Education
M.A./A.M.	Master of Arts
M.Div.	Master of Divinity
M.R.E.	Master of Religious Education
M.Th.	Master of Theology
Ph.D.	Doctor of Philosophy
S.T.B.	Bachelor of Sacred Theology
S.T.M.	Master of Sacred Theology
Th.D.	Doctor of Theology
Th.M.	Master of Theology

PREACHING STYLES

List 4-23. Preaching Styles

Preaching in the African American church is considered one of the culture's most established modes of communication. Ministers move their congregations to experience the sermon with a distinctive style of preaching. The style is often called "old-time" or "down-home" preaching. This preaching style is a blending of African culture, which emphasized healing, expression of possession by the spirit, and vivid imagery. The style emerged in the eighteenth century but remains popular today and has influenced public speaking and singing styles. While popular, it is not exclusive to African Americans nor is it inclusive of all styles used by them.

The approach to preaching has form and structure that generally begins in a conversational tone; gradually increases in rate, volume, and intensity; moves to an emotional peak or climax; and returns to a calm conversational closing. During the rhythmic, chanting section of the sermon, the minister sometimes lengthens vowels or compacts words to match his speech to a beat. The beat is occasionally accentuated by a gasp for air at the end of phrases or sentences. It is called "stylistic switching." The chanted sermon remains a very strong tradition. Additional characteristics follow:

- Charismatic performer
- Use of metrical, tonal, rhythmic chant
- Warm and supportive, healing tradition
- Strong verbal skills; storytellers
- Oratorical (characterized by stock phrases that appeal to the emotions)
- Builds sermon extemporaneously
- Persuasive oral form rather than literary form
- Uses symbolism, metaphors, and alliteration
- Text-context applications; relates text to day-to-day concerns
- Listener experiences the message emotionally and intellectually
- Heavy emphasis given to Jesus and the "Holy Spirit"
- Sermon has strong biblical basis, with scripture read by the minister
- Integrates music with text

MUSIC IN THE AFRICAN AMERICAN CHURCH

List 4-24. Musical Traditions

1600s   Negro spirituals begin in plantation praise houses or fields. Music is characterized by:

- call-response structure
- extensive melodic ornamentation (slides, slurs, bends, moans, shouts, wails, grunts)
- complex rhythmic structures
- integration of song and movement
- each component involved improvisation
- slave preachers established the foundation and form of black music

1680   Reverend Godwin objects to African American spirituals in the church.

1693   Enslaved African Americans in Boston agree to sing psalms during Sunday worship services.

1700   African American music is noticed and practiced in the northern colonies.

1724   Bishop of London surveys religious conditions among slaves in the U.S. and finds cultural and language barriers. As conditions improve, blacks are allowed to worship with whites.

1784   Bishop Porteus of London recommends that the clergy design new musical repertoire for slaves.

1800   John Watson, a Methodist minister, is critical of blacks' songs. Despite opposition, African Americans continue to recognize their customs drawn from African cultures.

1801   Richard Allen publishes a hymnal, *A Collection of Spiritual Songs and Hymns Selected from Various Authors.*

1840   The American Anti-Slavery Society commissions Edwin F. Hatfield to compile a hymnody of protest songs. It is titled "Freedom's Lyre; or Psalms, Hymns, and Sacred Songs, for the Slave and His Friends."

1841   Daniel Payne lobbies to change the style of worship in AME churches. He advocates the "right fit and proper way of serving God." Choral singing in northern AME churches results in congregational splits and withdrawals from the church.

1900   Black churches use spirituals and hymns, sung to the accompaniment of handclapping and tapping of the feet. Musical instruments such as tambourines, drums, piano, horns, guitar, and organs assist in creating black religious music known as Gospel.

1906   C.A. Tindley composes songs with melody and rhythm of gospel music.

Thomas Dorsey later develops a gospel style based on the blues, ragtime, and boogie-woogie piano accompaniment. This presentation of black music begins a new urban religious tradition.

1950   Traditional gospel involving choirs and congregational singing of commercial and contemporary repertoires emerges.

The freedom songs used during the 1950s and 1960s Civil Rights Movement are an extension and adaptation of Evangelical hymns.

List 4-25. Gospel Performers of the Twentieth Century

- Angelic Gospel Singers
- Rev. Shirley Caesar
- The Caravans
- The Clark Sisters
- Rev. James Cleveland
- Sam Cooke
- Dixie Hummingbirds
- The Fisk Jubilee Singers
- Five Blind Boys of Mississippi
- Aretha Franklin
- Theodore Frye
- Walter Hawkins
- Mahalia Jackson
- Queen Esther Marrow
- Sally Martin
- Mighty Clouds of Joy
- Whitney Phipps
- Della Reese
- Cleophus Robinson
- Sensational Nightingales
- Willie Mae Ford Smith
- Swan Silvertones
- Sister Rosetta Thorpe
- Clara Ward Singers
- The Winans
- Maceo Woods

List 4-26. Contemporary Gospel Singers and Groups

- Yolanda Adams
- Helen Baylor
- Andre Crouch
- Florida Mass Choir
- Kurt Franklin
- Al Green
- Fred Hammond
- Larnelle Harris
- Edwin Hawkins Singers
- Tremaine Hawkins
- Ron Kenoly

- Donnie McClurkin
- Mississippi Mass Choir
- Dottie Peoples
- Richard Smallwood
- Sounds of Blackness
- Staple Singers
- Take Six
- Albertina Walker
- BeBe Winans
- CeCe Winans
- Women of Worship

List 4-27. Music Resources

Name	Founded
Consortium of Musicians of the Metropolitan Area, Inc.	1867
Edwin Hawkins Music and Arts Seminar, Inc.	1981
Gospel Music Ministries International	1978
Gospel Music Workshop of America, Inc.	1966
Gospelrama Gospel Expo, Inc.	1982
Hampton University Ministers Conference, Choir Directors, Organists Guild	1914
International Praise Gospel Music Workshop	1982
Middle Atlantic Regional Gospel Music Festival	1972
National Coalition of Black Church Musicians	ND
National Convention of Gospel Choirs and Choruses, Inc.	1932
Youth Unlimited Community Christian Club, Inc.	1972

RELIGIOUS ORGANIZATIONS

List 4-28. Councils

- American Women's Clergy Association and Male Auxiliary
- Faith Hope Charity in Christ Outreach Center, Inc.
- Hampton University Ministers
- Marion City Ministerial Alliance
- National Black Evangelical Association
- North Carolina Association for Women in the Ministry, Inc.
- Southern Regional Council, Inc.

List 4-29. Nondenominational Organizations

- African Peoples' Christian Organizations
- Black Light Fellowship
- Center for Black Church Development
- Clergy Interracial Forum—Grace
- Coalition for Christian Outreach—Black Campus Ministry
- Congress of National Black Churches
- National Association of Black Seminaries
- United Black Church Appeal

List 4-30. Service Agencies and Organizations

- African Methodist Episcopal Church
- Afro-American Music Hall of Fame and Musicians, Inc.
- Afro-American Music Opportunities Association, Inc.
- Association of Black Directors of Christian Education
- Black Church Magazine
- Black Methodists for Church Renewal, Inc.
- Black Music Association
- Black Religious Broadcasters Association

- Commission for Racial Justice, United Church of Christ
- Glide Memorial United Methodist Church
- Improved Benevolent Protective Order of Elks of the World
- Leadership Conference on Civil Rights
- Martin Luther King, Jr. Center for Nonviolent Social Change
- National Baptist Convention, USA
- National Baptist Publishing Board, Inc.
- National Conference of Black Churchmen
- Operation PUSH
- Opportunities Industrialization Centers of America, Inc.
- Southern Christian Leadership Conference
- Successful Stewardship for Life Ministries, Inc.
- The Church of What's Happening Now
- The National Black Christian Education Resources Center
- United Church of Christ, Commission for Racial Justice
- United Outreach for Christ Mission Team, Inc.
- Women's International Religious Fellowship

MINISTERIAL LEADERSHIP

List 4-31. Ministers Who Became Civil Rights Leaders

Ralph D. Abernathy (1926-1990) (Baptist), one of the founders of the Southern Christian Leadership Conference (SCLC)

James L. Bevel (no dates) (Baptist), Minister of the American Baptist Church in the U.S.; a key leader of SCLC

Benjamin Chavis (1948-) (Baptist), Executive Director of the NAACP; co-organizer with Louis Farrakhan of the Million Man March in 1996

Benjamin L. Hooks (1925-) (Baptist), Executive Director of NAACP

Jesse L. Jackson (1941-) (Baptist), organized Operation PUSH (People United to Save Humanity) and the Rainbow Coalition

Martin L. King, Jr. (1929-1969) (Baptist), Pastor of Dexter Avenue Baptist Church, Montgomery Improvement Association, and President of SCLC

Martin L. King, Jr.

Joseph Lowery (1924-) (United Methodist), President of the SCLC

Henry H. Proctor (1868-1933) (Congregationalist), instrumental in creating the Interracial Committee of Atlanta; founded the *Georgia Congregationalist*, forerunner of the *Congregational Worker*

Fred L. Shuttlesworth (no dates) (Baptist), organized the Alabama Christian Movement for Human Rights (ACHR)

Wyatt T. Walker (no dates) (Baptist), Vice President and Executive Director of SCLC from 1964-1966

List 4-32. Ministers Elected to National Political Office

- **Walter Fauntroy** (1933-) (Baptist), former representative to the U.S. House of Representatives from Washington, D.C.

- **Floyd Flake** (1945-) (Methodist), former Congressman from New York, elected in 1986

- **William H. Gray III** (1941-) (Baptist), former Pennsylvania Congressman; presently president of the United Negro College Fund

- **Jesse L. Jackson** (1941-) (Baptist), elected as a representative from Washington, D.C. to the U.S. House of Representatives

- **Adam Clayton Powell, Jr.** (1908-1974) (Baptist), pastor of Abyssinian Baptist Church and elected to the U.S. Congress from New York in 1945

- **Andrew Young** (1932-) (United Church of Christ), former Georgia U.S. Congressman; Ambassador to United Nations; Mayor of Atlanta

List 4-33. Prominent Religious Leaders

- **Elroy Barber** (Baptist), president of the Florida Baptist Convention

- **John Branham** (Baptist), radio preacher

- **Calvin Butts** (Baptist), pastor of Abyssinian Baptist Church, Harlem, New York

- **Tony Evans**, senior pastor, Oak Cliff Bible Fellowship, Texas; president of Urban Alternative, broadcast on more than 200 radio stations

- **Louis Farrakhan** (Muslim), Nation of Islam minister; instrumental in the organization of the Million Man March

- **Charles F. Golden** (Methodist), bishop of United Methodist Church

- **Peter J. Gomes** (Baptist), Plummer Professor of Christian Morals, Harvard University

- **William H. Graves** (Methodist), bishop of Christian Methodist Episcopal Church

- **T.D. Jakes** (Nondenominational), pastor of the Potters House, Dallas, Texas

- **Lawrence N. Jones** (UCC), Dean Emeritus, Howard University School of Divinity

- **Harvey B. Kinchlow** (Methodist), televangelist; co-host of "700 Club"

- **Malcolm X** (Muslim), Nation of Islam minister; social activist; assassinated in 1965

- **Benjamin E. Mays** (Baptist), former president of Morehouse College; first black vice president of Federal Council of Churches

- **William McCary** (Mormon), prophet of the Latter-Day Saints in the mid nineteenth century

- **Elijah Muhammad** (Muslim), Nation of Islam leader

- **Johnnie Colemon Nedd** (Ecumenical), founder of Universal Foundation for Better Living, Inc.

- **Fred Price** (Pentecostal), televangelis; tenth highest rated religious personality on television

- **Dr. Samuel D. Proctor** (Baptist), Professor Emeritus, Rutgers University

- **George A. Stallings, Jr.** (Catholic), archbishop, Imani Temple

- **Cecil Williams** (Methodist), Glide Memorial United Methodist Church

List 4-34. Bishops and Archbishops (Catholic)

Bishop	Ordained/Appointed Bishop
James Augustine Healy	1875
Harold Perry	1944
Joseph Oliver Bowers	1953
Carlos Lewis	1965
Joseph Lawson Howze	1973
Eugene A. Marino	1974 (Archbishop of Atlanta, 1988)
Joseph Abel Francis	1976
Raymond R. Caesar	1978
James P. Lyke	1979 (Archbishop of Atlanta, 1991)
Moses B. Anderson	1982
Emerson J. Moore	1982
Wilton D. Gregory	1983
John H. Ricard	1984
J. Terry Steib	1984
Carl Anthony Fisher	1987
Curtis John Guillory	1988
Leonard Olivier	1988
Dominic Carmon	1993
Elliott Griffin Thomas	1993
George V. Murry	1995
Edward K. Braxton	1995
Gordon D. Bennett	1998
Joseph N. Perry	1998

List 4-35. Spotlight: JOHNNIE COLEMON NEDD

➤ Born in Columbus, Mississippi, date of birth not available

➤ Demonstrated leadership abilities in high school

➤ Graduated from Union Academy as class valedictorian

➤ Received B.A. degree from Wiley College

➤ Taught in the Chicago Public School System

➤ Price analyst for Chicago Market Center

➤ Founder and pastor of Christ Universal Temple, Chicago

➤ First black elected president of the Association of Unity Churches

➤ Organized Universal Foundation for Better Living, Inc. (UFBL) on June 14, 1974

➤ Served as District President of the International New Thought Alliance

➤ 1985—received the coveted "Par Excellence" Award

➤ 1987—received the Candace Award

➤ 1987—inducted into the Morehouse College Preacher's Hall of Fame

➤ TV highlights:

—"Daybreak"

—"Lee Phillip Show"

—Channel 2: "The People—A Woman Called Johnnie"

—Channel 26: "Better Living with Johnnie Colemon"

—Motivational Minute (ABC-TV)

➤ Awarded honorary Doctor of Divinity Degree

List 4-36. Spotlight: PETER JOHN GOMES

➤ Born in Plymouth, Massachusetts, 1942

➤ Ordained to the Christian Ministry by the First Baptist Church of Plymouth

➤ Taught at Tuskegee University

➤ Widely recognized as one of America's most distinguished preachers

➤ 1965—received A.B. degree from Bates College

➤ 1968—received S.T.B. degree from Harvard Divinity School

➤ 1974—Plummer Professor of Christian Morals at Harvard University and Minister at the Memorial Church

➤ Member of the faculty of Divinity and the faculty of Arts and Sciences at Harvard University

➤ Teaching and research interests include the history of the ancient Christian Church, Elizabethan Puritanism, homiletics, worship, church music, and history of the black American experience

➤ Published studies in several journals and wrote *The Good Book: Reading the Bible with Mind and Heart*

➤ Serves as Advisory Editor of *Pulpit Digest*

➤ Serves on the Advisory Board of *The Living Pulpit*

➤ Participated in the presidential inaugurations of Ronald Reagan and George Bush

➤ Honorary Chairman of North American Friends of Emmanuel College, the University of Cambridge, England

➤ Holds honorary degrees from New England College, Waynesbury College, Gordon College, Knox College, Bates College, Duke University, and Wooster College

ACRONYMS AND GLOSSARY

List 4-37. Acronyms

AA	African American
ACS	American Colonization Society
AMA	American Missionary Association
AME	African Methodist Episcopal
AMEZ	African Methodist Episcopal Zion
BWA	Baptist World Alliance
CMEC	Christian Methodist Episcopal Church; Colored Methodist Episcopal Church
MEC	Methodist Episcopal Church
NAACP	National Association for the Advancement of Colored People
NBCA	National Baptist Convention of America, Inc.
NBCU	National Baptist Convention Unincorporated
NBCUSA	National Baptist Convention United States of America
NMBC	National Missionary Baptist Convention
PCAF	Pentecostal Churches of Apostolic Faith
PNBC	Progressive National Baptist Convention, Inc.
PNC	Progressive National Convention
SCLC	Southern Christian Leadership Conference
SPG	Society for the Propagation of the Gospel
UCC	United Church of Christ
YMCA	Young Men's Christian Association
YWCA	Young Women's Christian Association

List 4-38. Glossary

ADVENTIST	Christian denomination believing in the second coming of Christ
AFRICAN AMERICAN (BLACK)	a person having origins in any of the Black racial groups of Africa
ALLAH	Supreme Being in Islamic religious traditions
ALTAR CALL	parishioners given the opportunity to come to the altar if they wish special prayer
BAPTISM	ceremony for inducting new believers by submersion, sprinkling, or the pouring of water over them
BAPTISTS	a Protestant denominational body with a church policy
BORN AGAIN	spiritual rebirth by recommitment or baptism
CATHOLIC	non-Protestant body with a church policy, with the Pope as the highest religious leader
CHRISTIAN	one who believes in Jesus as the Christ or follows religious practices based on the life of Jesus Christ
CHURCH	an organization of believers united in beliefs and religious practices
COMMUNION, LORD'S SUPPER	practice of taking bread and wine sacrament of the Lord's supper and unifying recipients in faith
CONFERENCE OR CONVENTION	meeting held to address relevant issues for denomination and its members
COVENANT	an agreement between God and man as expressed in the Bible
CULT	a group with practices centered around an exclusive ideology
DENOMINATION	a religious body with shared doctrinal beliefs; established organizational structure
ECUMENICAL	pertaining to universal Christian church without regard to denominational distinctions
EPISCOPAL	Protestant denomination governed by Bishops
FILLED WITH THE HOLY SPIRIT	in the Holiness/Pentecostal religion, a declaration of liturgical identity signifying that the saint has experienced total initiation into the worshiping community by a personal confession or manifestation of spirit possession

GLOSSOLALIA	speech pattern that occurs when one is filled with the Holy Spirit; also known as "speaking in tongues" or "ecstatic speech"
GRACE	the unmerited gift of God to humanity
HOLY TRINITY	Father, Son, and Holy Ghost (Holy Spirit)
INCARNATE	embodiment of God in the form man, Jesus Christ, to provide means for salvation
JUDGMENT	time of accounting for righteous or sinful behavior
LAYING ON OF HANDS	practice of church elders praying for and placing their hands on the heads of believers during special services
METHODIST	Protestant denomination with a hierarchical structure based on the methods of John Wesley
MISSIONARY	one sent by the church to promote the growth of the religious faith
ORDINATION	ritual for the appointment to a ministerial office
PENTECOSTAL	religious experience and tradition in which believers speak in tongues
PRESBYTERIAN	Protestant denomination with roots to the reformer John Calvin and is ruled by a presbytery, a court of local congregational elders and ministers
RELIGION	the organized faith, denomination, or sect to which a person adheres, believes, or practices
RELIGIOUS	person belonging to or connected to a religion or religious teaching
SAVED OR SALVATION	in the Holiness/Pentecostal religion, a sign that one has repented, asked forgiveness of sins, and confessed Jesus Christ as Savior and Lord; a basic entry level of liturgical identity that distinguishes the saint from the unbeliever
TRINITY	belief that the Godhead exists in three separate but equal forms: the Father, the Son, and the Holy Spirit
VODOUN	religion of African origin practiced by people in Haiti, it combines elements of Catholic and traditional West African religions
YAHWEH	name of God in the Hebrew text of the Old Testament

Section 5

MEDICINE, SCIENCE, AND TECHNOLOGY

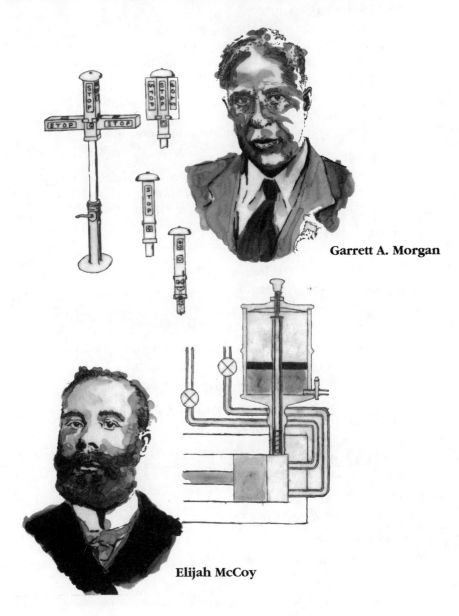

Garrett A. Morgan

Elijah McCoy

SECTION 5

MEDICINE, SCIENCE, AND TECHNOLOGY

African Americans were pioneers in virtually every aspect of medicine, science, and technology. Enslaved Africans came to America armed with proven methods of relieving pain and treating diseases that significantly influenced medical procedures in the United States. African Americans have contributed to the development of blood plasma, open heart surgery, and other aspects of health care. They invented products such as the ironing board, clothes dryer, shoe lasting machine, hearing aid, and heart monitor. African American scientists and engineers played a substantial role in the development of solid state devices, high-powered and ultra-fast lasers, hypersonic flights, and elementary particle science. These contributions have touched each of our lives.

The achievements of African Americans in medicine, science, and technology have been obscured or largely unknown due to racial discrimination and prejudice. Restrictions by the federal government on giving patents to slaves, others taking credit for slave inventions, and corporations capitalizing on the work of employees are other reasons that knowledge of African Americans' contributions is scarce. It has only been in recent years that history textbooks and other historical works acknowledged the contributions of African Americans.

Section 5 paints a picture of some contributions made by African Americans in medicine, science, technology, health, and wellness. Because they were faced with so many barriers to their development, the achievements made are even more remarkable.

FIRSTS IN SCIENCE

List 5-1. Firsts in Medicine, Science, and Technology

Lilia Ann Abron-Robinson	earned doctorate in chemical engineering
Edwin Adom	blind physician and psychiatrist
Alexander T. Augusta	surgeon
William H. Barnes	chief of Otolaryngology at Frederick Douglass Hospital
Emmett Bassett	dairy technology
David H. Blackwell	National Academy of Sciences mathematician
Guion S. Bluford	African American in space
St. Elmo Brady	received Ph.D. in chemistry
Mattie D. Brewer	midwife
Ben Carson	separated conjoined twins at the head
Rebecca Cole	awarded medical degree in the U.S.
Arthur Craig	electrical engineer graduate in the U.S.
Rebecca L. Crumpler	female doctor in the U.S.
Walter Daniel	earned Ph.D. in engineering
James Derham	male doctor in the U.S.
Charles Drew	director of American Red Cross Blood Bank
Harold Ellis	obtained degree in neurology
John Frederick	forensic pathologist
Solomon Carter Fuller	found Alzheimer's disease caused by other than arteriroscleroses
Ulysses Grant	International College of Surgeons
Ida Gray	dentist
William Hinton	wrote *Syphilis and Its Treatment,* first medical textbook
Algernon Brashear Jackson	President of American College of Physicians
Richard F. Jones	Diplomate, American Board of Urology
Roseau F. Lee	oral surgeon
Miles V. Lynk	medical journal publisher
Howard M. Payne	President, National Tuberculosis Association

David J. Peck	graduate of American medical school
Henry R. Peters	D.C. Pharmacy Board
Samuel Proctor, Jr.	National Science Foundation
John B. Slaughter	National Science Director
James McCune Smith	received American medical degree
Frederick D. Stubbs	thoracic surgeon
Clarence Sumner	Diplomate, American Board of Neurosurgery
Levi Watkins	implantation of automatic defibrillator
Harold D. West	President, Meharry Medical College
Daniel Hale Williams	heart surgeon

List 5-2. Firsts in Nursing

James B. Abram	Nursing Department Head, Walter Reed Army Medical Center
Clara Adams-Ender	Nursing Department Chief, Walter Reed Army Medical Center
Margaret E. Bailey	nurse, Lt. Colonel
Marie Rozina Boyd	nurse, Medical Inspection Team Chief
James Rankin Cowan	Commissioner of Health
Frances R. Elliott	nurse, American Red Cross
Warren Hatcher	male Ph.D. nurse
Beatrice J. Holmes	nurse midwife graduate in Mississippi
Hazel W. Brown Johnson	Chief, Army Nurse Corps
Elizabeth Lipford Kent	Ph.D. nurse
Nancy C. Lefenant	nurse in Army Nurse Corps
Mary Elizabeth Mahoney	nurse professional, first graduate nurse, 1879
Barbara Lauraine Nichols	President, American Nursing Association
Estelle M. R. Osborne	Board of Directors, American Nurses Association
Jessie C. Sleet	public health nurse
Eunice Lewis Smith	Director of Nursing, St. Elizabeth's Hospital, Washington, D.C.

INNOVATIVE CONTRIBUTIONS

List 5-3. Inventions in Science, Medicine, and Technology

James S. Adams—airplane propeller, 1920

John H. Allen—Doppler operation test set

A.P. Ashbourne—biscuit cutter, 1875

L.C. Bailey—folding bed, 1899

C.O. Baillift—shampoo headrest, 1898

Benjamin Banneker—wooden clock, 1754; almanac, 1791

William H. Barnes—pituitary gland instrument, 1931

James Bauer—coin changer, 1970

Andrew Beard—automatic railcar coupler, 1897

G.E. Becket—letter box, 1892

Miriam E. Benjamin—gong-and-signal chair, 1888

Edmond Berger—spark plug, 1889

Henry Blair—corn and cotton planters, 1836; seed planter, 1834

Lockrum Blue—corn sheller, 1884

Sarah Boone—ironing board, 1892

Henrietta Bradberry—torpedo discharger, 1945; bed rack, 1943

C.B. Brooks—street sweeper, 1896

Solomon Brown—assisted Samuel Morse with code, 1840

J.A. Burr—lawn mower, 1899

David N. Campbell—dispenser to prevent tuberculosis

George Washington Carver—peanut butter, 1896; agricultural discoveries/patents, 1943

M.A. Cherry—tricycle, 1886

Leander M. Coles—mortician's table

Cap B. Collins—portable electric light, 1938

A.L. Cralle—ice cream scooper, 1897

Joseph H. Dickinson—record player arm, 1819; player piano, 1900

Charles Drew—blood bank, 1940; blood plasma bag, 1945

James Earl—antenna feed for tracking radar

T. Elkins—chamber commode, 1897

Robert Flemming, Jr.—patent for the guitar, 1886

James Forten—sail-raising device, 1850

Albert Gainer—flame retardant

Sarah E. Goode—folding cabinet bed, 1885

Meredith C. Gourdine—electradyne paint spray gun, 1974, 1984, 1985 (27 patents)

George Grant—golf tee, 1899

Julia F. Hammonds—yarn skeins holder, 1896

Edward Hawthorne—heart monitor

M. Headen—foot power hammer, 1886

Harry Hopkins—hearing aid

J.H. Hunter—portable scales, 1896

Augusta Jackson—ice cream

B.F. Jackson—clothes dryer, 1862; gas burner, 1899

Thomas Jennings—dry-cleaning process, 1821

I.R. Johnson—bicycle frame, 1899

John A. Johnson—monkey wrench

P. Johnson—eye protector, 1880

W. Johnson—eggbeater, 1884

Frederick McKinley Jones—refrigerated trucks for long distance; portable X-ray machine, 1960; ticket-dispensing machine, 1939; motor, 1939; air conditioning unit, 1949

Marjorie Joyner—permanent waving machine, 1928

Percy L. Julian—chemical patents, 1936, 1953; glaucoma treatment, 1935

Lewis Latimer—incandescent electric lamp, 1882

W.A. Lavalette—printing press, 1878

Joseph Lee—dough-kneading machine, 1894, 1895

J.L. Love—pencil sharpener, 1897

T. Marshall—fire extinguisher, 1872

Elijah McCoy—lawn sprinkler, 1899; lubricating oil cap, 1872

D. McCree—portable fire escape, 1890

Alexander Miles—patent for first elevator, 1887

Benjamin Montgomery—steamboat propeller with angled blades, 1850

Garrett A. Morgan—gas mask; four-way traffic signal, 1923

W.B. Purvis—handstamp, 1883; machine to make paper bags, 1890; fountain pen, 1890

A.C. Richardson—casket lowering device, 1894

W.H. Richardson—patent for child's carriage, 1899

Charles Richey—device to detect unauthorized use of telephone, 1897

Norbert Rilieux—sugar refiner, 1846

Archia Ross—wrinkle-preventing trouser stretcher, 1899

Lawrence P. Roy—dust pan, 1897

William C. Ruth—bombsight

G.T. Sampson—clothes dryer, 1862; sled propeller, 1885

Dewey S.C. Sanderson—urinalysis meter

S.R. Scrottron—curtain rod, 1889

J.H. Smith—lawn sprinkler, 1897

Richard Spikes—gear shift; automatic directional light, 1913; beer keg tap, 1932

John Standard—refrigerator, 1891

T.W. Stewart—mop, 1893

Rufus Stokes—air purification device, 1968

E.H. Sutton—cotton cultivator, 1898

Lewis Temple—improved whaling harpoon, 1848

Hyram S. Thomas—potato chips

M. Toland—float-operated circuit closer, 1920

Madeline M. Turner—fruit press, 1916

Ubert C. Vincent—varicocele procedure in surgery

Madame C.J. Walker—hair straightener, 1904

J.W. West—wagon, 1870

Ozzie S. Williams—radar search beacon, 1875

Granville T. Woods—phone transmitter, 1884; railroad telegraph, 1887

Louis T. Wright—intradermal smallpox vaccination, 1918; treatment for head and neck injuries, 1918

List 5-4. Contemporary Inventions (1950-Present)

George E. Alcorn—semiconductor, 1984

Tanya Allen—Forever Fresh disposable panties

Virgie M. Ammons—fireplace damper activating tool, 1975

Dr. Patricia Bath—laserphaco probe to remove cataracts, 1988

Alfred Bishop—nuclear core flow distributor, 1978

Bessie J. (Griffin) Blount—device to aid those without limbs to feed themselves, 1951

Otis Boykin—guided missile device; simulator for artificial heart; burglar-proof cash register, 1959

Marie Von Brittain Brown and Albert Brown—home security system, 1969

Paul Brown—Whizzer (spinning top)

I.O. Carter—nursery chair, 1960

Mark Dean—ISA systems bus, 1997, with Dennis Moeller

Linneaus C. Dormon—chemical patents for Dow Chemical, 1960, 1983

Gertrude Downing—baseboard cleaning attachment for rotary floor treatment machine, 1973

Clarence L. Eldor—occustat system (uses motion detectors to lower temperatures in unoccupied room), 1975

Dawn Francis—Way-t'Gro! (fertilizer)

Betram O. Fraser-Reid—method for making nonsugar compounds from sugars, 1975

Joanne Hardin—keyboard stand, 1993

Betty Harris—spot test for explosives called TATB

L.M. Holmes—knockdown wheeled toy, 1950

Ruane Sharon Jeter—toaster, 1987; medical waste disposal, 1999

Lonnie G. Johnson—Super Water Blaster, 1982

Mary Kenner—sanitary belt, 1956; carrier attachment for invalid walker, 1976; bath tissue holder, 1982

Joseph G. Logan—jet engine; small, low-fuel engines for missiles and helicopters, 1950

Michael Molaire—laser printing and optical recording, 1983

Mary Moore—pain-relief composition, 1979

Edwin R. Russell—eleven atomic energy processes, 1996

Henry Sampson—cellular phone, 1971

Maxine Snowden—rain hat, 1983

Valerie L. Thomas—illusion transmitter, 1980

Dennis Weatherby—lemon formula in cleaning products

Rufus J. Weaver—stairclimbing wheelchair, 1968

Jane Cooke Wright—tissue culture tests for anticancer drugs, 1960, 1970

List 5-5. Research Contributions

Scientist	Field	Contribution
Benjamin Alexander	Organic Chemistry	synthesis of pesticides
St. Elmo Brady	Chemistry	ricinoleic acid and magnolia seeds
Louis Cason	Organic Chemistry	medicinal chemistry and organometallic compounds
Joseph C. Dacons	Organic Chemistry	electronic spectra
Lincoln Diuguid	Organic Chemistry	amalgamated aluminum
Irvin W. Elliott	Organic Chemistry	synthesis of isoquinoline and dibenzopyrrocoline alkaloids
Billy J. Evans	Inorganic Chemistry	low-temperature synthesis routes for high-temperature materials
Sylvester J. Gates	Physics	Einstein's unified field type theories
Paula T. Hammond	Chemical Engineering	molecular aspects of chemical engineering
Gary Harris and Michael Spencer	Electrical Engineering	microelectronics and semi-conductor technology
John E. Hodge	Organic Chemistry	carbohydrates
Percy L. Julian	Organic Chemistry	synthesis of physostigmine
Katheryn Lawson	Inorganic Chemistry	quantitative television microscopy
William A. Lester	Computational and Theoretical Chemistry	electronic structure and nuclear motion of molecules
Henry C.R. McBay	Chemistry	radical chemistry
Dolphus Milligan	Chemistry	spectroscopy of free radicals and reactive molecules
Ida Owens	Biochemistry	genetics of detoxification enzymes
Benjamin F. Peery, Jr.	Astronomy	physics of stellar structure, evolution, and nucleosynthesis
Jewel Plummer	Cell Biology	melanoma cancer
Samuel Proctor	Organic Chemistry	phenothiazines, organometallics
Edwin R. Russell	Chemistry	radioactive waste treatment
Dotsevi Y. Sogah	Polymer Chemistry	living polymerization methods

List 5-6. Spotlight: MAE C. JEMISON

➤ Born in Decatur, Alabama, 1956

➤ Attended Stanford University majoring in chemical engineering and Afro-American studies

➤ While in college, participated in dance and theater; represented Stanford in Carifesta '76 in Jamaica

➤ Graduated from Stanford in 1977 and was accepted to Cornell Medical School

➤ Volunteered for a summer experience at a Thai refugee camp while at Cornell

➤ Studied health issues in Kenya, 1979

➤ Organized New York City-wide health and law fair for the National Student Medical Association, 1979

➤ Graduated with an M.D. degree from Cornell Medical School, 1981

➤ Completed internship at Los Angeles County/University of Southern California Medical Center

➤ Joined Peace Corps as medical officer in Sierra Leone and Liberia, 1985

➤ Manager of health care for Peace Corps volunteers and U.S. Embassy personnel

➤ Developed and participated in research projects on hepatitis-B vaccine, schisto-somaisis, and rabies

➤ Speaks Swahili, Japanese, and Russian

➤ Accepted into NASA's astronaut training program, 1987

➤ First African American woman as part of the crew on space shuttle *Endeavor,* 1992

➤ Professor in Environmental Studies; director, Jemison Institute, Dartmouth College

List 5-7. Contributions to Aerospace

Charles Anderson . . . . . completed the first round-trip transcontinental flight

Jessie L. Brown . . . . . . recipient of Distinguished Flying Cross and Air Medal

Jill Brown. . . . . first female pilot of a major airline

Willa B. Brown. . . . . . officer in the Civil Air Patrol

Eugene Bullard. . . . . . combat aviator

George Carruthers . . . . developed the cameras used on Apollo 16 and Skylab 4

Cornelius Coffey . . . . . started the National Airmen's Association of America

Bessie Coleman . . . . . pilot

Col. Benjamin Davis. . . . commander of 99th Fighter Squadron

Gregory F. Drew . . . . . space shuttle commander

Capt. David Harris. . . . . captain of American Airlines

Daniel Chappy James . . . Four-Star General, head of North America Defense Command

Irene Long . . . . Female chief, NASA's Human Resource Branch

Gustavas A. McLeod. . . . piloted open-cockpit aircraft over the North Pole

Ronald E. McNair . . . . . conducted experiments in space

John C. Robinson . . . . . organized Challenger Air Pilots Association

Warren Wheeler . . . . . . airline owner

Woodrow Whitlow. . . . . received a Ph.D. in aeronautics and astronautics from MIT

Edward Wright . . . . accepted into the U.S. space program

KEY DATES

List 5-8. Science, Medicine, and Technology (1966-Present)

1966	Samuel Nabrit	first African American to serve on the Atomic Energy Commission
1981	James Mitchell	received the Percy Julian Outstanding Research Award
1989	Louis W. Sullivan	confirmed as Health and Human Services Secretary
1992	Mae C. Jemison	first African American female astronaut
1993	Michael Espy	appointed Secretary of Agriculture
1993	Jocelyn Elders	confirmed as U.S. Surgeon General

1994	Captain Donnie Cochran	commanded the Blue Angels
1995	Henry W. Foster, Jr.	nominated for U.S. Surgeon General
1995	Bernard Harris	first African American to walk in space
1995	Shirley Jackson	appointed Chair of Nuclear Regulatory Commission
1995	Harold Amos	won the National Academy of Science highest honor: the Public Welfare Medal
1997	David Satcher, M.D.	U.S. Surgeon General

List 5-9. Years of Birth of African American Scientists (1900-1956)

Name	Year	Name	Year
Hildrus A. Poindexter	1901	Jane C. Wright	1920
Lloyd E. Alexander	1902	Benjamin H. Alexander	1921
Leonidas Berry	1902	Marie M. Daly	1921
Flemmie P. Kittrell	1904	Geraldine P. Woods	1921
Charles Drew	1904	James B. Drew	1922
Warren E. Henry	1909	J. Ernest Wilkins, Jr.	1923
Walter L. Hawkins	1911	Jewell P. Cobb	1924
Herman R. Branson	1914	Thomas Craft, Sr.	1924
Margaret M. Lawrence	1914	Evelyn B. Granville	1924
Henry C. McBay	1914	Emmett W. Chappelle	1925
Louis F. Cason	1916	Irving W. Elliott, Jr.	1925
Moddie D. Taylor	1912	Angela D. Ferguson	1925
Lincoln Diuguid	1917	Randolph W. Bromery	1926
James H.M. Henderson	1917	Carl A. Rouse	1926
Clarence F. Stephens	1917	Katheryn E. Lawson	1926
Lloyd N. Ferguson	1918	John L. Gwaltney	1928
David H. Blackwell	1919	Emmanuel B. Thompson	1928
Samuel P. Massie	1919	Meredith C. Gourdine	1928
Welton I. Taylor	1919	Dolphus E. Milligan	1928
Carroll M. Leevy	1920	Don N. Harris	1929

Name	Year	Name	Year
Theodore R. Williams, Jr.	1930	Christine M. Darden	1942
Samuel L. Kountz	1930	Slayton A. Evans, Jr.	1943
Mack Gipson, Jr.	1931	John K. Haynes	1943
Ralph Lewis	1931	Ronald E. Mickens	1943
Tyson Tildon	1931	James W. Mitchell	1943
Samuel von Winbush	1930	Gerald V. Stokes	1943
Harry Morrison	1932	Margaret E. M. Tolbert	1943
William R. Wiley	1932	Joseph C. Dunbar, Jr.	1944
Leodis Davis	1933	Ambrose Jerald, Jr.	1944
James King, Jr.	1933	George M. Langford	1944
Joan Murrell Owens	1933	Kennedy J. Reed	1944
Louis W. Sullivan	1933	Fitzgerald B. Bramwell	1945
Bertram Fraser-Reid	1934	George Campbell, Jr.	1945
Wade M. Kornegay	1934	Renty B. Franklin	1945
Ivory V. Nelson	1934	Lilia A. Abron-Robinson	1945
John B. Slaughter	1934	Carolyn B. Brooks	1946
Linneaus C. Dorman	1935	Walter A. Hill	1946
William M. Jackson	1936	Shirley A. Jackson	1946
Juanita S. Scott	1936	Xavier Creary	1946
Warren M. Washington	1936	Herman Eure	1947
William A. Lester, Jr.	1937	Sandra Murray	1947
Gloria Anderson	1938	Willie Williams, Jr.	1947
Frank E. Gainer	1938	Mary S. Harris	1949
Walter E. Massey	1938	Freeman A. Hrabowski	1950
Earl D. Mitchell, Jr.	1938	Ronald E. McNair	1950
George R. Carruthers	1938	Benjamin S. Carson, Sr.	1951
John W. Macklin	1939	Gregory L. Florant	1951
Cornelia D. Gillyard	1941	Faye V. Harrison	1951
Wesley L. Harris	1941	Joseph S. Francisco	1955
Robert W. Harrison III	1941	A. Oveta Fuller	1955
James H. Wyche	1942	Mae C. Jemison	1956

HEALTH ISSUES

List 5-10. Children's Health Issues

- Access to health care
- Smoking during pregnancy causing low birth weight by mother
- Drinking alcohol during pregnancy
- AIDS
- Asthma
- Improper diet of mother
- Lead poisoning
- Sickle cell anemia
- Children needing a second vaccination against measles
- Flu shots not given to children
- Lack of health insurance

Clara McBride "Mother" Hale (1905-1992) — Founder of Hale House, a home for the treatment of infants born to drug-addicted mothers, in 1975. Mother Hale nurtured over 500 of these children. She also raised 40 children in 27 years, sometimes 7 or 8 foster children at a time in her home.

List 5-11. Black Infant Mortality

- African American mortality rate double that of whites
- Black:white infant death ratios show little change in 50 years
- Poor nutrition
- Tobacco; parents who smoke
- Drug abuse by mother
- Alcoholism and Fetal Alcohol Syndrome (FAS)
- Sudden Infant Death Syndrome (SIDS)
- Low-weight births
- Infections
- Lack of prenatal care

List 5-12. Warning Signs of Drug Use in Children

- Red eyes
- Being overly defensive about privacy
- Chronic cough
- Odd hours coming and going
- Constant lying
- Constant fatigue
- Hostility
- Stealing
- Long periods of "the silent treatment"
- Mood swings
- New friends
- Change in school progress; declining grades; cutting school
- Change in overall appearance

List 5-13. Women's Health Issues

- Access to health care

- Heart disease—leading cause of death

- Cancer (breast)—second leading cause of death

- Diabetes

- Hypertension

- Epidemics

  ➤ Victims of homicide
  ➤ AIDS
  ➤ Poverty (poor health maintenance, drug use, sexually transmitted disease)

- Fibroids

  ➤ Fibroid-related anemia
  ➤ Fibroid-related infertility

- Lesser known health issues

  ➤ Systemic Lupus Erythematosus
  ➤ Depression and other mental diseases
  ➤ Diet, improper nutrition, high cholesterol
  ➤ Poor lifestyle, lack of exercise, obesity
  ➤ Pneumonia and influenza
  ➤ Sarcoidosis
  ➤ Substance abuse

- Empowerment and self-esteem

- Stress

- Stroke

- Liver disease

- Lung cancer

- Kidney disease

- Septicemia (a bacterial infection of the bloodstream)

- Homicide

- Drug-induced causes

- Alcohol-induced causes

- Social support

- Increased stress from racism and discrimination

- Obesity

- Less aggressive treatment or medical records

List 5-14. Men's Health Issues

- Access to health care
- Prostrate cancer
- Heart disease
- Hypertension
- Kidney and urinary tract diseases
- Keloids
- Obesity
- Smoking, substance abuse—serious social and mental health problems
- Accidents and adverse effects
- Homicide and lack of legal intervention
- Diet—poor nutrition, high cholesterol, lack of exercise
- Stroke
- Cancer
- Chronic obstructive pulmonary disease
- Lung cancer
- Pneumonia and influenza
- AIDS
- Septicemia (a bacterial infection of the bloodstream)
- Unintentional injuries
- Suicide
- Homicide
- Drug-induced causes
- Alcohol-induced causes
- Racism
- Exposure to severe environmental risk factors
- Less aggressive treatment or medical referrals

List 5-15. Elderly Health Issues

- Abuse by children
- Hypertension
- Heart disease
- Cardiovascular disease
- Cancer
- Diabetes
- Depression
- Chronic diseases including chronic obstructive lung disease
- Risk factors and life styles
  - ➤ Smoking
  - ➤ Use of drugs
  - ➤ Unhealthy diets
  - ➤ Lack of exercise
  - ➤ Poor stress management
  - ➤ Under reporting of illness
  - ➤ Delay reporting
  - ➤ Consider physiological changes as part of aging
  - ➤ See sickness as weakness
- Long-term care
- Insurance
- Poor quality health care
- Poverty
- Non-medical compliance
- Grandparents caring for grandchildren without adequate assistance

List 5-16. Screening Tests for African Americans

- Blood pressure
- Breast exam—monthly (home), annually by physician
- Cholesterol
- Colonoscopy
- Dental exam
- Electrocardiogram
- Eye exam

- Mammogram
- Gynecology exam
- Physical—annually after 40
- Prostate exam
- Rectal exam
- Sigmoidoscopy
- Testicular exam

RESEARCH

List 5-17. Tuskegee Syphilis Experiment (1932-1972)

- Sponsored by the U.S. government
- Announced as a new health care program in Macon County, Alabama
- Distributed announcement only to African Americans
- Based at Tuskegee Institute Hospital
- Designed as short-term (6-8 months) project
- Purpose was to gain a greater scientific understanding of syphilis by studying the untreated progression of the disease
- Involved 623 men, most with syphilis; noninfected were control subjects
- Provided men with aspirin and iron supplements in 1935
- None of the men consented to participate in study (never were told it was an experiment)
- Denied medical treatment for 40 years to 412 men with syphilis while pretending to treat them, even after penicillin became available
- Assumed black men would not get treatment because they were black and poor
- Nurse Eunice Rivers Laurie was major contact for patients:

  —Worked directly with white doctors from Washington, D.C.
  —Worked on project for 30 years

- On November 16, 1972 Health Education and Welfare ordered the experiment closed and treatment for surviving participants
- The 1998 HBO movie "Miss Evers' Boys" was a dramatization of the study
- President Bill Clinton apologized to survivors on May 16, 1999

List 5-18. Spotlight: DR. BENJAMIN CARSON

➢ Born in 1951 in Detroit, Michigan

➢ Poor student in elementary school and developed a bad temper during adolescence

➢ Mother made him read two books a week and limited the amount of television

➢ Became an outstanding student by the time he completed high school in 1968

➢ Attended Yale University on an academic scholarship

➢ Attended University of Michigan Medical School

➢ Performed his residency and internship in neurosurgery at Johns Hopkins Hospital in Baltimore, Maryland

➢ 1982—chief resident of neurosurgery at Johns Hopkins

➢ 1984—assistant professor of neurosurgery and oncology at Johns Hopkins University

➢ 1984—appointed chief of pediatric neurosurgery at Johns Hopkins Medical Center

➢ 1987—assistant professor of pediatrics at Johns Hopkins University

➢ 1985-1991—director of pediatric neurosurgery at Johns Hopkins Medical Center

➢ Recognized for performing brain surgery on children

➢ 1987—led a team of 70 medical professionals in separating conjoined twins joined at the back of the head

➢ Published studies in several journals and authored two books:

   Think Big

   Gifted Hands

➢ Established foundation to assist African American medical students

List 5-19. Spotlight: DR. CHARLES R. DREW

➤ Born June 3, 1904 in Washington, D.C. to Charles and Nora Drew, the eldest of five children

➤ Active in basketball, baseball, football, and track, Dunbar High School in Washington

➤ Attended Amherst College on an athletic scholarship and graduated with highest honors in 1926

➤ Athletic director and football coach, Morgan College, Baltimore; taught biology and chemistry for two years; although interested in sports, real love was medicine

➤ Entered McGill University Medical School, Montreal, Canada, 1928; graduated second in class of 137 with a Doctor of Science and Master of Surgery degrees in 1933; received Doctor of Science in Medicine degree from Columbia University, 1940; at McGill, became interested in blood research and continued research at two hospitals in Montreal, Canada

➤ Taught for a short period at the Medical School at Howard College (now Howard University) before moving to Columbia Presbyterian Hospital, New York; at Columbia, developed technique for long-term preservation of blood plasma

➤ Discovery came when most needed—during World War II; his method critical in getting blood products to injured soldiers. U.S. shared the technology with Britain; Dr. Drew directed that effort as medical supervisor of the Blood for Britain program; established several blood banks in Europe; drafted by the American Red Cross to establish the blood bank program in the U.S.

➤ 1941, U.S. War Department issued order declaring "it is not advisable to collect and mix Caucasian and Negro blood indiscriminately...." Dr. Drew fought the move, calling the order indefensible; resigned his post as Assistant Director of the national blood program in 1941.

➤ Recipient of numerous awards including NAACP's Spingarn Medal, 1944

➤ Died in an automobile accident April 1, 1950

➤ U.S. Postal Service honored Dr. Drew with commemorative stamp, 1981

FOLK MEDICINE AND HEALERS

List 5-20. Folk Medicines

- Roots, herbs, minerals, plants

- Teas were known as "first medicines"

- Vaccination of smallpox with a live virus discovered by Onesimus, 1706, a slave; contribution documented in diary of slave owner, Boston Puritan minister Cotton Mather

- Cure for rattlesnake bite discovered by Caesar, a slave, 1792

- Dr. Lucas Santomée, first non-American black physician, practiced folk medicine among the Africans, Dutch, and English in New Amsterdam

- Infusions/decoctions

- Tinctures

- Extracts

List 5-21. Folk Practitioners and Traditional Healers

- Bonesetter

- Fetish priest or priestess

- Herbalist

- Medicine man

- Root doctor

- Traditional birth attendant

- Voodoo doctor

- Witch doctor

List 5-22. Faith and Spiritual Healing Practices

- Use of prayer

- Laying on of hands

- Rubbing with holy oil

- Fasting

List 5-23. Home Remedies

Honey, lemon, and whiskey tea . . . . cold

Warm salt water . . . . fever

Garlic cloves . . . . blood pressure

Eucalyptus oil and honey . . . . cold

Fat meat or potatoes. . . . . boils

Raw eggs . . . . boils

Penny and chewed tobacco. . . . . . . rusty nail wound

String tied on leg. . . . . cramps

Coins, keys . . . . bleeding nose

Beer . . . . worms

Turpentine and sugar . . . . healing of open wounds

Kerosene and sugar . . . . cold

Silver dollar and belly band. . . . . . . protruding navel

Mustard seed . . . . asthma

Dirt and clay rocks. . . . . headache

Standing on head . . . . headache

List 5-24. Folk Practices for Various Ailments

- Breathing problem or asthma
    - ➢ mixture of honey, lemon juice, and whiskey
- Stomach disorders, burns, cleaning teeth
    - ➢ baking soda
- Aching bones
    - ➢ honey, vinegar, and "moonshine" (corn whiskey)
- Cuts
    - ➢ turpentine
- Whooping cough and diarrhea
    - ➢ a glass of mare's (horse) milk and a cup of flour water
- Bee stings, bronchial ailment (known as croup)
    - ➢ coal oil

ORGANIZATIONS AND ASSOCIATIONS

List 5-25. Medicine, Science, and Research

African AIDS Project (Pasadena, California)

African Medical & Research Foundation USA (New York, New York)

Alliance for Alternatives in Health Care (Thousand Oaks, California)

American Foundation for Alternative Health Care (Monticello, New York)

American Holistic Medical Association (Catasauqua, Pennsylvania)

Association of Black Cardiologists (Atlanta, Georgia)

Association of Black Nursing Faculty (Liste, Illinois)

Association of Minority Health Professors Schools (Washington, D.C.)

Association of Third World Anthropologists (Baltimore, Maryland)

Auxiliary to the National Medical Association (Washington, D.C.)

Committee for Freedom of Choice in Medicine (Chula Vista, California)

Complementary Medicine Networking and Referral Service (Tucson, Arizona)

Delta Health Center, Inc. (Mound Bayou, Mississippi)

Institute for International Health & Development (Washington, D.C.)

National Association of Health Services Executives (Columbia, Maryland)

National Association of Medical Minority Educators (Milwaukee, Wisconsin)

National Association for Sickle Cell Disease, Inc. (Los Angeles, California)

National Black Child Development Institute (Washington, D.C.)

National Black Nurses Association, Inc. (Washington, D.C.)

National Black Women's Health Project (Atlanta, Georgia)

National Center for the Advancement of Blacks in Health Professions (Detroit, Michigan)

National Medical Association (Washington, D.C.)

National Minority Health Association (Harrisburg, Pennsylvania)

Research Foundation for Ethnic Related Diseases (Los Angeles, California)

Sammy Davis, Jr. National Liver Institute (Newark, New Jersey)

Sickle Cell Disease Association of America (Culver City, California)

List 5-26. Science and Technology

American Association of Blacks in Energy (Denver, Colorado)

Atlanta Council of Black Professional Engineers (Atlanta, Georgia)

Carver Research Foundation of Tuskegee Institute, Inc. (Tuskegee, Alabama)

Chemical Industry for Minorities in Engineering (Wilmington, Delaware)

Los Angeles Council of Black Professional Engineers (Los Angeles, California)

National Action Council for Minorities in Engineering (New York, New York)

National Association of Black Consulting Engineers (Washington, D.C.)

National Institute of Science (Prairie View, Texas)

National Organization for the Professional Advancement of Black Chemists and Chemical Engineers (Washington, D.C.)

National Society of Black Engineers (Brooklyn, New York)

National Society of Black Physicists (Murray Hill, New Jersey)

National Society of Minority Women in Science (Washington, D.C.)

Negro Airmen International (Tuskegee, Alabama)

Organization of Black Airline Pilots, Inc. (Flushing, New York)

Organization of Black Scientists, Inc. (Washington, D.C.)

Tuskegee Airmen, Inc. (Denver, Colorado)

MEDICAL AND HEALTH WEBSITES

List 5-27. Medical and Health Websites

- African American Health
  http://www.888Antiage.com

- Dr. Marcellus Walker
  http://www.walkermd.com

- FeMiNa: Health and Wellness
  http://www.femina.com/femina/healthandwellness

- Algy's Herb Page
  http//www/aalgy.com/herb/index.html

- Dr. Bowers Complementary and Alternative Medicine Home Page
  http://www.galen.med.virginia.edu/-pjb3s/

- The Alternative Medicine Homepage
  http://www.pitt.edu/-cbw/altm.html

- Detox Help
  http://www.detoxhelp.com

- Ask Dr. Weil
  http://www.ddrweil.com

- "Bones Are Us"
  http://www.cosortho.com

- Between the Lines
  http://members.aol.com/pbchowka

- Ask the Dietitian
  http://www.hoptechno.com/rdindex.htm

- Yahoo!'s Alternative Medicine Page
  http://www.yahoo.com/health/aaalternative_medicine

- Yahoo! Health: Women's Health
  http://www.yahoo.com/health/women_s_health

- Women's Medical Health Page
  http://www.bet.com/~sirlou/wmhp.html

- General Complementary Medicine References
  http://www.forthrt.com/~chronicl/archiv.htm

- Southwest School of Botanical Medicine
  http://www.chili.rt66.com/hrbmore/HOMEPAGE/HomePage.html

- HealthGate
  http.//www.healthgate.com

- OncoLink, University of Pennsylvania Cancer Center Resource
  http://www.oncolink.org

- Health World Online
  http://www.health.net

- NEW AGE Online
  http://www.newage.com

- Homeopathic Home Page
  http://www.dungeon.com/~cam/homeo.html

- National Association of People with AIDS
  http://www.thecure.org

- Institute for Traditional Medicine
  http://www.europa.com/~itm

- MedWeb
  http://www.cc.emory.edu/WHSCL/medweb.html

- The MedAccess Site
  http://www.medaccess.com

AFRICAN AMERICAN HOSPITALS

List 5-28. African American Hospitals

(Hospitals that served primarily African Americans. Some are named for African Americans.)

- Atlanta Mac Vicor Infirmary (Atlanta, Georgia)
- Charity Hospital of Louisiana (New Orleans, Louisiana)
- Cook County Hospital (Chicago, Illinois)
- Cuyahoga County Hospital (Cleveland, Ohio)
- Drew/King Hospital (Los Angeles, California)
- D. C. General Hospital (District of Columbia)
- Fairview Medical Center (Montgomery, Alabama)
- George W. Hubbard Hospital, Meharry Medical College (Nashville, Tennessee)
- Grady Memorial Hospital (Atlanta, Georgia)
- Howard University Center (District of Columbia)
- Jackson Park Hospital (Chicago, Illinois)
- L. Richardson Memorial Hospital (Greensboro, North Carolina)
- Norfolk Community Hospitals (Norfolk, Virginia)
- Provident Hospital (Chicago, Illinois & Baltimore, Maryland)
- Richmond Community Hospital (Richmond, Virginia)
- Roseland Community Hospital (Chicago, Illinois)
- Southwest Detroit Hospital (Detroit, Michigan)
- St. Luke Colored Hospital (Marlin, Texas)
- Westland Medical Center (Westland, Michigan)

HISTORICAL SITES

List 5-29. Historical Sites

- Benjamin Banneker Circle and Foundation (Washington, D.C.)
- The Daniel Chappie James Center for Aerospace Science (Tuskegee University)
- Dr. Charles R. Drew Home (Arlington, Virginia)
- Dr. Daniel Hale Williams Home (Chicago, Illinois)
- Dunbar Hospital (Detroit, Michigan)
- Eighth Regiment Army Armory (Chicago, Illinois)
- First National Black Historical Society of Kansas (Wichita, Kansas)
- Fisk University/Meharry Medical School (Nashville, Tennessee)
- The George Washington Carver National Monument (Diamond, Missouri)
- I. P. Stanback Museum and Planetarium (Orangeburg, South Carolina)
- Lloyd Hall Home (Chicago, Illinois)
- Moorland-Spingarn Research Center (Howard University)
- Moton Field, Tuskegee Army Air Field (Tuskegee University)
- National Museum of the Tuskegee Airmen at Historic Fort Wayne (Detroit, Michigan)
- North Carolina Central University (Raleigh, North Carolina)
- Provident Hospital Training School (Chicago, Illinois)
- Shaw University (Raleigh, North Carolina)
- Southern Museum of Flight (Birmingham, Alabama)

LITERATURE

List 5-30. Science Books for Children and Young Adults

- *African American Medical Pioneers,* Charles Epps & David G. Johnson
- *African American Scientists,* Jetty Kahn
- *African American Scientists,* Patricia McKissack & Frederick McKissack
- *Against All Opposition: Black Explorers in America,* Jim Haskins
- *Ben Carson: Medicine Man,* Alex Simmons
- *Benjamin Banneker: Scientist,* Garnet N. Jackson
- *Bessie Coleman: She Dared to Fly,* Dolores Johnson
- *Black First: 2,000 Years of Extraordinary Achievement,* Jessie C. Smith
- *Black Stars in Orbit: The Story of NASA's African American Astronauts,* Khephra Burns & William Miles
- *Blacks in Science and Medicine,* Vivian O. Sammons
- *Carter G. Woodson,* Robert Franklin Durden
- *Charles Drew: Doctor,* Garnet N. Jackson
- *Chemistry Quickies,* Vivian W. Owens
- *Contributions of Black Women to America,* Edited by Marianna W. Davis
- *Contributions of African Americans to Science: Diversity in the Science Curriculum,* Belinda Thien, Judith Pryor, & Vera Kolb
- *Encyclopedia of Black America,* W. Augusta Low & Virgil A. Clift
- *Garrett Morgan: Inventor,* Garnet N. Jackson
- *George Washington Carver: The Peanut Scientist,* Patricia McKissack & Frederick McKissack
- *Madam C. J. Walker: Pioneer Businesswoman,* Marian W. Taylor
- *Mae Jemison: Astronaut,* Garnet N. Jackson
- *Outward Dreams: Black Inventors and Their Inventions,* Jim Haskins
- *The Real McCoy: The Life of an African American Inventor,* Wendy Towle
- *Red-Tail Angels: The Story of the Tuskegee Airmen of World War II,* Patricia McKissack & Frederick McKissack
- *The Story of George Washington Carver,* Eva Moore
- *Sure Hands, Strong Heart: The Life of Daniel Hale Williams,* Lillie Patterson

Section 6

BUSINESS AND INDUSTRY

Robert Johnson

AFRICAN AMERICANS IN BUSINESS AND INDUSTRY

SECTION 6

BUSINESS AND INDUSTRY

Africans brought to America a history of entrepreneurial experience. Whether that experience was based on bartering within or between villages or trading on a larger scale among nations, they understood the concepts of supply and demand. That knowledge of enterprise—combined with highly developed skills in areas ranging from agriculture to astronomy—provided the formula for successful business development. African Americans carried on that entrepreneurial spirit and began to establish commerce even before the outbreak of the Civil War, and the tradition continues today.

Early business development was conducted by two distinct groups of African Americans: free and enslaved. Free African Americans were able to establish businesses mostly in crafts or service areas not in competition with white businesses, including bakers, blacksmiths, cabinet makers, metal workers, tanners, tailors, dressmakers, weavers, caterers, and hairdressers. The second group were slaves who were allowed to make and sell products or services during their free time or received monies when their skills were leased to others. Enslaved Africans would often use those funds to purchase freedom for themselves and family members.

In either case, developing a business during slavery for an African American was more than a challenge. Existing laws controlled enslaved blacks and restricted the movement of free blacks as well. African Americans were segregated, prohibited from meeting in groups, and could be kidnapped and sold into slavery without cause. All those conditions limited free enterprise, but African Americans were motivated to have personal and economic freedom. Striving against the odds, they created organizations such as the National Negro Business League to support and encourage business development.

Starting with Madame C. J. Walker who developed a system and equipment for hair care, African Americans focused on a limited range of businesses to include small restaurants, funeral services, cleaning establishments, shoe repair, and gas stations. Shortly after the signing of the Emancipation Proclamation, manufacturing, insurance, and banking businesses quickly emerged. These businesses focused on delivery of services to the African American community. Steady progress was made in business over the past century in spite of Jim Crow laws and segregation. Fast forward to the 1980s and 1990s and you find African American businesses in all industries. These enterprises continue to face challenges when competing in the broader market. Two of the primary challenges are discrimination or disparity in the availability of venture capital and competition from larger white businesses for the African American market and its estimated multibillion-dollar purchasing power.

Section 6 identifies medium- and large-scale businesses in a wide range of industries and some of the pioneers in the field.

AFRICAN AMERICANS IN BUSINESS AND INDUSTRY

List 6-1. Firsts in Business and Industry

1810	African Insurance Company of Philadelphia	first African American insurance company; Joseph Randolph, President
1818	Thomas Day	first furniture maker in the South
1846	William Leidesdorff	opened hotel in San Francisco; organized first horserace (1847); chair of Board of Education that opened California's first public school (1848)
1850	Samuel R. Ward	first president, American League of Colored Workers
1858	Association of Black Caulkers	first labor organization on record
1866	Biddy Mason	first African American woman property owner in Los Angeles, California
1888	Tree Reformers' Bank, Richmond, Virginia; Capital Savings Bank, Washington, D.C.	first banks founded and operated by African Americans
1893	North Carolina Mutual Life Insurance Company	insurance company to reach $100 million in assets
1910	Madam C. J. Walker	built manufacturing plant in Indianapolis, first female millionaire
1925	A. Phillip Randolph	founded Brotherhood of Sleeping Car Porters
1932	Asa Spaulding	actuary
1936	National Negro Congress	first attempt at organizing to improve conditions of black workers
1938	Ferdinand C. Smith	founder and vice president, National Maritime Union
1943	Ferdinand C. Smith	member, National Congress of Industrial Organizations (CIO) Executive Board
1957	Cirilo A. McSween	sold $1 million in life insurance in a major white-owned insurance company
1959	Ruth J. Bowen	established booking and talent agency in New York City
1960	Charles F. Harris	established Zenith Books, presenting minority histories to the general public

1961	Dempsey J. Travis	established Sivart Mortgage Company in Chicago, Illinois
1962	Harvey C. Russell, Jr.	vice president, Pepsico
1962	Nelson J. Edwards	member of International Executive Board of United Autoworkers
1965	Freedom National Bank	first commercial bank, Harlem, New York
1970	Clarence C. Findley	division president of a major firm, Char-Tred-Monticello (branch of Burlington Industries)
1970	Joseph L. Searles III	first African American to become a member of the New York Stock Exchange
1971	Willie L. Daniels and Travers Bell, Jr.	first African American company on the New York Stock Exchange
1972	John H. Johnson	received Henry Johnson Fisher Award of the Magazine Publishers Association; publisher of *Jet, Ebony, Ebony Man,* and *Ebony Jr.*
1977	E. G. Bowman Company	African American-owned insurance firm on Wall Street
1981	Barbara B. Hutchinson	female member, AFL-CIO Executive Council
1983	Ben F. Branch	established the nation's first black-owned soft drink company, Chicago, Illinois
1987	Barbara J. Wilson	female automobile dealer; received Candace Award as Business Woman of the Year
1988	John N. Sturdivant	president, American Federation of Government Employees
1990	Bertram M. Lee	member of Board of Directors of Reebok International
1993	Pearline Motley	honored as American Business Woman of the Year
1994	Henry Hampton	received Heinz Award in the Arts and Humanities for Blackside, Inc., his independent film and television company (1968); produced documentaries *Eyes on the Prize* I and II
1998	Cushcity.com	first African American bookstore online
1998	Blackstocks.com	Internet site devoted to providing investment services and financial education
2000	Donald V. Adderton	editor of the *Delta Democrat-Times* in Greenville, Mississippi, becoming the first black editor of a major daily newspaper in Mississippi

List 6-2. Largest Industrial/Service Companies
(Top 20 of *Black Enterprise* 100s)

	Year Started
World Wide Technology, Inc.	1990
The Philadelphia Coca-Cola Bottling Co.	1985
Johnson Publishing Co.	1942
Active Transportation Co.	1987
The Bing Group	1980
BET Holdings II, Inc.	1980
Washington Cable Supply, Inc.	1984
Spiral Inc.	1989
H. J. Russell & Company	1952
Fuci Metals USA, Inc.	1986
Granite Broadcasting Corp.	1988
Hawkins Food Group	1995
Simeus Foods International, Inc.	1996
Sayers	1982
Anderson-Dubose Co.	1991
Rush Communications	1991
Mays Chemical Co.	1980
Barden Companies, Inc.	1981
Global Automotive Alliance LLC	1999
Midwest Stamping, Inc.	1993

For further information, see *Black Enterprise,* 30 (11), June 2000, pp. 107-129.

List 6-3. Young Entrepreneurs

Dwan Andre Brown. . . . . . . Brown Investments (real estate, Tennessee)

Damon John, Keith Perrin,
Carl Brown, J. Alex Martin . . . FUBU (For Us By Us)

Jasmine A. Jordan . . . . *Tools for Living* Magazine

Anthony Kirkland . . . . Mass Sound Recording

Jerry & Sindy Lewis . . . . Allied Personnel, Inc.

Marvin & Malcolm Miles . . . . J & R Beauty and Barber Supplies

Daniel Miller, Jr. . . . . Custom Postcards (printing)

Desiree Sanders . . . . Afrocentric Bookstore

Sedessia Spivey . . . . S & W Innovative Solutions

Alisa and Danzell Starks . . . . Multiplex Movie Theaters

Lolita Sweet . . . . Bay Area Young Entrepreneurs

Omar Wason . . . . New York Online (NYO)

List 6-4. African American Business Schools

Alabama A&M University, Normal, Alabama

Clark Atlanta University, Atlanta, Georgia

Fayetteville State University, Fayetteville, North Carolina

Grambling State University, Grambling, Louisiana

Jackson State University, Jackson, Mississippi

Lincoln University, Jefferson City, Missouri

BUSINESSES

List 6-5. Construction/Manufacturing

A.L.L. Construction, St. Louis, Missouri

A.W. Steel Contractors, St. Louis, Missouri

Alves Contracting Company, Ltd., Washington, D.C.

Bing Steel, Detroit, Michigan

C.D. Moody Construction, Inc., Lithonia, Georgia

H.J. Russell & Co., Atlanta, Georgia

J & L Service Construction, Fairbanks, Alaska

Mays Chemical Company, Indianapolis, Indiana

Midwest Stamping Company, Bowling Green, Ohio

Ozanne Construction Company, Inc., Cleveland, Ohio

Powers & Sons Construction Co., Inc., Gary, Indiana

Solo Construction Corp., North Miami Beach, Florida

List 6-6. Cosmetics and Hair Care

Bronner Brothers, Inc., Marietta, Georgia

Carson's Products, Inc., Savannah, Georgia

Dudley Products, Inc., Kernersville, North Carolina

Epitomi, Miami, Florida

Fashion Fair, Chicago, Illinois (now owned by IVAX Corporation)

Iman Cosmetics, New York, New York

Luster Products Company, Chicago, Illinois

M & M Products, Atlanta, Georgia

Naomi Sims Beauty Products Limited, Amityville, Wyoming

Pro-Line, Dallas, Texas

Soft-Sheen Products, Chicago, Illinois

Walker Enterprises, Indianapolis, Indiana

List 6-7. Educational Products and Services

African American Images, Chicago, Illinois

African Publishing, New York, New York

Afrikids, Cincinnati, Ohio

Career Communications Group, Baltimore, Maryland

Dudley Accelerated Learning Systems, Phoenix, Arizona

Intelligent Era Computing & Tutoring, Inc., Bowie, Maryland

KNC Software LLC, Los Angeles, California

Learn*Learn*Learn Education Corporation, Lanham, Maryland

List 6-8. Engineering

Bay Associates, Boston, Massachusetts

Capsonic Automotive, Inc., Elgin, Illinois

Integrated Management Services (IMS), Woodbridge, Virginia

Integrated Systems Analysts, Inc., Arlington, Virginia

Navcom Systems Group, Manassas, Virginia

Polytech, Inc., Cleveland, Ohio

Sentel Corporation, Alexandria, Virginia

Systems Engineering and Management Associates, Alexandria, Virginia

United Energy, Inc., Portland, Oregon

List 6-9. Entertainment

Production Companies

Amen Ra Films, Wesley Snipes, Los Angeles, California

40 Acres and a Mule, Shelton Jackson "Spike" Lee, Los Angeles, California

Blackside, Inc., Henry Hampton, Boston, Massachusetts

Tony Brown Productions, Inc., Tony Brown, New York, New York

Don Cornelius Productions, Inc., Don Cornelius, New York, New York

Edmonds Entertainment, Kenneth & Tracey Edmonds, Los Angeles, California

Gordy\dePasse Productions, Berry Gordy and Suzanne dePasse, Los Angeles, California

Harpo Productions, Oprah Winfrey, Chicago, Illinois

Inner City Broadcasting Corp., Harold Jackson, New York, New York

Don King Productions, Don King, Los Angeles, California

MJJINC, Michael Jackson, Los Angeles, California

Eddie Murphy Productions, Eddie Murphy, Los Angeles, California

New Millennium Studios, Tim and Daphne Maxwell Reid, Petersburg, Virginia

Sisterlee Productions, Hollywood, California

United Image Entertainment, Robert Johnson, Washington, D.C.

Radio and Television Stations

American Urban Radio Networks, Sydney Small, New York, New York

Barden Companies, Detroit, Michigan

Black Entertainment Television, Robert Johnson, Washington, D.C.

Granite Broadcasting, Don Cornwell, New York, New York

Radio One, Cathy Hughes, Washington, D.C.

Roberts Broadcasting, St. Louis, Missouri

Rush Communications, New York, New York

Sutton's Inner City Broadcasting, Percy Sutton, Philadelphia, Pennsylvania

Record Labels

48th/49th Records, Washington, D.C.

Dick Griffey Productions/ADPIC, Sherman Oaks, California

Jimmy Jam and Terry Lewis, Minneapolis, Minnesota

Flavor Unit Records and Management Co., Los Angeles, California

LaFace Records, Atlanta, Georgia

Moore Entertainment Group, Upper Saddle River, New Jersey

No Limit Records, Richmond, California

Paisley Park, Chanhassen, Minnesota

Qwest Records, Los Angeles, California

Wondirection Records, Los Angeles, California

Promotions

African Heritage Networks Group, New York, New York

Chisholm-Mingo Group, Inc., New York, New York

Don Coleman Advertising, Inc., Southfield, Michigan

E. Morris Communications, Chicago, Illinois

Fantasy Entertainment, Los Angeles, California

Headhunta Entertainment, Los Angeles, California

Magic Johnson Enterprises, Los Angeles, California

Matlock and Associates, Atlanta, Georgia/New York, New York

No Limit Enterprises, Baton Rouge, Louisiana

Pro-Indi Entertainment LLC, Los Angeles, California

Quincy Jones Entertainment, Los Angeles, California

SRB Productions, Inc., Washington, D.C.

Stowe Communications, Inc., Long Island, New York

Sykes Communications, Inc., Houston, Texas

Theater/Ballet

Alvin Ailey American Dance Theater, New York, New York

American Dance Theater of Harlem, Harlem, New York

Dallas Black Theater, Dallas, Texas

Dance Theater of Harlem, New York, New York

Dayton Contemporary Dance Company, Dayton, Ohio

Philadelphia Dance Company (Philadanco), Philadelphia, Pennsylvania

Soul In Motion Players, Inc., Washington, D.C.

List 6-10. Ethnic Collectibles

Asanti Collections, Raleigh, North Carolina

Great Hours of Dolls, Virginia Beach, Virginia

Keepsake Expressions, Lithonia, Georgia

Roberta's Collectibles, Lauderhill, Florida

Roger's Originals, Los Angeles, California

List 6-11. Food Industry

Baldwin Richardson Foods Company, Matteson, Illinois

Beatrice International Holdings, New York, New York

Branch Products, Chicago, Illinois

Bridgeman Foods, Louisville, Kentucky

Brooks Food Group, Inc., Bedford, Virginia

Convenience Corporation of America, West Palm Beach, Florida

Elephant Walk, Lewmert Park Village, California

Fair Oaks Farms LLC, Pleasant Priarie, Wisconsin

Fedco Foods, Los Angeles, California

Glory Foods, Columbus, Ohio

Gourmet Companies, Inc., Atlanta, Georgia

H.G. Parks Sausage Company, Inc., Baltimore, Maryland

Mojo Highway Brewing Company, New York, New York/Washington, D.C.

Olajuwon Group of Companies, Houston, Texas

Philadelphia Coca-Cola Bottling Company, Philadelphia, Pennsylvania

RLLW, Inc., Las Vegas, Nevada

Stop Shop Save Food Markets, Baltimore, Maryland

Thompson Hospitality Service, Sterling, Virginia

V and J Holding Companies, Milwaukee, Wisconsin

Vendemmia, Inc., Atlanta, Georgia

List 6-12. Graphic Design

Destee Design and Publishing, Mobile, Alabama

Dover Graphics, Dover, Delaware

Mec Efx, Raleigh, North Carolina

List 6-13. Health and Nutrition

Advantage Enterprises, Inc., Toledo, Ohio

Akbari's Hair Nutrition System, Memphis, Tennessee

AMASSI, Los Angeles, California

Health Resources, Inc., Lemoyce, Pennsylvania

Mosiac Advisory Committee, San Mateo, California

R.O.W. Sciences, Inc., Rockville, Maryland

Ugly Duckling Enterprise Plus, Kershaw, South Carolina

List 6-14. Information Technology

Advanced Resource Technologies, Inc., Alexandria, Virginia

Computer Consulting Associates International, Inc., Southport, Connecticut

Digital Systems Research, Inc., Arlington, Virginia

Edge Systems, Inc., Downers Grove, Illinois

INNOLOG (Innovative Logistics Techniques, Inc.), McLean, Virginia

Intelli Systems Technology Corporation, Fairfax, Virginia

Management Technology, Inc., Clinton, Maryland

McNeil Technologies, Springfield, Virginia

Metters Industries, Inc., McLean, Virginia

Pulsar Data Systems, Lanham, Maryland

Ronson Communications and Information Systems, LLC, Alexandria, Virginia

R.S. Information Systems, Inc., McLean, Virginia

Sylvest Management Systems Corporation, Lanham, Maryland

UNITECH, Fairfax, Virginia

United Communications Systems, Inc., McLean, Virginia

List 6-15. Investment Firms

Blaylock and Partners L.P., New York, New York

Chapman Company, Baltimore, Maryland

Edgar Lomax Company, Springfield, Virginia

M.R. Beal & Co., New York, New York

Paradigm Asset Management, New York, New York

Pryor, Counts & Company, Inc., Philadelphia, Pennsylvania

Rideau Lyons & Co., Inc., Los Angeles, California

SBK Brooks Investment Corp., Cleveland, Ohio

Siebert Brandford Shank & Company LLC, San Francisco, California

Smith, Graham and Company, Houston, Texas

The Williams Capital Group L.P., New York, New York

Wordford Capital Management, New York, New York

List 6-16. Marketing and Advertising

Black Sheep, Atlanta, Georgia

Burrell Communications Group, Chicago, Illinois

Deborah Minor, Tuscaloosa, Alabama

Diane Wilson Onwuchekwa, Danville, Virginia

Don Coleman Advertising, Southfield, Michigan

E. Morris Communications, Chicago, Illinois

Sykes Communications, Houston, Texas

Uniworld Group, New York, New York

Vision Accomplished, Charlotte, North Carolina

List 6-17. Publishing

Africa World Press, Trenton, New Jersey

Allied Productions, Inc., Tallahassee, Florida

Anlise Press, Seattle, Washington

Black Classic Press, Baltimore, Maryland

Broadside Press, Detroit, Michigan

Chistell Publishing, Bensalem, Pennsylvania

Earl G. Graves Publishing Company, New York, New York

Essence Communications, New York, New York

Howard University Press, Baltimore, Maryland

Johnson Publishing Company, Inc., New York, New York/Chicago, Illinois

Lushena Books, Inc., New York, New York

Mind Productions, Inc., New York, New York

Red Sea Press, Lawrenceville, New Jersey

R.R. Donnelley & Sons Printing Co., Chicago, Illinois

The FIRE! Press, Elizabeth, New Jersey

Third World Press, Chicago, Illinois

Urban Research Press, Inc., Chicago, Illinois

List 6-18. Telecommunication

Alternative Communications, Columbia, South Carolina

Black Star Communications, Melbourne, Florida

Calhoun Enterprises, Montgomery, Alabama

Dynamics Concepts, Inc., Washington, D.C.

Pacific Network Supply, San Jose, California

PRWT, Inc., Philadelphia, Pennsylvania

Russell Rowe Communications, Macon, Georgia

Telecommunication System, Annapolis, Maryland

TLC Next Generation, St. Louis, Missouri

Universal Systems & Technology, Fairfax, Virginia

Washington Cable Supply, Inc., Lanham, Maryland

Wireamerica of Indiana, Inc., Fort Wayne, Indiana

List 6-19. Web Development

AHA Communications, Inc., New York, New York

Global Web Development, San Leandro, California

Imagestic Productions, Tuskegee, Alabama

KemNet Technologies, Shrewsbury, New Jersey

Savoy Website Designs, Cleveland, Ohio

Web Masterpieces, Orange County, California

FINANCIAL COMPANIES

List 6-20. African American Financial Companies

**Year
Started**

1894	First Tuskegee Bank (Tuskegee, Alabama)
1903	Consolidated Bank and Trust Co. (Richmond, Virginia)
1921	Citizens Trust Bank (Atlanta, Georgia)
1921	Mutual Community Savings Bank, SSB (Durham, North Carolina)
1925	Mutual Federal Savings & Loan Assn. of Atlanta (Atlanta, Georgia)
1934	Industrial Bank of Washington (Washington, D.C.)
1946	Broadway Federal Savings & Loan Assn. (Los Angeles, California)
1957	Citizens Federal Savings Bank (Birmingham, Alabama)
1968	Independence Federal Savings Bank (Washington, D.C.)
1971	North Milwaukee State Bank (Milwaukee, Wisconsin)
1975	First Texas Bank (Dallas, Texas)
1982	Boston Bank of Commerce (Boston, Massachusetts)
1982	The Harbor Bank of Maryland (Baltimore, Maryland)
1991	Tri-State Bank of Memphis (Memphis, Tennessee)

INSURANCE COMPANIES

List 6-21. African American Insurance Companies

**Year
Started**

1898   The Pilgrim Health & Life Insurance Company (Augusta, Georgia)

1899   North Carolina Mutual Life Insurance Co. (Durham, North Carolina)

1905   Atlanta Life Insurance Co. (Atlanta, Georgia)

1915   Mammoth Life and Accident Insurance Company (Louisville, Kentucky)

1921   Supreme Life Insurance Company (Chicago, Illinois)

1923   Universal Life Insurance Co. (Memphis, Tennessee)

1925   Golden State Mutual Life Insurance Co. (Los Angeles, California)

1927   Chicago Metropolitan Assurance Co. (Chicago, Illinois)

1932   Booker T. Washington Insurance Company (Birmingham, Alabama)

1941   Gertrude Geddes Willis Life Insurance Co. (New Orleans, Louisiana)

1942   Wright Mutual Insurance Co. (Detroit, Michigan)

1947   Majestic Life Insurance Co. (New Orleans, Louisiana)

1958   Golden Circle Life Insurance (Brownsville, Tennessee)

INDUSTRIAL/SERVICE COMPANIES

List 6-22. African American Industrial/Service Companies

**Year
Started**

1883   C.H. James & Co. (Charleston, West Virginia)

1942   Johnson Publishing Co. Inc. (Chicago, Illinois)

1952   H.J. Russell & Co. (Atlanta, Georgia)

1954   Johnson Products Co., Inc. (Chicago, Illinois)

1964   Soft Sheen Products Inc. (Chicago, Illinois)

1967   Powers & Sons Construction Co. Inc. (Gary, Indiana)

1969	Essence Communications, Inc. (New York, New York)
1970	Pro-Line Corp. (Dallas, Texas)
1970	Systems Management American Corp. (Norfolk, Virginia)
1971	Burrel Communications Group (Chicago, Illinois)
1972	Inner City Broadcasting Corp. (New York, New York)
1974	Automated Sciences Group Inc. (Silver Spring, Maryland)
1975	The Gourmet Co. (Atlanta, Georgia)
1977	Technology Applications, Inc. (Alexandria, Virginia)
1978	Consolidated Beverage Corp. (New York, New York)
1979	Network Solutions Inc. (Herndon, Virginia)
1980	The Bing Group (Detroit, Michigan)
1980	Black Entertainment Television Holdings (Washington, D.C.)
1981	Advanced Systems Technology Inc. (Atlanta, Georgia)
1981	Metters Industries Inc. (McLean, Virginia)
1982	Pulsar Systems, Inc. (New Castle, Delaware)
1983	Wesley Industries, Inc. (Flint, Michigan)
1983	R.O.W. Sciences Inc. (Rockville, Maryland)
1984	Calhoun Enterprises (Montgomery, Alabama)
1984	Crest Computer Supply (Skokie, Illinois)
1984	Premium Distributors Inc. (Washington, D.C.)
1985	Brooks Sausage Co., Inc. (Kenosha, Wisconsin)
1985	Coca-Cola Bottler Co. Inc. (Philadelphia, Pennsylvania)
1986	Navacom Systems Inc. (Manassas, Virginia)
1987	TLC Beatrice International Holdings (New York, New York)
1989	Garden State Cable TV (Cherry Hill, New Jersey)

AUTO DEALERS

List 6-23. African American Auto Dealers (Top 20 of *Black Enterprise* 100s)

Year Started	
1975	Mel Farr Automotive Group
1998	March/Hodge Holding Company
1989	Prestige Automotive
1993	Chicago Truck Center, Inc.
1992	Village Auto Group, Inc.
1985	Martin Automotive Group
1995	Family Automotive Group
1973	S & J Enterprises
1984	Ray Wilkinson Buick Cadillac, Inc.
1990	32 Ford Mercury, Inc.
1989	Roundtree Automotive Group
1994	Southgate Automotive Group
1991	The Matthews Automotive Group
1986	Hubbard Automotive L.L.C.
1992	Avis Ford
1990	Armstrong Holdings
1984	B & G Associates
1991	Barnett Auto Group L.P.
1992	Legacy Automotive, Inc.
1989	Brandon Dodge, Inc.

For further information, see *Black Enterprise,* 30 (11), June 2000, pp. 139-156.

SPOTLIGHTS

List 6-24. Spotlight: WARREN THOMPSON

➤ Born in the Tidewater area of Virginia in 1959

➤ Resident of Virginia and the Washington D.C. metropolitan area

➤ Received a Bachelor of Arts degree in managerial economics from Hampden-Sydney College and earned an M.B.A. from the University of Virginia's Colgate Darden Graduate School of Business Administration

➤ Served as Vice President of Host International, a food service division of Marriott

➤ In 1992 purchased 32 Bob's Big Boy restaurants and converted them to Shoney's

➤ Became President and CEO, Thompson Hospitality Services

➤ Now owns several Shoney's, Bob's Big Boy restaurants, America's Best Dinérs, and TJ's Roadhouse Grill and Saloons

➤ Runs a contract food service business with a catering division and a lodging division that manages campus housing at a major university in northern Virginia

➤ Served on a number of boards: Board of Directors of University of Virginia's Darden School of Business, Bowie State University, Chamber of Commerce, Virginia Restaurant Association, YMCA of Metropolitan Washington, Campaign to Rebuild Education in Washington, D.C., and Ronald H. Brown Minority Business Roundtable Inaugural Committee of the Ronald H. Brown Foundation

List 6-25. Spotlight: ROBERT JOHNSON

➤ Born and raised in Mississippi, 1946

➤ Spent undergraduate years at University of Illinois and received a Masters of Arts from Princeton University

➤ Former congressional aide

➤ Worked for the Washington Urban League; as a press secretary; as an executive for a cable television trade association; and finally as a cable lobbyist in Washington, D.C.

➤ In 1979 borrowed $15,000 to start Black Entertainment Television (BET)

➤ Launched the cable network as a weekly music video program; five years later, BET was broadcasting 24 hours a day

Robert Johnson

➤ By 1987 BET offered diverse programs including news, music videos, movies, and sports

➤ Investors in BET include Tele-Communications, Inc., Great American Broadcasting, and Home Box Office (HBO)

➤ First and only cable network with solely African American programming

➤ BET holdings went public in 1991, becoming the first black-controlled company on the New York Stock Exchange

➤ BET ventured into new arenas:

—Publishing *Emerge* and *Young Sisters and Brothers (YSB)* magazines

—Formed United Image Entertainment, a movie production company

—Launched a direct-marketing firm, BET Direct

—Second cable television channel, BET on Jazz

—Partnered with Microsoft and Encore Media Corporations to move to the Internet and movie productions

—Restaurants in the D.C. metropolitan area, BET on Jazz and BET Soundstage

➤ Recently bought back outstanding shares and took the company private

➤ Awards and honors include National Cable Television Association's Presidential Award, Image Award from the NAACP, Pioneer Award from the Capitol Press Club, and Business of the Year Award from the Washington, D.C. Chamber of Commerce

List 6-26. Spotlight: MADAM C. J. WALKER

➤ Born Sarah Breedlove, December 23, 1867, Delta, Louisiana, daughter of former slaves who died before she was eight years old

➤ Married to Mr. McWilliams, 1882; had one daughter; moved with her to St. Louis, 1888, after husband's death

➤ Did laundry to earn money; created black hair-care products from formula envisioned in dream; sold products door-to-door that were eventually sold by agent-operators

➤ Before starting own business, worked as sales agent with Mrs. Annie M. Turnbo Malone's thriving hair-care business

➤ Moved to Denver, Colorado, 1905, with proven products, successful marketing techniques

➤ Married newspaperman Charles J. Walker; kept his name after marriage ended in divorce; known thereafter as Madam C. J. Walker

➤ Developed hair-care process—The Walker Method or The Walker System; opened second office and cosmetology school, Lelia College, Pittsburgh, 1908 (now closed)

➤ Combined operations and established new headquarters, Indianapolis, Indiana, 1910, with plant to serve as center of all ventures (Walker College of Hair; Walker Manufacturing Company)

➤ Became large employer; developed business strategies widely used today (multi-level marketing and door-to-door sales techniques); feminist; involved daughter in business; stipulated in will that company always be headed by women

➤ Generous contributor to black charities; encouraged agent-operators to do same, issuing bonuses to those with greatest community service

➤ Social activist; was denied appointment with President Woodrow Wilson to discuss views against lynching, 1917; subsequently gave $5,000 to NAACP's anti-lynching campaign, largest donation to that date; contributed to many causes, Tuskegee Institute and National Association of Colored Women to purchase and preserve the Frederick Douglass home

➤ Daughter, A'Lelia Walker Robinson Wilson Kennedy, managed many aspects of business. After mother's death, known for hosting white intellectuals and talented black authors, critics, musicians, and artists in a café/salon in home, "the Dark Tower"—place for blacks and whites to come together across racial barriers. Attendees were central "Harlem Renaissance" figures.

➤ Madam C. J. Walker died at 51, May 25, 1919, at home, Villa Lewaro, a 32-room country mansion built in New York, by Vertner Woodson Tandy, first licensed African American architect. House completed one year before her death.

➤ Madam Walker Manufacturing Company building, 1927, is a national historic landmark called Madam Walker Urban Life Center, Indianapolis, Indiana. Villa Lewaro, willed to NAACP following A'Lelia's death, is listed on National Register of Historic Places, 1976.

➤ Madam Walker's hair-care products and cosmetics manufactured today by Walker Enterprises of Indianapolis, Indiana

➤ U.S. Postal Service issued stamp in honor of Madam Walker, 1998

List 6-27. Spotlight: ARTHUR GEORGE (A. G.) GASTON

➢ Born July 4, 1892 in log cabin built by grandparents, former slaves, on their farm near Demopolis, Alabama

➢ Raised by his grandparents; father worked on the railroad, mother lived in a neighboring town with white family for whom she was the cook

➢ When adolescent, mother moved with employer, A. B. Loveman of Loveman's Department Store, to Birmingham and took her son along

➢ Matriculated at Tuggle Institute in Birmingham, Alabama, school for black children founded by former slave Carrie Tuggle; learned great deal watching Mrs. Tuggle manage money. Before leaving Tuggle, tenth grade, met his idol, Booker T. Washington. First book he owned: *Up From Slavery* by Washington. The two had similar ideas about hard work and the power of money.

➢ Served with distinction during World War I in the 92nd Rainbow Division, all-black army unit

➢ Returning to Birmingham, worked at menial jobs. While employed as laborer *Tennessee Coal and Iron Company (TCI),* began to sell boxed lunches made by his mother; made loans to other steelworkers and allowed them to repay bi-weekly; operated a popcorn and peanuts stand.

➢ Got idea for a business watching workers donate money to help preachers bury their members. Started burial society for TCI's black employees, 1923. Several of his business ventures were:

   1932   Bought a mortuary (Smith & Gaston Funeral Directors) and later formed the Booker T. Washington Insurance Company

   1939   Established Booker T. Washington Business College

   1946   Opened Brown Belle Bottling Company

   1947   Bought New Grace Hill Cemetery

   1954   Opened A. G. Gaston Motel

   1957   With investors, started Citizens Federal Savings and Loan Association

   Added a radio station to his business holdings around mid-1960s. Of particular note is that A. G. Gaston accomplished all the above in the segregated South.

➢ Appeased whites in public but was a quiet, consistent supporter of the civil rights struggle behind the scenes. Provided loans for black activists whose banks threatened foreclosure, provided lodging for Martin Luther King, Jr. and other civil rights workers, and put up money for bail for jailed demonstrators. Was attacked by blacks and whites for his stance. Blacks criticized him for not being openly active in the movement and white hate groups bombed his home and motel.

➤ At end of the civil rights movement while Birmingham was recovering, was invited to join the Chamber of Commerce and other influential organizations.

➤ Remained grounded in his philosophy and continued to work well beyond his 100th birthday. His business acumen widely acknowledged; holdings currently valued at over $100 million. Recipient of ten honorary degrees and numerous other awards although he never finished high school.

➤ Quintessential businessman and civic leader died January 19, 1996 at age 103.

Section 7

LAW AND GOVERNMENT

Thurgood Marshall

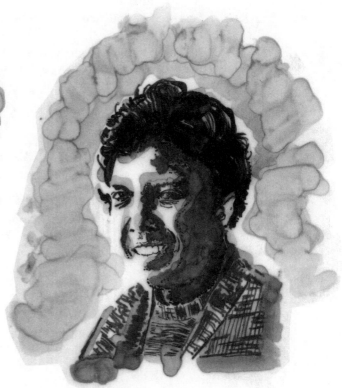

Barbara Jordan

SECTION 7

LAW AND GOVERNMENT

In the areas of law and government, African Americans have provided a rich legacy. Historically, slaves were considered "property" and, therefore, not participants in the political structure. However, they creatively developed methods to express their views and opinions. One such method was the "Negro Election Day" festivals. Free blacks, who made up one-tenth of the entire black population, made more definite attempts to participate in political affairs. The majority of them, however, found that their efforts were not successful and they were not able to establish a power base or influence within the system. Free blacks found that they were able to make more gains through community activities, such as rallies and petitions.

During the Reconstruction period, over 1,500 African Americans held offices on the national, state, and local levels. Pioneers such as attorney John Rock, U.S. Marshal Frederick Douglass, and diplomat Ebenezer Don Carlos Bassett were only a few of the pioneers during this period. The majority of political offices were held in southern states: South Carolina, Mississippi, Louisiana, North Carolina, Alabama, and Georgia. From the period of 1869-1901, there were 20 black representatives and 2 black senators in the U.S. Congress. Due to nonacceptance by whites, these positions were gradually eliminated toward the end of the century.

Due to strong efforts by African American lawyers and civil rights leaders, there was a resurgence of elected and appointed officials, beginning in the 1960s. Supreme Court Justice Thurgood Marshall, Congressman Adam Clayton Powell, and Senator Edward Brooke are examples of the contemporary leaders in the areas of law and government.

Section 7 presents firsts and notable personalities, prominent federally appointed and elected officials, and organizations supporting the political and legal structures.

FIRSTS IN LAW AND GOVERNMENT

List 7-1. Firsts in Law and Government

1845	Macon B. Allen	formally admitted to the Bar
1855	John Mercer Langston	elected to public office; Clerk of Brownhelm Township, Ohio
1861	William C. Nell	federal civilian job
1865	John S. Rock	approved to argue cases before the Supreme Court, but did not*
1865	Henry Garnet	spoke in Nation's Capitol
1867	Monroe Baker	mayor, St. Martin, Louisiana
1868	John W. Menard	elected to Congress (denied his seat)
1869	Ebenezer Don Carlos Bassett	diplomat
1870	Hiram Rhodes Revels	appointed U.S. Senator (unexpired term)
1870	Joseph H. Rainey	member, House of Representatives
1870	Thomas M. Petersen	first voter following passage of Fifteenth Amendment
1872	Charlotte Ray	female lawyer
1873	Pinckney Pinchback	governor of Louisiana (served one month)
1873	Mifflin W. Gibbs	judge
1875	Blanche Kelso Bruce	appointed U.S. Senator (full-term)
1877	Frederick Douglass	appointed as U.S. Marshal, Washington, D.C.
1884	John R. Lynch	chairman, Republican National Convention
1911	William Lewis	Assistant Attorney General of U.S.
1921	Charles H. Houston	Harvard Law Review
1926	Violette N. Anderson	woman admitted to practice before Supreme Court
1928	Oscar De Priest	seat in House in twentieth century
1935	Charles H. Houston	argued a Supreme Court case*
1935	Arthur W. Mitchell	democrat in the U.S. House of Representatives

---

*John Rock was first given permission to argue, but did not. Charles Houston was the first to actually *argue* before the Supreme Court.

1937	William A. Hastie	federal judge, Virgin Islands
1938	Crystal Fauset	woman state legislator
1939	Jane Bolin	woman judge, Court of Domestic Relations, New York
1949	William A. Hastie	served on federal appeals court
1949	William T. Coleman	U.S. Supreme Court Clerk
1949	William Dawson	headed standing committee of Congress
1950	Ralph J. Bunche	Nobel Peace Prize
1950	Edith S. Sampson	alternate delegate to United Nations General Assembly
1955	E. Frederic Morrow	executive position in the White House (administrative aide to President Eisenhower)
1958	Clifton R. Wharton, Sr.	diplomat (Minister to Romania)
1961	James B. Parsons	federal district court judge in continental U.S.
1961	Robert C. Weaver	administrator, Housing and Home Agency
1965	Patricia Roberts Harris	woman ambassador
1966	Edward Brooke	U.S. Senator elected by popular vote
1966	Lucius Amerson	elected sheriff
1966	Constance Baker Motley	woman to serve on federal bench
1966	Robert C. Weaver	secretary, Housing and Urban Development
1966	Andrew Brimmer	governor, Federal Reserve Board
1967	Thurgood Marshall	U.S. Supreme Court justice
1967	Carl Stokes	elected mayor of a major city (Cleveland)
1968	Barbara Watson	assistant Secretary of State
1968	Shirley Chisholm	woman to serve in U.S. Congress
1970	Kenneth Gibson	mayor of Newark, New Jersey
1972	Benjamin Hooks	member, Federal Communications Commission
1972	Frank Wills	discovered Watergate break-in
1972	Shirley Chisholm	ran for President of the United States
1975	Cardiss Collins	chair, House Government Operations, and chair, Congressional Black Caucus
1976	Barbara Jordan	African American and woman to give keynote address at the Democratic National Convention
1976	Kenneth Gibson	President, U.S. Conference of Mayors

1977	Patricia Roberts Harris	woman cabinet member, Secretary of Housing and Urban Development
1977	Andrew Young	ambassador to United Nations
1977	Eleanor Holmes Norton	chair, Equal Education Opportunity Act
1980	Ronald Brown	chief counsel, State Judiciary Committee
1981	Arnette R. Hubbard	woman president of National Bar Association
1982	Loretta T. Glickman	woman mayor of a city of 100,000 or more (Pasadena, California)
1988	Colin Powell	chairman, Joint Chiefs of Staff
1988	Lenora Falani	African American and woman to be on the Presidential ballot in all 50 states
1989	L. Douglas Wilder	Governor of Virginia
1989	Ronald Brown	chair, National Democratic Party
1989	Louis Sullivan	Secretary, Health and Human Services
1990	David Dinkins	mayor of New York, New York
1992	Willie Williams	Chief of Police of Los Angeles, California
1992	Bobby Rush	former Black Panther elected to Congress
1992	Jacquelyn Barrett	elected female sheriff (Fulton Co., Georgia)
1992	Carol Moseley-Braun	woman elected as U.S. Senator (Illinios)
1992	Pamela Fanning Carter	state attorney general (Indiana)
1992	Mike Espy	Secretary of Agriculture
1993	Hazel O'Leary	Secretary of Energy
1993	Ronald Brown	Secretary of Commerce
1993	Ronald Dellums	chair, House Armed Services Committee
1993	Jocelyn Elders	African American and woman Surgeon General
1993	Alexis Herman	Secretary of Labor
1996	Lee Brown	mayor of Houston, Texas
1998	David Satcher	African American and male Surgeon General
1999	Carolyn Jefferson-Jenkins	president, League of Woman Voters
2000	Johnnie Rawlinson	African American female judge for Appellate Circuit (9th U.S. Circuit Court of Appeals)

NOTABLE PERSONALITIES

List 7-2. Past and Present Notable Personalities

Marion Barry (1936-)	cofounded Student Nonviolent Coordinating Committee (SNCC); mayor, Washington, D.C. (1979-1990; 1994-1998)
Mary F. Berry (1938-)	commissioner and vice chair, U.S. Commission on Civil Rights, 1980
Derrick Bell (1930-)	first black tenured professor, Harvard Law School (1971)
Julian Bond (1940-)	Georgia House of Representatives (1966); Georgia State Senate (1974-1986); Chair, National Association for the Advancement of Colored People (NAACP) (1998)
Thomas Bradley (1917-)	mayor, Los Angeles, California (1973-1993)
Carol Moseley Braun (1947-)	U.S. Senator (1992-1998); Ambassador, New Zealand (1999)
Edward Brooke (1919-)	Massachusetts Attorney General (1962); U.S. Senator (1967-1979)
Ronald Brown (1941-1996)	Chair, Democratic National Committee (1989); Secretary of Commerce (1993-1996)
Willie Brown (1934-)	first black mayor, San Francisco (1995)
Blanche K. Bruce (1841-1898)	U.S. Senator (1875-1880); Register, U.S. Treasury Department (1881-1885; 1897-1898)
Ralph J. Bunche (1904-1971)	winner, Nobel Peace Prize (1950); Undersecretary, Special Political Affairs (1957-1967); Undersecretary General, United Nations (1968-1971)
Yvonne B. Burke (1932-)	House of Representatives (1973-1979); Los Angeles Board of Supervisors (1979-1980; 1992-2000)
Stokely Carmichael (1941-1998) (Kwame Ture)	director, Student Nonviolent Coordinating Committee (1966-1967); Prime Minister, Black Panther Party (1968)
Shirley Chisholm (1924-)	U.S. House of Representatives (1969-1982)
William Clay (1931-)	U.S. House of Representatives (1968-present)
Johnnie Cochran, Jr. (1937-)	lead attorney in the O. J. Simpson trial
Cardiss Collins (1931-)	U.S. House of Representatives (1973-1997), Democratic Whip-at-Large
John Conyers (1929-)	U.S. House of Representatives (1965-present)
Ronald Dellums (1935-)	U.S. House of Representatives (1971-1998)

Oscar S. DePriest (1871-1951)	U.S. Representatives (1929-1935)
David Dinkins (1927-)	mayor, New York City (1989-1993)
Julian Dixon (1934-)	U.S. House of Representatives (1971-present)
Oscar Dunn (1820-1871)	Lieutenant Governor, Louisiana
Michael Espy (1953-)	U.S. House of Representatives (1987-1992); secretary, Department of Agriculture (1993-1994)
Walter Fauntroy (1933-)	U.S. House of Representatives (1971-1990)
Gary Franks (1953-)	U.S. House of Representatives (1991-1997)
Lani Guinier (1950-)	chosen to head Justice Department's Civil Rights division (1993), nomination withdrawn; author
Patricia R. Harris (1924-1985)	secretary, Department of Health and Human Services (1979); secretary, Department of Housing and Urban Development (1979-1981); ambassador, Luxembourg (1965)
William H. Hastie (1904-1976)	Judge, Federal District Court, Virgin Islands (1937); U.S. Court of Appeals, 3rd District (1949)
Alexis Herman (1947-)	secretary, Department of Labor (1993-present)
A. Leon Higginbotham, Jr. (1928-1998)	Federal Trade Commission (1962-1964); federal district court judge (1964-1978); U.S. Court of Appeals (1978-1993)
Anita Hill (1956-)	law professor/author; honored with Anita Faye Hill Professorship Endowed Chair, University of Oklahoma (1995)
Oliver W. Hill, Sr. (1907)	civil rights attorney; played pivotal role in dismantling legalized segregation; recipient of Presidential Medal of Freedom (1999)
Eric Holder (1941-)	Deputy Attorney General (1997); Attorney General for the District of Columbia (1993)
Charles Houston (1895-1950)	civil rights lawyer; argued case of *Hollins* v. *Oklahoma* (1935); legal counsel to NAACP
Jesse Jackson, Sr. (1941-)	founded People United to Save Humanity (Operation PUSH); bid for Democratic presidential nomination (1984, 1988); president, National Rainbow Coalition (1984); Shadow Senator for the District of Columbia (1990-present); awarded Presidential Medal of Freedom (2000)
Jesse Jackson, Jr. (1965-)	U.S. House of Representatives (1995-present)

Maynard Jackson (1938-)	mayor of Atlanta (1974-1982; 1989-1993)
Barbara Jordan (1936-1996)	U.S. House of Representatives (1973-1978); first African American speaker at the Democratic National Convention (1976)
Vernon Jordan (1935-)	Executive Director, United Negro College Fund (UNCF); head, Urban League (1972-1981); chair, President Clinton's Transition Team (1992)
Sharon P. Kelly (1944-)	mayor, Washington, D.C. (1990-1994); NAACP Presidential Award (1983); UNCF District Leadership Award (1985)
John M. Langston (1829-1897)	elected to Congress, 1888 (served 1890-1892)
George "Mickey" Leland (1944-1989)	U.S. House of Representatives (1979-1989); killed in plane crash delivering food and goods to a refugee camp in Ethiopia (1989)
John Lewis (1940-)	U.S. House of Representatives (1986-present); 40 years of political activism
Kweisi Mfume (1948-)	U.S. House of Representatives (1987-1996); president and CEO of the NAACP (1995-present)
Arthur W. Mitchell (1883-1968)	argued case that declared "Jim Crow" practices illegal (1941); U.S. House of Representatives (1935-1943)
Eleanor Holmes Norton (1938-)	head, EEOC (1979-1981); U.S. House of Representatives (1991-present)
Hazel O'Leary (1937-)	secretary of Energy (1993-present)
Clarence M. Pendleton, Jr. (1930-1988)	first African American to chair the U.S. Civil Rights Commission (1981)
Pinckney Pinchback (1837-1921)	appointed interim governor of Louisiana (1872); first African American governor
Adam Clayton Powell, Jr. (1908-1972)	U.S. House of Representatives (1945-67); re-elected to seat in 1969, denied seniority
Joseph Rainey (1832-1887)	U.S. House of Representatives (1871); first African American to serve as U.S. congressional representative
Charles Rangel (1930-)	U.S. House of Representatives (1970-present)
Hiram Rhodes Revels (1822-1901)	appointed to vacant Senate seat
Al Sharpton (1954-)	political and civil rights activist; first African American candidate for New York State Senate (1978)
Robert Smalls (1839-1915)	U.S. House of Representatives (1875-1886)

Clarence Thomas (1948-)	Supreme Court Judge (1991-present)
Harold Washington (1922-1987)	U.S. House of Representatives (1980-1982); first African American mayor of Chicago (1982-1987)
Maxine Waters (1938-)	California State Assembly (1976-1990); U.S. House of Representatives (1990-present)
Robert Weaver (1907-1997)	secretary, Department of Housing and Urban Development (1966-1968); HUD building named in his honor: Robert C. Weaver Federal Building (2000)
L. Douglas Wilder (1931-)	first elected governor, Virginia (1989-1993)
Andrew Young (1932-)	U.S. House of Representatives (1972); Ambassador to the United Nations (1977-1979); mayor, Atlanta, Georgia (1982-1988)
Coleman Young (1918-1997)	mayor of Detroit, Michigan (1974-1994)

RECONSTRUCTION

List 7-3. African Americans in Politics During Reconstruction (1865-1877)

1865	Henry H. Garnet	delivered address in the House of Representatives
1865	John Rock	admitted to practice before the Supreme Court
1866	Edward G. Walker	elected to a northern state legislature
1866	Charles L. Mitchell	elected to a northern state legislature
1866	Thaddeus Stevens	Congressman
1867	Charles Sumner	Senator (Massachusetts)
1867	Monroe Baker	Mayor of St. Martin, Louisiana
1868	Oscar J. Dunn	Lieutenant Governor of Louisiana
1868	John W. Menard	elected to Congress (Louisiana); denied his seat
1868	P.B.S. Pinchback	active in politics; appointed interim Governor of Louisiana, 1872
1868	James J. Harris	delegate to Republican Convention
1868	Francis L. Cardozo	appointed Secretary of State in South Carolina

1869	Ebenezer Don Carlos Bassett	U.S. Minister to Haiti
1860s	Hiram Reeves	served in U.S. Senate
1870	Joseph H. Rainey	seated as Congressman (South Carolina); spoke at Republican National Convention (1872)
1870	Robert C. DeLarge	elected to Congress (South Carolina)
1870	Robert B. Elliott	elected to Congress (South Carolina); spoke at Republican National Convention (1872)
1870	Benjamin S. Turner	elected to Congress (Alabama)
1870	Josiah T. Walls	elected to Congress (Georgia)
1870	Jonathan J. Wright	elected to South Carolina Supreme Court
1871	Jefferson F. Long	seated as Congressman (Georgia)
1872	John R. Lynch	spoke at Republican National Convention
1874	Blanche K. Bruce	elected to full term in the Senate

VOTING RIGHTS LEGISLATION

List 7-4. Voting Rights Legislation (1865-1993)

1865	Thirteenth Amendment ratified
1866	Civil Rights Act
1868	Fourteenth Amendment ratified
1870	Fifteenth Amendment ratified
1870	First Enforcement Act (Force Act)
1871	Second Force Act
1875	*United States* v. *Reese*
1884	ex parte Yarborough
1898	*Williams* v. *Mississippi*
1903	*James* v. *Bowman*
1904	*Giles c. Harris, Giles* v. *Teasley*
1915	*Guinn* v. *United States*
1920	Nineteenth Amendment ratified
1927	*Nixon* v. *Herndon*

1932   *Nixon* v. *Condon*

1935   *Grovey* v. *Townsend*

1938   *Lane* v. *Wilson*

1944   *Smith* v. *Allwright*

1949   *Davis* v. *Schnell*

1953   *Terry* v. *Adams*

1957   Civil Rights Act of 1957

1960   Civil Rights Act of 1960

1960   *United States* v. *Raines*

1960   *Gomillion* v. *Lightfoot*

1961   Twenty-third Amendment ratified

1964   Twenty-fourth Amendment ratified

1965   Voting Rights Act of 1965

1966   *South Carolina* v. *Katzenback*

1969   *Allen* v. *Board of Elections*

1975   *Richmond* v. *United States*

1976   *United Jewish Organization* v. *Carey*

1980   *Mobile* v. *Bolden*

1980   *Rome* v. *United States*

1990   President George Bush vetoed Civil Rights Bill

1993   *Shaw* v. *Reno*

JUDICIARY SYSTEM

List 7-5. Chronology of Cases, Laws, and Legal Decisions

1639   Case of Hugh Davis, white person who had sexual relations with a black person

1640   Case of John Punch, white man who fathered a child with a black servant

1641   Case of Graweere, black servant who secured freedom for his child

1705   prohibited the practice of intermarriage between blacks and whites

1712   Decline of Rights: required slaves to have a written pass when leaving slaves' quarters

1780   gradual abolition of slaves

1787   Northwest Ordinance: outlawed slavery in territories that would become Ohio, Indiana, Illinois, Michigan, and Wisconsin

1793   Fugitive Slave Act

1863   Emancipation Proclamation

1865   Thirteenth Amendment: abolished slavery

1866   Civil Rights Act: granted all African Americans civil rights, without vote

1867   Reconstruction Act: admitted confederate states to the Union

1868   Fourteenth Amendment: guaranteed African Americans equal protection as citizens in the United States

1869   Louisiana Law: forbade black and white passengers on same public transportation

1870   Fifteenth Amendment: right of citizens to vote

1871   Civil Rights Act: combat violence

1875   Civil Rights Act: equal access to public accommodations

1876   *U.S.* v. *Craikshank*: Supreme Court ruled Fourteenth Amendment did not protect right to peaceful assembly

1896   *Plessy* v. *Ferguson*: man arrested when refused to ride in the colored section of a Louisiana train

1932   *Powell* v. *Alabama*: nine Scottsboro boys were denied counsel for the alleged rape of two white women

1946   Executive Order 9808: protection of Civil Rights

1948   Executive Order 9981: desegregation of Armed Forces

1950   *Sweatt* v. *Painter*: University of Texas Law School opened doors to a black applicant

1954   *Brown* v. *Board of Education*: segregated educational facilities "inherently unequal"

1957   Civil Rights Act: citizens given right to vote regardless of race, color, religion, national origin

1960   Civil Rights Act: outlawed literacy tests as a qualification for voting

1964   trial of Bobby Seale, Black Panther leader

1965   *Loving* v. *Virginia*: law against marriages between African American and European American unconstitutional

1968   Civil Rights Act: banned discrimination in housing and penalties for crossing state lines to incite a riot

1971   *Swann* v. *Charlotte-Meckelburg*: busing issue related to desegregation

1978   *Bakke* case: race could not be used by public schools in affirmative-action programs to ensure minority representation

1989   *City of Richmond* v. *J.A. Croson Co.*: unconstitutional for a city to create a plan to award public contracts to minority contractors without a pattern of prior discrimination

1991   Civil Rights Act: limited ability for victims of discrimination to sue for discrimination

List 7-6. Supreme Court Justices

1967-1991   Thurgood Marshall

1991-   Clarence Thomas

List 7-7. Spotlight: THURGOOD MARSHALL

- Born 1908 in Baltimore, Maryland
- Named after his paternal grandfather, Thoroughgood
- Attended Lincoln University in Chester County, Pennsylvania
- Participated in a sit-in while attending college to protest segregation
- Graduated with honors from Lincoln University
- Rejected by Maryland School of Law because of his race; attended Howard University Law School in Washington, D.C.
- 1933—Graduated first in class from Howard Law School
- 1936—Closed private law practice in Baltimore and moved to New York City
- 1939-1961—Served as director and chief counsel for the NAACP Legal Defense Fund
- Developed and implemented strategies to fight racial segregation
- Argued and won several cases before the Supreme Court. Among his cases were:

  —*Chambers* v. *Florida* (1940)

  —*Smith* v. *Allwright* (1944)

  —*Shelley* v. *Kraemer* (1948)

  —*Sipuel* v. *University of Oklahoma* (1948)

  —*Sweatt* v. *Painter* (1950)

- Most notable case was the *Brown* v. *Board of Education of Topeka* (1954) which declared segregation in public schools unconstitutional

- Also argued cases that led to desegregation of public parks, swimming pools, local bus systems, and athletic facilities

- 1961—Appointed to United States Second Circuit Court of Appeals by President John F. Kennedy

- 1965—Appointed Solicitor General of the United States by President Lyndon B. Johnson

- 1967—Confirmed as Associate Justice to the Supreme Court by President Johnson

- During his tenure as a Supreme Court Justice, wrote and proposed many decisions including:

  —*Stanley* v. *Georgia* (1969)

  —*Grayned* v. *City of Rockford* (1972)

  —*San Antonio Independent School District* v. *Rodriguez* (1973)

  —*Florida* v. *Bostick* (1991)

- 1991—Retired from the Supreme Court due to failing health

- 1993—Died of heart failure and buried in Arlington National Cemetery

List 7-8. Federal Judges

1937	William H. Hastie	District of Virgin Islands
1938	Herman E. Moore	District of Virgin Islands
1945	Irwin C. Mollison	Customs Court
1949	William H. Hastie	Third Circuit (Pennsylvania)
1957	Scovel Richardson	Customs Court
1958	Walter A. Gordon	Third Circuit (Virgin Islands)
1961	Thurgood Marshall	Second Circuit (New York)
1961	Wade H. McCree	Eastern District of Michigan
1961	James B. Parsons	Northern District of Illinois
1964	A. Leon Higginbotham	Third Circuit (Pennsylvania)
1964	Spottswood W. Robinson	D.C. Circuit
1965	William B. Bryant	D.C. Circuit
1966	Wade H. McCree	Sixth Circuit (Michigan)
1966	Constance B. Motley	Southern District of New York
1966	Aubrey E. Robinson	District of Columbia
1966	James L. Watson	Customs Court
1967	Damon Keith	Sixth Circuit
1967	Thurgood Marshall	U.S. Supreme Court
1967	Joseph C. Waddy	District of Columbia
1969	Almeric L. Christian	Third Circuit
1969	Barrington Parker	District of Columbia
1969	David W. Williams	Southern District of California
1971	Clifford Scott Green	Eastern District of Pennsylvania
1971	Lawrence W. Pierce	Southern District of New York
1972	Robert L. Carter	Southern District of New York
1972	Robert M. Duncan	Military Court of Appeals
1974	Henry Bramwell	Eastern District of New York
1974	Robert M. Duncan	Southern District of Ohio
1976	Matthew Perry, Jr.	Military Court of Appeals
1976	George N. Leighton	Northern District of Illinois
1976	Cecil F. Poole	Northern District of California

1977	A. Leon Higginbotham	Third Circuit
1977	Damon Keith	Eastern District of Michigan
1978	Robert F. Collins	Eastern District of Louisiana
1978	Julian A. Cooke, Jr.	Eastern District of Michigan
1978	Mary Johnson Lowe	Southern District of New York
1978	Theodore McMillian	Eighth Circuit (Missouri)
1978	David S. Nelson	District of Massachusetts
1978	Paul Simmons	Western District of Pennsylvania
1978	Jack E. Tanner	Western District of Washington
1979	J. Jerome Farris	Ninth Circuit
1979	Benjamin F. Gibson	Western District of Michigan
1979	James T. Giles	Eastern District of Pennsylvania
1979	Alcee L. Hastings*	Eleventh Circuit (Florida)
1979	Joseph W. Hatchett	Eleventh Circuit (Florida)
1979	Terry Hatter, Jr.	D.C. Circuit
1979	Joseph C. Howard	D.C. Circuit
1979	Nathaniel R. Jones	Sixth Circuit (Ohio)
1979	Amalya L. Kearse	Second Circuit (New York)
1979	Gabrielle Kirk McDonald	Southern District of Texas
1979	John Garrett Penn	District of Columbia
1979	Matthew Perry, Jr.	District of South Carolina
1979	Cecil F. Poole	Ninth Circuit
1979	Anna Diggs Taylor	Eastern District of Michigan
1979	Anne E. Thompson	District of New Jersey
1979	Horace T. Ward	Northern District of Georgia
1980	Clyde S. Cahill, Jr.	Eastern District of Missouri
1980	U. E. Clemon	Northern District of Alabama
1980	Harry T. Edwards	D.C. Circuit
1980	Richard C. Erwin	Middle District of North Carolina
1980	Earl B. Gilliam	Southern District of California

---

*impeached, 1989

1980	Thelton E. Henderson	Northern District of California
1980	Odell Horton	Western District of Tennessee
1980	George Howard, Jr.	Eastern District of Arizona
1980	Norma H. Johnson	District of Columbia
1980	Consuela B. Marshall	Central District of California
1980	Myron H. Thompson	Middle District of Alabama
1980	George White	Northern District of Ohio
1981	Lawrence W. Pierce	Second Circuit
1982	Reginald Gibson	U.S. Court of Claims
1984	John R. Hargrove	District of Maryland
1985	Ann C. Williams	Northern District of Illinois
1985	Henry T. Wingate	Southern District of Missouri
1986	James R. Spencer	Eastern District of Virginia
1988	Kenneth M. Hoyt	Southern District of Texas
1988	Henry J. Hutton	Eastern District of Pennsylvania
1990	Clarence Thomas	D.C. Circuit
1990	James Ware	Northern District of California
1991	Saundra Brown Armstrong	Northern District of California
1991	Fernando Gaitan	Western District of Missouri
1991	Donald Graham	Southern District of Florida
1991	Curtis Joyner	Eastern District of Pennsylvania
1991	Joe McDade	Central District of Illinois
1991	Clarence Thomas	U.S. Supreme Court
1992	Garland Burrell	Eastern District of California
1992	Carol E. Jackson	Eastern District of Missouri
1992	Sterling Johnson	Eastern District of New York
1992	Timothy Lewis	Third Circuit
1993	Henry Lee Adams	Middle District of Florida
1993	Wilkie Ferguson	Southern District of Florida
1993	Raymond Jackson	Eastern District of Virginia
1993	Gary Lancaster	Western District of Pennsylvania
1993	Reginald Lindsay	District of Massachusetts

1993	Charles Shaw	Eastern District of Missouri
1994	Deborah Batts	Southern District of New York
1994	James Beaty, Jr.	District Court, North Carolina
1994	Franklin Burgess	Western District of Washington
1994	David Coar	District Court, Illinois
1994	Audrey Collins	Central District of California
1994	Clarence Cooper	Northern District of Georgia
1994	Michael Davis	District of Minnesota
1994	Raymond Finch	District of Virgin Islands
1994	Vanessa Gilmore	Southern District of Texas
1994	Ancer Haggerty	District of Washington
1994	Denise Page Hood	District Court, Michigan
1994	Napoleon Jones	District Court, California
1994	Blance Manning	District Court, Illinois
1994	Theodore McKee	Third Circuit
1994	Vicki Miles-LaGrange	District Court, Oklahoma
1994	Solomon Oliver, Jr.	Northern District of Ohio
1994	Barrington Parker, Jr.	District Court, New York
1994	Judith Rogers	Circuit Court, District of Columbia
1994	W. Louis Sands	District Court, Georgia
1994	Carl Stewart	Circuit Court, Fifth Circuit
1994	Emmet Sullivan	Circuit Court, District of Columbia
1994	William Walls	District Court, New Jersey
1994	Alexander Williams	District Court, Maryland
1995	R. Guy Cole	Circuit Court, Sixth Circuit
1995	Curtis Collier	District Court, Tennessee
1995	Wiley Daniel	District Court, Colorado
1995	Andre Davis	District Court, Maryland
1995	Bernice B. Donald	District Court, Tennessee
1996	Charles Clevert, Jr.	District Court, Wisconsin
1996	Joseph A. Greenaway, Jr.	District Court, New Jersey
1997	Eric L. Clay	Circuit Court, Sixth Circuit

1997	Martin J. Jenkins	District Court, California
1997	Henry H. Kennedy, Jr.	District Court, District of Columbia
1997	Algenon L. Marbley	District Court, Ohio
1998	Lynn Bush	Court of Federal Claims
1998	Raner Collins	District Court, Arizona
1998	Gerald Bruce Lee	District Court, Virginia
1998	Ivan L. R. Lemelle	District Court, Louisiana
1998	Sam A. Lindsay	District Court, Texas
1998	Stephan P. Mickle	District Court, Florida
1998	Johnnie B. Rawlinson	District Court, Nevada
1998	Richard Roberts	District Court, District of Columbia
1998	Victoria Roberts	District Court, Michigan
1998	Margaret Seymour	District Court, South Carolina
1998	Gregory Sleet	District Court, Delaware
1998	Ralph Tyson	District Court, Louisiana
1999	William Hibler	District Court, Illinois
2000	Johnnie B. Rawlinson	9th U.S. Circuit Court of Appeals

GOVERNMENT LEADERS

List 7-9. Governors

| 1872-1872 | P. B. S. Pinchback | (by default) | Louisiana |
| 1989-1993 | L. Douglas Wilder | (elected) | Virginia |

List 7-10. Senators

1870-1871	Hiram R. Revel	Republican
1875-1881	Blanche K. Bruce	Republican
1967-1979	Edward W. Brooke	Republican
1992-1998	Carol Moseley-Braun	Democrat

List 7-11. Presidential Cabinet Members

1969	Robert C. Weaver, Secretary of Housing and Urban Development
1977	Patricia R. Harris, Secretary of Housing and Urban Development
1979	Patricia R. Harris, Secretary of Health, Education and Welfare
1981	Samuel R. Pierce, Jr., Secretary of Housing and Urban Development
1989	Louis Sullivan, Secretary of Health and Human Services
1993	Hazel O'Leary, Secretary of Energy
1993	Mike Espy, Secretary of Agriculture
1993	Jesse Brown, Secretary of Veteran Affairs
1993	Ron Brown, Secretary of Commerce
1997	Alexis Herman, Secretary of Labor
1997	Rodney Slater, Secretary of Transportation
1998	Togo West, Secretary of Veteran Affairs

List 7-12. Ambassadors

1949	Edward R. Dudley—Liberia
1953	Jessie D. Locker—Liberia
1955	Richard L. Jones—Liberia
1959	John Howard Morrow—Guinea
1961	Mercer Cook—Niger
1961	Clifton R. Wharton—Norway
1963	Carl T. Rowan—Finland
1964	Mercer Cook—Niger
1964	Clinton E. Knox—Dahomey
1965	Mercer Cook—Gambia
1965	Patricia Roberts Harris—Luxembourg
1965	Hugh Smythe—Syrian Arab Republic
1965	Franklin H. Williams—Ghana
1966	Elliot P. Skinner—Upper Volta
1967	Hugh Smythe—Malta
1968	Samuel C. Adams—Niger
1969	Clinton E. Knox—Haiti

1969	Terence A. Todman—Chad
1969	Samuel Z. Westerfield—Liberia
1970	Jerome Heartwell Holland—Sweden
1970	Clarence Clyde Ferguson, Jr.—Uganda
1971	Charles J. Nelson—Botswana, Lesotho, Swaziland
1971	John E. Reinhardt—Nigeria
1972	W. Beverly Carter—Tanzania
1972	Terence A. Todman—Guinea
1973	O. Rudolph Aggrey—Senegal and Gambia
1974	David R. Bolen—Botswana, Lesotho, Swaziland
1974	Theodore R. Britten, Jr.—Barbados and Grenada
1974	Terence A. Todman—Costa Rica
1976	W. Beverly Carter—Liberia
1976	Ronald D. Palmer—Togo
1976	Charles A. James—Niger
1977	O. Rudolph Aggrey—Romania
1977	Maurice D. Bean—Burma
1977	David B. Bolen—German Democratic Republic
1977	Richard K. Fox, Jr.—Trinidad and Tobago
1977	Ulrich Haynes—Algeria
1977	William B. Jones—Haiti
1977	Wilbert LeMelle—Kenya
1977	Mable M. Smythe—Cameroon
1977	Andrew Young—United Nations
1977	Terence A. Todman—Spain
1979	Horace G. Dawson—Botswana
1979	Anne F. Holloway—Mali
1979	Donald F. McHenry—United Nations
1980	Walter C. Carrington—Senegal
1980	Barbara Watson—Malaysia
1981	Melvin H. Evans—Trinidad and Tobago
1981	Ronald D. Palmer—Malaysia
1981	Gerald E. Thomas—Guyana
1982	Howard K. Walker—Togo
1983	Arthur W. Lewis—Sierra Leone

1983	George E. Moose—Benin
1983	Gerald E. Thomas—Guyana
1983	Terence A. Todman—Denmark
1985	Irvin Hicks—Seychelles
1985	Edward J. Perkins—Liberia
1986	Ronald D. Palmer—Mauritius
1986	Edward J. Perkins—South Africa
1986	Cynthia Shepard Perry—Sierra Leone
1988	John A. Burroughs, Jr.—Uganda
1988	George E. Moose—Senegal
1988	Leonard O. Spearman, Sr.—Rwanda
1989	Cynthia Shepard Perry—Burundi
1989	Stephen Rhodes—Zimbabwe
1989	Terence A. Todman—Argentina
1989	Howard K. Walker—Madagascar
1989	Ruth V. Washington—Gambia*
1989	Johnny Young—Sierra Leone
1990	Aurelia Erskine Brazeal—Micronesia
1990	Arlene Render—Gambia
1990	Leonard O. Spearman, Sr.—Lesotho
1991	Charles R. Baquet III—Djibouti
1991	Johnnie Carson—Uganda
1992	Ruth A. Davis—Benin
1992	Kenton Wesley Keith—Qatar
1992	Edward J. Perkins—United Nations
1992	Joseph Monroe Segars—Cape Verde
1998	Charles Stith—Tanzania
1998	George W. B. Haley—Gambia
1998	Shirley Barnes—Madagascar
1999	Carol Moseley-Braun—New Zealand
1999	Delano E. Leewis—Republic of South Africa
2000	Sidney Poitier—Japan

*killed in accident on route to post

List 7-13. Members of Congress (1870-1999)

1870-1879	Joseph H. Rainey
1870-1871	Jefferson F. Long
1871-1874	Robert B. Elliott
1871-1873	Robert C. De Large
1871-1873	Benjamin S. Turner
1871-1873	Josiah T. Walls
1873-1875/1877-1879	Richard H. Cane
1873-1877/1882-1883	John R. Lynch
1873-1875	James T. Rapier
1873-1875	Alonzo J. Ransier
1875-1877	Jeremiah Haralson
1875-1877	John A. Hyman
1875-1877	Charles E. Nash
1875-1878	Robert Smalls
1883-1887	James E. O'Hara
1889-1893	Henry P. Cheatham
1890-1891	John M. Langston
1890-1891	Thomas E. Miller
1893-1895/1896-1897	George W. Murray
1897-1901	George W. White
1929-1935	Oscar DePriest
1935-1943	Arthur W. Mitchell
1943-1970	William L. Dawson
1945-1967/1969-1971	Adam Clayton Powell, Jr.
1955-1980	Charles C. Diggs, Jr.
1958-1978	Robert N. Nix
1963-1990	Augustus F. Hawkins
1965-	John Conyers, Jr.
1969-	William L. Clay
1969-1998	Louis Stokes
1969-1982	Shirley Chisholm
1970-	Charles B. Rangel
1970-1972	George W. Collins
1971-1998	Ronald V. Dellums

Adam Clayton Powell, Jr.

1971-1978	Ralph H. Metcalfe
1971-1987	Parren H. Mitchell
1971-1990	Walter E. Fauntroy
1973-1979	Yvonne B. Burke
1973-1997	Cardiss Collins
1973-1978	Barbara C. Jordan
1973-1977	Andrew Young
1975-	Harold E. Ford
1978-1980	Melvin Evans
1979-	Julian C. Dixon
1979-1991	William H. Gray
1979-1989	Mickey Leland
1979-1980	Bennett McVey Steward
1980-1990	George W. Crockett
1981-1992	Mervyn M. Dymally
1981-1992	Gus Savage
1981-1983	Harold Washington
1982-1984	Katie Hall
1983-	Major Owens
1983-	Edolphus Towns
1983-1995	Alan Wheat
1983-1992	Charles Hayes
1986-1987	Alton R. Waldon, Jr.
1987-1997	Mike Espy
1987-1997	Floyd Flake
1987-	John Lewis
1987-1996	Kweisi Mfume
1988-	Donald Payne
1989-	William Jefferson
1989-1995	Craig Washington
1990-1997	Barbara Rose Collins
1990-1997	Gary Franks
1990-	Eleanor Holmes Norton
1991-1995	Lucien Blackwell
1991-	Maxine Waters
1993-	Stanford D. Bishop

1993-	Corrine Brown
1993-	Eva Clayton
1993-	James Clyburn
1993-	Alcee Hastings
1993-	Earl F. Hilliard
1993-	Eddie Bernice Johnson
1993-	Cynthia McKinney
1993-	Carrie Meek
1993-	Bobby Rush
1993-	Robert (Bobby) C. Scott
1993-	Bennie Thompson
1993-	Melvin L. Watt
1993-	Albert R. Wynn
1995-	Chaka Fallah
1995-	Jesse Jackson, Jr.
1995-	Sheila Jackson-Lee
1995-	Julius Watts
1996-	Elijah Cummings
1996-	Juanita Millender-McDonald
1997-	Julia Carson
1997-	Danny Davis
1997-	Harold Ford
1997-	Carolyn Kilpatrick
1998-	Barbara Lee
1998-	Gregory Meeks
1999-	Stephanie Tubbs Jones

List 7-14. Spotlight: BARBARA JORDAN

- A powerful personality

- Born in Houston, Texas on February 21, 1936

- Honor student in high school, graduating in 1952 at age 16

- B.A. in history and political science from Texas Southern University and J.D. from Boston University in 1959

- Taught at Tuskegee Institute for one year

- Practiced law in Houston

- Elected to Texas Senate in 1966; first African American woman to serve in that body and as president pro tem; authored Texas's first minimum wage bill

- Elected to U.S. House of Representatives and served from 1972-1978

- Instrumental in enacting amendments to strengthen the 1964 Civil Rights Bill, including measures for printing bilingual ballots

- Perhaps best known for her role on the House Judiciary Committee considering the impeachment of Richard M. Nixon in 1974

- In 1976 became first African American and first woman to keynote the Democratic National Convention

- Resigned from Congress and served as professor at University of Texas; appointed to Lyndon Baines Johnson Centennial Chair of National Policy

- Throughout her career, was a consummate soldier against racism and intolerance and a protector of civil rights for all

- Received many honors and awards

- Member of Board of Directors of several corporations

- Eleanor Roosevelt Humanities Award (1984)

- Texas Women's Hall of Fame

- *Ladies Home Journal*'s "100 Most Influential Women in America"

- *Time*'s "Ten Women of the Year" in 1976

- Received 27 honorary doctoral degrees

- Died in 1996

MAYORS

List 7-15. Mayors Representing Major Cities (populations of 50,000 or more)

Floyd Adams, Jr. (Savannah, Georgia)

Dennis Archer (Detroit, Michigan)

Richard Arrington (Birmingham, Alabama)

Martin G. Barnes (Paterson, New Jersey)

Sharon Belton (Minneapolis, Minnesota)

Sara Bost (Irvington, New Jersey)

Robert L. Bowser (East Orange, New Jersey)

Omar Bradley (Compton, California)

Lee Brown (Houston, Texas)

Willie Brown (San Francisco, California)

Bill Campbell (Atlanta, Georgia)

Emanuel Cleaver II (Kansas City, Missouri)

Ernest D. Davis (Mt. Vernon, New York)

David Dinkins (New York City)

Roosevelt F. Dorn (Inglewood, California)

Loretta T. Glickman (Pasadena, California)

Clarence Harmon (St. Louis, Missouri)

W.W. Herenton (Memphis, Tennessee)

Chris Holden (Pasadena, California)

James Holley (Portsmouth, Virginia)

Sharpe James (Newark, New Jersey)

Harvey Johnson (Jackson, Mississippi)

W. Johnson (Rochester, New York)

Ron Kirk (Dallas, Texas)

Gary Loster (Saginaw, Michigan)

David Moore (Beaumont, Texas)

Walter Moore (Pontiac, Michigan)

Marc Morial (New Orleans, Louisiana)

Lorraine Morton (Evanston, Illinois)

Elzie Odom (Arlington, Texas)

Douglas Palmer (Trenton, New Jersey)

Abe Pierce (Monroe, Louisiana)

Kurt Schmoke (Baltimore, Maryland)

James Sills, Jr. (Wilmington, Delaware)

Woodrow Stanley (Flint, Michigan)

Wellington E. Webb (Denver, Colorado)

Michael R. White (Cleveland, Ohio)

Anthony Williams (Washington, D.C.)

List 7-16. Women Mayors

Sharon Belton (Minneapolis, Minnesota)

Sara Bost (Irvington, New Jersey)

Doreatha D. Campbell (Willingboro, New Jersey)

Audrey L. Carey (Newburgh, New York)

Rosalyn R. Dance (Petersburg, Virginia)

Loretta T. Glickman (Pasadena, California)

Jean L. Harris (Eden Prairie, Minnesota)

Patsy J. Hilliard (East Point, Georgia)

Charlene Marshall (Morgantown, West Virginia)

Lorraine H. Morton (Evanston, Illinois)

Clara K. Williams (Riviera Beach, Florida)

PRESIDENTIAL MEDAL-OF-FREEDOM HONOREES

List 7-17. Presidential Medal-of-Freedom Honorees

1963	Marian Anderson (singer)
1963	Ralph J. Bunche (scholar, diplomat—with distinction)
1964	Lena F. Edwards (physician, humanitarian)
1964	John Lewis (congressman)
1964	Leontyne Price (singer)
1964	A. Philip Randolph (trade unionist)
1969	Ralph Ellison (writer)
1969	Roy Wilkins (civil rights leader)
1969	Whitney M. Young (social worker)
1969	Edward Kennedy "Duke" Ellington (pianist, composer)
1976	Jesse Owens (athlete, humanitarian)
1977	Martin Luther King, Jr. (civil rights leader [posthumously])
1980	Andrew Young (public servant)
1980	Clarence M. Mitchell, Jr. (lawyer, civil rights activist)
1981	James H. "Eubie" Blake (ragtime pianist and composer)
1983	James Edward Cheek (educator, scholar)
1983	Mabel Mercer (singer)
1984	Jack Roosevelt "Jackie" Robinson (baseball player [posthumously])
1985	William "Count" Basie (jazz pianist)
1985	Jerome H. Holland (educator, ambassador [posthumously])
1988	Pearl Bailey (entertainer)
1992	Ella Fitzgerald (singer)
1993	Colin Powell (General, U.S. Army)
1994	Dorothy Height (civil rights leader)
1994	Barbara Jordan (lawyer, congressional leader)
1995	William Coleman, Jr. (lawyer, civil rights defender)
1995	John Hope Franklin (historian)
1995	A. Leon Higginbothem, Jr. (federal judge)
1996	John H. Johnson (business leader)
1996	Rosa Parks (civil rights activist)
1999	Oliver W. Hill, Sr. (lawyer, civil rights activist)
2000	Marian Wright Edelman (founder and president of Children's Defense Fund)
2000	Rev. Jesse Jackson, Sr. (civil rights leader)
2000	Gardner C. Taylor (minister, author, civil rights supporter)

PRESIDENT AND VICE PRESIDENT CANDIDATES/NOMINEES

List 7-18. Presidential Candidates/Nominees

1864	John Fremont (nominated, declined)
1968	Channing E. Phillips (nominated from floor at Democratic National Convention)
1972	Shirley Chisholm
1984	Jesse Jackson
1984	Lenora Fulani
1988	Jesse Jackson
1988	Lenora Fulani
1992	L. Douglas Wilder
1996	Alan Keyes
2000	Alan Keyes

List 7-19. Vice Presidential Candidates/Nominees

1936	James W. Ford, Communist Party
1968	Julian Bond (nominated from the floor at the Democratic convention, declined)
1980	Angela Davis
1984	Angela Davis
2000	Ezola Foster

ATTORNEYS AND LAWYERS

List 7-20. Pioneering Attorneys

1834	George Ruffin	first to graduate from U.S. university law school (Harvard); won seat in Massachusetts legislature (1869); Massachusetts judge (1883)
1845	Macon Bolling Allen	first licensed attorney admitted to Maine bar; elected judge in South Carolina (1873)
1849	Robert Morris, Jr.	attorney in Sarah Roberts case, challenging Boston school segregation; although unsuccessful, an important case

1854	John Mercer Langston	first elected to public office; elected to U.S. Congress from Virginia (1888)
1865	John S. Rock	first attorney admitted to practice before the Supreme Court
1870	Robert Brown Elliot	elected to 42nd Congress from South Carolina
1872	Charlotte E. Ray	first woman to graduate from law school
1885	Everett J. Waring	admitted to bar of Supreme Bench in Baltimore, Maryland; challenged segregation, handled many racial issues
1889	Thomas E. Miller	elected as South Carolina state senator (1880); served in House of Representatives (1890-1891)
1926	Violette Nearly Anderson	first woman prosecutor in Chicago (1922-1923); first woman admitted to practice before the Supreme Court
1927	Sadie R. M. Alexander	lawyer and activist

List 7-21. Outstanding Lawyers

Nineteenth Century

John S. Rock	Admitted to practice before the U.S. Supreme Court, 1865; physician and civil rights advocate
John M. Langston	1867, one of the first deans of Howard University; 1877, United States Minister to Haiti
James C. Napier	Howard University law graduate
Richard T. Greener	First Harvard Law School graduate, 1870
Edward A. Morris	Admitted to the Illinois bar, 1879
J.T.V. Hill	Began practice in Indianapolis, 1882
Judson W. Lyons	Howard University Law graduate, 1884
Frederick L. McGhee	Admitted to the Illinois bar, 1885
James H. Lott	Began practice in Indianapolis, 1890s
Robert L. Bailey	Began practice in Indianapolis, 1890s
Simuel McGill	Served as counsel for Knights of Pythias
Perry Howard	Mississippi
George Hall	New York
William H.H. Hart	Taught criminal law at Howard University for 25 years
Walter Moran Farmer	First African American Washington University law graduate
Homer G. Phillips	St. Louis, Missouri

Civil Rights Lawyers (Male)

Ashby Hawkins	Baltimore NAACP, counsel in *Buchanan* v. *Warley*, 1917
Scipio Africanus	Representative with NAACP in the Arkansas Jones sharecroppers case, 1919
Charles Hamilton Houston	Civil Rights
William H. Hastie	Civil Rights
James M. Nabrit	Civil Rights
Leon Ransom	Civil Rights
Raymond Pace Alexander	Civil Rights
Lloyd Lionel Gaines	Civil Rights
Herman Sweatt	Civil Rights
Louis Redding	Lawyer in Wilmington, Delaware
Oliver W. Hill, Sr.	Civil Rights
Leonard W. Holt	Served as counsel for school integration
Howard Moore, Jr.	Defended Martin Luther King, Jr.
Fred Gray	Defended Rosa Parks, 1955
Sidney Redmond	Civil Rights
Loren Miller	Civil Rights
Thurgood Marshall	Civil Rights

Civil Rights Lawyers (Female)

Charlotte Ray	First African American woman lawyer, 1872
Jan Bolin	New York, New York
Juanita Jackson Mitchell	Baltimore, Maryland
Frankie Muse Freeman	St. Louis, Missouri
Constance Baker Motley	New York, New York
Patricia Roberts Harris	Washington, D.C.
Juanita Kidd Stout	Philadelphia, Pennsylvania
Ruby Martin	Washington, D.C.
Eleanor Holmes Norton	Washington, D.C.
Edith Miller	New York, New York
Ada Sipuel	Civil Rights

POLICE CHIEFS

List 7-22. Police Chiefs of Major Cities

Terry G. Hilliard (Chicago, Illinois)

Bernard C. Parks (Los Angeles, California)

Harold L. Hurtt (Phoenix, Arizona)

Clarence O'Neal Bradford (Houston, Texas)

Arthur Jones (Milwaukee, Wisconsin)

Benny N. Napoleon (Detroit, Michigan)

James G. Jackson (Columbus, Ohio)

Charles H. Ramsey (Washington, D.C.)

Ronald Henderson (St. Louis, Missouri)

Beverly J. Harvard (Atlanta, Georgia)

Richard J. Pennington (New Orleans, Louisiana)

Walter J. Winfrey (Memphis, Tennessee)

Emmett H. Turner (Nashville, Tennessee)

Major T. Berry, Jr. (Oklahoma City, Oklahoma)

Bennie R. Holder (Tampa, Florida)

Dr. Charles A. Moose (Portland, Oregon)

Dr. Gwendolyn V. Boyd (Prichard, Alabama)

ORGANIZATIONS

List 7-23. Organizations

- Alliance of Black Women Attorneys
- Alliance for Justice
- American Bar Association
- American Civil Liberties Union
- American Political Science Association
- Association of Black American Ambassadors
- Association of Black Women Attorneys

- The Black Agenda
- Blacks in Government
- Center for Constitutional Rights
- Center for Democratic Renewal
- Charles Houston Bar Association
- Congressional Black Associates
- Congressional Black Caucus
- Congressional Black Caucus Foundation, Inc.
- Joint Center for Political and Economic Studies
- Lawyers' Committee for Civil Rights Under Law
- NAACP Legal Defense and Education Fund
- National Alliance of Black Organizations
- National Association for the Advancement of Colored People
- National Association of Blacks in Criminal Justice
- National Bar Association
- National Black Caucus
- National Black Caucus of Local Elected Officials
- National Black Caucus of State Legislators
- National Black Law Student Association
- National Black Leadership Roundtable
- National Conference of Black Lawyers
- National Conference of Black Mayors, Inc.
- National Political Congress of Black Women, Inc.
- National Political Science Association
- National Prison Project of the ACLU Foundation
- National Urban League
- The Sentencing Project

Section 8

ARTS, LETTERS, AND MEDIA

SPOTLIGHTS

PERFORMING ARTS ORGANIZATIONS AND FACILITIES

TRADE PUBLICATIONS AND RESOURCE GUIDES

SECTION 8

ARTS, LETTERS, AND MEDIA

The first Africans arrived in the United States with a rich history in the arts. In the cultures from which the slaves originated, music, dance, and drama accompanied almost every public activity. The Africans brought this love of music and dance and when possible, made them integral parts of daily life in America. Consequently, African Americans inherited an oral and dramatic tradition in which music and dance were expected.

Art has been the least-known contribution of African Americans to American culture. There were African American painters, sculptors, printmakers, and other artisans from the beginning, but their work was largely ignored or not credited. While some patrons appreciated their work, it was not until the nineteenth century that African American artists were allowed to emerge and fully express artistic talents.

The Arts evolved through several periods beginning in the 1700s, with the best known being the Harlem Renaissance (1920-1940), and the second African American Renaissance (1980s to the present). Artists found their voices as they focused on the issues important to people of color. Art, music, dance, and literature reflected the concerns, hopes, and dreams of people during each of those evolutionary periods. For example, the evolution of music reflected the tenor of society over time: spirituals, blues, cool jazz, bebop, soul, rock and roll, avant garde, rap, and hip hop. The messages are clear.

Section 8 explores aspects of art, dance, music, theater, films, literature, and more.

FIRSTS IN ARTS, LETTERS, AND MEDIA

List 8-1. Firsts in Arts, Letters, and Media

Date	Pioneer/Event	Contribution
1770	Phillis Wheatley	first black woman to be published
1778	Jupiter Hammon	published poem, "To Miss Phillis Wheatley"
1833	Ira Aldridge	performed Othello on stage in London
1843	Frank Johnson	published sheet music; gave formal band concerts; produced first racially integrated concert
1850s	Robert S. Duncanson	noted muralist and studio painter
1852	*Uncle Tom's Cabin*	novel by Harriet Beecher Stowe, first major American work to have African American man as the central character
1853	Elizabeth T. Greenfield	concert singer; make a command performance before royalty
1858	Thomas G. Bethune	blind pianist and composer
1861	Harriet Jacobs	published first novel by African American woman
1878	James Bland	published official state song, "Carry Me Back to Old Virginny"
1898	*Trip to Coontown*	show organized, produced, and managed by African Americans
1899	Charles W. Chessnut	published collection of short stories
1900s	William E. Braxton (1878-1932)	expressionist painter
1900s	Edmonia Lewis	female sculptor
1912	W.C. Handy	published first blues composition
1914	Egbert "Bert" Williams	comedian, starred in Ziegfield Follies; in 1920, first to be allowed to join Actor's Equity (show business labor union)
1916	*Rachel*	drama written and interpreted on stage by African American actors
1917	Broadway plays	*Granny Maumee; The Rider of Dreams;* and *Simon and Cyrenian*
1919	Oscar Micheaux	produced first film, "The Homesteader"
1920	Charles S. Gilpin	starred in major American play *The Emperor Jones;* Spingarn recipient (in 1921)
1920	Mamie Smith	recorded a blues record, "Crazy Blues"

1920s	Florence Mills	attained international fame as female superstar
1921	Ethel Waters	performing artist to first record for Black Swan, W.C. Handy's record label
1923	Willis Richardson	Broadway play, *The Chip Woman's Fortune*
1923	Paul Revere Williams	member of American Institute of Architecture
1928	Norma M. Sklarek	woman licensed as an architect in the U.S.
1932	Don Redman	led all African American band on a sponsored radio series, "Chipso"
1934	Aaron Douglas	recognized as illustrator and leading artist during Harlem Renaissance; known as "father of Black American art"
1935	Langston Hughes	*Mulatto,* first long-running Broadway hit by African American author; first author to make a living with earnings from his writing
1939	Billie Holiday	recorded "Strange Fruit," song with a political message about lynchings
1917-2000	Jacob Lawrence	represented in mainstream gallery and in art textbooks
1943	Paul Robeson	played Othello on American stage with a white cast
1945	Richmond Barthe	elected to the American Academy of Arts and Letters
1950	Gwendolyn Brooks	won the Pulitzer Prize
1955	Marian Anderson	performed at the Metropolitan Opera in New York
1956	Alice Childress	won an OBIE for her play, *Trouble in Mind*
1959	Lorraine Hansberry	won New York Drama Critics Award for *A Raisin in the Sun*
1959	Ella Fitzgerald and Count Basie	won Grammy Awards
1960	Harry Belafonte	won Emmy Award for "Tonight With Belafonte"
1963	Sidney Poitier	won Academy Award for best actor in *Lilies of the Field*
1965	Ruby Dee	appeared on Broadway in *The Taming of the Shrew; King Lear; A Raisin in the Sun* (1959)
1966	Leontyne Price	opened the Metropolitan Opera season
1968	Henry Lewis	conductor of a major American orchestra (New Jersey symphony, Newark) and first to lead the Metropolitan Opera

1971	Maya Angelou	*Georgia,* first movie screenplay by African American woman to be produced
1978	Max Robinson	anchor on a network news program
1979	"Rapper's Delight"	became first top-40 rap single in America by the Sugar Hill Gang
1980	Robert Johnson	BET—first black-owned company listed on New York Stock Exchange
1982	Charles Fuller	won Pulitzer Prize and a New York Drama Critics Award for "A Soldier's Play"
1982	Bryant C. Gumbel	co-host of "The Today Show," a major television news show
1982	Michael Jackson	all-time bestselling video, "Thriller"
1983	Alice Walker	Pulitzer Prize for *The Color Purple*
1984	Paula Giddings	published *When and Where I Enter: The Impact of Black Women and Race and Sex in America,* first narrative history of African American women
1984	Bill Cosby	"The Cosby Show" premiered on NBC
1986	Salt-N-Pepa	female rappers received platinum award for debut album, "Hot, Cool, and Vicious"
1989	Oprah Winfrey	purchased Harpo Productions, becoming the first African American and the third woman to own a major studio facility
1989	*Emerge*	a news magazine, first published
1992	Terry McMillan	*Waiting to Exhale* on the bestseller list for extended period
1992	Awadagin Pratt	won first prize in Naumburg Competition in New York as classical pianist
1993	Rita Dove	first woman to be named Poet Laureate, and the youngest, at age 40
1993	Toni Morrison	Nobel Prize for Literature
1996	George Wolfe and Savior Glover	won four Tony Awards for *Bring in 'Da Noise, Bring in 'Da Funk*
1997	Wynton Marsalis	"Blood on the Fields" is first jazz composition to win Pulitzer Prize for music
1998	Dr. Walter J. Turnbull	received the Heinz Award in the Arts and Humanities for his creation of the Boys Choir of Harlem
1999	*Black Issues Book Review*	first consumer magazine devoted to books

ART AND ARTISTS

Many of the artists listed here work in more than one medium, such as painting and photography, or sculpture and conceptual art. The list includes major, influential artists from the past, and well-known contemporary artists.

List 8-2. Painting, Drawing, Printmaking

Allen, Tina (1955-)

Alston, Charles H. (1907-1977)

Amos, Emma (1938-)

Andrews, Benny (1930-)

Bailey, Malcolm (1937-)

Banks, Ellen (1941-)

Bannister, Edward M. (1828-1901)

Barnes, Ernie (1938-)

Basquiat, Jean Michel (1960-1987)

Bearden, Romare (1911-1988)

Beasley, Phoebe (1943-)

Benoit, Rigaud (1911-1987)

Biggers, John T. (1924-)

Billops, Camille (1933-)

Birch, Willie (1942-)

Blayton-Taylor, Betty (1937-)

Bolton, Shirley (1945-)

Bradley, Peter (1940-)

Braxton, William E. (1878-1932)

Brown, Grafton Tyler (1841-1918)

Chandler, Dana (1941-)

Chaplin, John G. (1828-1907)

Coleman, Floyd (1937-)

Colescott, Robert H. (1925-)

Cortor, Eldzier (1916-)

Crichlow, Ernest (1914-)

Crite, Allan Rohan (1918-)

Cruz, Emilio (1938-)

Davis, Alonzo (1943-)

Davis, Bing (Willis) (1937-)

DeKnight, Avel (1933-)

Delaney, Beauford (1901-1979)

Delaney, Joseph (1904-1991)

Denmark, James (1936-)

DePillars, Murry (1938-)

Douglas, Aaron (1898-1979)

Driskell, David (1931-)

Duncanson, Robert Stuart (1823-1872)

Edwards, Melvin (1939-)

Farrow, William McKnight (1885-1967)

Favorite, Malaika (1949-)

Fletcher, Gilbert (1948-)

Freeman, Robert (1946-)

Gammon, Reginald (1921-)

Gilliam, Sam (1933-)

Godwin, Michelle (1961-)

Goodnight, Paul T. (1946-)

Gordon, Russell (1936-)

Grigsby, J. Eugene, Jr. (1918-)

Hammons, David (1943-)

Harden, Marvin (1935-)

Harper, William A. (1873-1910)

Harris, Michael D. (1948-)

Hayden, Palmer C. (1893-1973)

Heath, Thomas (1949-)

Hendricks, Barkley (1948-)

Herring, James V. (1887-1969)

Hicks, Leon (1933-)

Hines, Felrath (1918-)

Hoard, Adrienne (1949-)

Holder, Robin (1952-)

Hollingsworth, Alvin C. (1928-)

Honeywood, Varnett (1950-)

Hughes, Manuel (1945-)

Hutson, Bill (1936-)

Iams, Gerald, (c. 1970-)

Jackson, Suzanne (1944-)

Johnson, Daniel LaRue (1938-)

Johnson, Lester (1937-)

Johnson, Malvin Gray (1896-1934)

Johnson, William Henry (1901-1970)

Johnston, Joshua, (c. 1765-1830)

Jones, Lois Mailou (1905-1998)

Lacy, Jean (1932-)

Lam, Wilfredo (1902-)

Lawrence, Jacob (1917-2000)

Lee, Ron (1951-)

Lee-Smith, Hughie (1915-1999)

LeVa, Barry (1941-)

Lewis, Joseph S. III (1953-)

Lewis, Norman (1909-1979)

Lewis, Samella (1924-)

Ligon, Glenn (1960-)

Logan, Juan (1946-)

Loving, Alvin (1935-)

Marshall, Kerry James (1955-)

Mason, Phillip (1942-)

Mayhew, Richard (1924-)

Miller, Tom (1945-)

Mills, Lev (1940-)

Mitchell, Dean (1957-)

Moorhead, Scipio, (active 1770s)

Morgan, Norma (1928-)

Morrison, Keith (1940-)

Motley, Archibald, Jr. (1891-1981)

Nefertiti (born Cynthia Freeman) (1949-)

Norman, Joseph E. (1957-)

O'Neal, Mary Lovelace (1942-)

Olugebefola, Ademola (1941-)

Oubre, Hayward (1916-)

Overstreet, Joe (1934-)

Parks, James Dallas (1907-)

Phillips, James (Charles) (1945-)

Pindell, Howardena (1943-)

Pippin, Horace (1888-1946)

Platt, Michael B. (1948-)

Pogue, Stephanie (1944-)

Porter, Charles Ethan (1847-c. 1923)

Porter, James A. (1905-1971)

Priestly, Debra (no date)

Proctor, Joseph (1816)

Reid, Robert (1924-)

Rickson, Gary (1942-)

Riddle, John (1933-)

Ringgold, Faith (1934-)

Roberts, (Lucille) Malkia (1917-)

Robinson, Christopher Wade (1965-)

Rozzelle, John (no date)

Ryder, Mahler (1937-1992)

Saunders, Raymond (1934-)

Scott, William Edouard (1844-1964)

Searles, Charles (1937-)

Sebree, Charles (1914-1985)

Sills, Thomas (1914-)

Smith, Alfred J., Jr. (1948-)

Smith, Vincent (1929-)

Snowden, Gilda (1954-)

Snowden, Sylvia (1946-)

Tanner, Henry Ossawa (1859-1937)

Thomas, Alma W. (1896-1978)

Thompson, Robert (1937-)

Tyler, Grafton (1841-1918)

Valentim, Rubem (1922-1991)

Walker, Annie E. (1855-1929)

Waring, Laura Wheeling (1887-1948)

Wells, James Lesesne (1902-1993)

West, Pheoris (1950-)

White, Charles (1918-1979)

Williams, Frank J. (1959-)

Williams, Philemona (1951-)

Williams, William T. (1942-)

Wilson, Ellis (1899-1977)

Wilson, John (1922-)

Woodruff, Hale A. (1900-1980)

Mixed Media

Bailey, Radcliff (1968-)

Baynes, Gloretta (1954-)

Carter, Carol Ann (1947-)

Carter, Nanette (1954-)

Howard, Mildred (1945-)

Johnson, Stephanie A. (1952-)

Jones, Benjamin (1942-)

Jones-Henderson, Napoleon (1943-)

Maynard, Valerie (no date)

Piper, Adrian (1948-)

Warmack, Gregory (Mr. Imagination) (1948-)

List 8-3. Photography

Amari, Amalia (1949-)

Bey, Dawoud (1953-)

Brathwaite, Kwame (1938-)

Burns, Millie (1950-)

Charles, Roland (1970-)

Cox, Renée (1958-)

DeCarava, Roy (1919-)

Grogion, Tyrone (1947-)

Higgins, Chester, Jr. (1946-)

Hinton, Milton J. (1910-)

Jones, Brent M. (1945-)

McLemore, LaMonte (1940-)

Moutousamy-Ashe, Jeanne (1951-)

Muhamad, Ozjer (1950-)

Parks, Gordon (1912-)

Pinderhughes, John (1946-)

Polk, Prentice Herman (1898-1984)

Rowe, Sandra (1939-)

Simpson, Coreen (1942-)

Simpson, Lorna (1960-)

Sleet, Moneta, Jr. (1926-1996)

Van Der Zee, James (1886-1983)

Walker, Christian (1954-)

Weems, Carrie Mae (1953-)

Williams, Pat Ward (1948-)

List 8-4. Sculpture, Installation, Performance Art

Adkins, Terry K. (1953-)

Artis, William E. (1914-1977)

Barthé, Richmond (1901-1989)

Brown, Everald (1917-)

Brown, James Andrew (1953-)

Buchanan, Beverly (1940-)

Burke, Selma (1900-1995)

Byard, Carole (1941-)

Catlett, Elizabeth (1915-)

Chase-Riboud, Barbara (1936-)

Conwill, Houston (1947-)

Davis, Bing (Willis) (1937-)

Drew, Leonardo (1961-)

Edwards, Mel (1937-)

Eversley, Frederick (1941-)

Fuller, Meta Vaux Warrick (1877-1968)

Green, Renée (1959-)

Hassinger, Maren (1947-)

Howard, Mildred (1945-)

Hunt, Richard (1935-)

Jackson-Jarvis, Martha (1952-)

Johnson, Sargent Claude (1888-1967)

Lewis, Edmonia (1843-c. 1909)

Lloyd, Tom (1929-)

Love, Ed (1936-)

Negudi, Senga (1943-)

Outterbridge, John (Wilfred) (1933-)

Perkins, Marion (1908-1961)

Pigatt, Anderson J. (1928-)

Prophet, Nancy Elizabeth (1890-1960)

Purifoy, Noah (1917-)

Puryear, Martin (1941-)

Ramsaran, Helen (1943-)

Ravarra, Patricia (1947-)

Rhoden, John (1918-)

Saar, Alison (1956-)

Saar, Betye (1926-)

Savage, Augusta (1892-1962)

Scott, Joyce (1945-)

Simmons, Gary (1964-)

Simms, Carroll H. (1924-)

Staton, Therman (1953-)

Stout, Renee (1958-)

Sullivan, Twotrees (Kaylynn) (1945-)

Thrash, Dox (1892-1965)

Toone, Lloyd (no date)

Warburg, Eugene (1826-1859)

Ward, Barbara (1940-)

Ward-Brown, Denise (1953-)

Washington, James W., Jr. (1911-)

Williams, Grace (no date)

Williams, Michael Kelly (1950-)

Wilson, Ed (1925-1996)

Wilson, Fred (1954-)

List 8-5. Self-Taught Artists

Bailey, Xenobia (no date), artist and designer

Dial, Richard (1955-), carver

Dial, Thorton, Sr. (1928-), carver/painter

Edmondson, William (1882-1951), stone sculpture

Evans, Minnie (1892-1987), painter

Ferguson, Amos (1920-), carver

Flemister, Frederick (1917-1976), painter

Gudgell, Henry (1826-1899), carver

Hampton, James (1909-1964), assemblage

Manigault, Mary (c. 1910), basket-maker

Morgan, Sister Gertrude (1900-1980), painter

Pierce, Elijah (1892-1984), carver

Pippin, Horace (1888-1946), painter

Powers, Harriet (1837-1911), quilt-maker

Rogers, Sultan (1922-), carver

Traylor, Bill (1854-1947), painter

Webster, Derek (1934), yard decorations

List 8-6. Spiral Group

The Spiral Group, founded in 1963 by Romare Bearden and Norman Lewis, deals with issues of aesthetic excellence while retaining the unique characteristics of African American art.

Alston, Charles (1907-1977)

Amos, Emma (1938-)

Bearden, Romare (1911-1988)

Douglas, Calvin (no date)

Ferguson, Perry (no date)

Gammon, Reginald (1921-)

Hines, Felrath (1918-)

Hollingsworth, Alvin (1928-)

Hutson, Bill (1936-)

Lewis Norman (1909-1979)

Loving, Alvin (1935-)

Majors, William (no date)

Mayhew, Richard (1924-)

Miller, Earle (no date)

Morgan, Norma (1928-)

Pritchard, William (no date)

Reid, Robert (1924-)

Simpson, Merton (1928-)

Thompson, Robert (1937-)

Williams, William T. (1942-)

Woodruff, Hale (1900-1980)

Yeargans, James (no date)

List 8-7. Harlem Renaissance, 1920s-1940

Barthé, Richmond (1901-1989)

Delaney, Beauford (1901-1979)

Douglas, Aaron (1898-1979)

Hayden, Palmer (1893-1973)

Johnson, Malvin Gray (1896-1934)

Johnson, Sargent Claude (1888-1967)

Johnson, William H. (1901-1970)

Jones, Lois Mailou (1905-1998)

Loving, Al (1935-)

Porter, James A. (1905-1971)

Prophet, Elizabeth (1890-1960)

Savage, Augusta (1892-1962)

Van Der Zee, James (1886-1983)

Woodruff, Hale (1900-1980)

List 8-8. Expressionist Painters

Andrews, Benny (1930-)

Bailey, Malcolm (1937-)

Chandler, Dona (1941-)

DePillars, Murry (1939-)

Edwards, Melvin (1939-)

Hammonds, David (1943-)

Mason, Phillip (1942-)

Overstreet, Joe (1934-)

Rickson, Gary (1942-)

Riddle, John (1933-)

Ringgold, Faith (1934-)

Searles, Charles (1937-)

Smith, Vincent (1929-)

List 8-9. Some African American Artists and Their Artworks

Alston, Charles, 1907-1977, painter. *The Family,* 1955, Whitney Museum of American Art, New York City

Andrews, Benny, 1930, painter. *Black,* 1971, Collection of the artist

Bannister, Edward Mitchell, 1828-1901, painter. *Landscape,* 1882, Museum of Art, Rhode Island School of Design; *Sabin Point, Narragansett Bay,* 1885, Brown University, Providence, Rhode Island

Barthé, Richmond, 1901-1989, sculptor. *The Boxer,* 1942, Metropolitan Museum of Art, New York City

Bearden, Romare, 1911-1988, painter. *The Intimacy of Water,* 1973, St. Louis Art Museum; *The Migration of the Negro,* 1940-1941, Museum of Modern Art, New York

Biggers, John, 1924, painter & muralist. *Shotguns, Third Ward,* 1987 (Mural, Christia V. Adair Park), Harris County, Texas; *Starry Crown,* 1987, Dallas Museum of Art, Dallas, Texas

Blayton-Taylor, Betty, 1937, painter/mixed media. *Improvisation # 5,* 1977, Collection of the artist

Brown, Everald, 1917, painter. *Instrument for Four People,* 1986, National Gallery of Jamaica, Kingston

Brown, Grafton Tyler, 1841-1918, painter. *Grand Canyon of the Yellowstone from Hayden Point,* 1891, The Oakland Museum, Oakland, California

Catlett, Elizabeth, 1915, sculptor. *Malcolm X Speaks for Us,* 1969, Museum of Modern Art, New York City; *Sharecropper,* 1968, National Museum of American Art, Washington, D.C.

Chase-Riboud, Barbara, 1936, sculptor. *Monument to Malcolm X (#11),* 1969, Newark Museum, New Jersey

Conwill, Houston, 1947, sculptor. *Installation, 1995,* Bernstein Associates, Mt. Vernon, New York

Cortor, Eldzier, 1916, painter/printmaker. *Southern Gate,* 1942-1943, National Museum of American Art, Washington, D.C.

Crite, Allan Rohan, 1918, painter. *Harriett and Leon,* 1941, The Boston Atheneum, Boston, Massachusetts

Douglas, Aaron, 1899-1979, painter. *The Negro in the African Setting*: Panel 1, 1934, Collection of The New York Public Library, New York City; *The Creation,* 1935, The Howard University Gallery of Art, Washington, D.C.

Duncanson, Robert Stuart, 1823-1872, painter. *The Blue Hole, Flood Waters, Little Miami River,* 1851, Cincinnati Art Museum; *The Land of the Lotus-Eaters,* c. 1861, His Majesty's Royal Collection, Stockholm

Edmondson, William, 1870-1951, carver. *Turtle,* limestone, 1940, Collection of Mr. and Mrs. Robert L. Gwinn; *Eve,* early twentieth century, Tennessee Botanical Gardens & Fine Arts Center, Nashville, Tennessee

Evans, Minnie, 1892-1987, painter. *Design Made at Arlie Gardens,* 1967, National Gallery of American Art, Washington, D.C.

Ferguson, Amos, 1920, carver. *Polka Dot Junkanoo,* 1984, Collection of Geoffrey Holder; *Untitled (Mermaid),* 1983, International Folk Art, Museum of New Mexico, Santa Fe

Fuller, Meta Vaux Warrick, 1877-1968, sculptor. *Richard B. Harrison as "De Lawd,"* c. 1935, Howard University Gallery of Art, Washington, D.C.

Hayden, Palmer, 1893-1973, painter. *John Henry on the Right, Steam Drill on the Left,* 1947, Collection of Museum of African Art, Los Angeles; *The Janitor Who Paints,* 1937, National Museum of American Art, Washington, D.C.

Johnson, Malvin Gray, 1896-1934, painter. *Self-Portrait,* 1934, National Museum of American Art, Washington, D.C.

Johnson, Sargent Claude, 1887-1967, sculptor. *Forever Free,* 1935, San Francisco Museum of Modern Art; *Mask,* 1935, San Francisco

Johnson, William Henry, 1901-1970, painter. *Street Musicians,* c. 1940, Oakland Museum of Art, California

Johnston, Joshua, c. 1765-1830, painter. *Portrait of a Cleric,* c. 1805, Bowdoin College Museum of Art, Brunswick, Maine

Jones, Ben, 1942, painter, scultor, printmaker, and mixed media. *Stars II* (15 elements), 1983, Collection of the Newark Museum, Newark, New Jersey

Jones, Lois Mailou, 1905-1998, painter. *Symbols d'Afrique II,* 1983, Collection of the artist; *Parade des Paysans,* 1965, Collection of Max Robinson, Washington, D.C.

Lacy, Jean, 1932, painter. *Little Egypt Condo/New York City,* 1987, Collection of the artist

Lawrence, Jacob, 1917-2000, painter. *Builders #1,* 1972, St. Louis Art Museum, St. Louis, Missouri; *The Migration of the Negro,* Panel 1, 1940-1941, Phillips Collection, Washington, D.C.

Lee-Smith, Hughie, 1915-1999, painter. *Two Girls,* 1966, New Jersey State Museum, Trenton, New Jersey

Lewis, Edmonia, 1843-c. 1909, sculptor. *Hagar,* 1869, National Museum of American Art, Washington, D.C.

Lewis, Norman, 1909-1979, painter. *Yellow Hat,* 1936, Collection of Ouida B. Lewis, New York

Lewis, Samella, 1924, painter. *Boy With a Flute,* oil, 1968, Collection of the artist

Love, Ed, 1936 sculptor. *Mask for Mingus,* welded steel, 1974, Collection of the artist

Miller, Dave, Sr., 1872-1969, carver. *Talisman,* wood, 1940, Collection of the estate of David Miller, Jr.

Motley, Archibald, Jr., 1891-1980, painter. *Chicken Shack,* 1936, Harmon Foundation Collection, the National Archives; *Mending Socks,* 1924, Ackland Art Museum, University of North Carolina at Chapel Hill, North Carolina

Pigatt, Anderson, 1928, sculptor. *Caught in the Middle Earth,* wood and paint, 1970, New York Public Library

Pindell, Howardena, 1943, painter. *Autobiography: Water/Ancestors, Middle Passages/Family Ghosts,* 1988, The Wadsworth Atheneum, Hartford, Connecticut

Pippin, Horace, 1888-1946, painter. *The Holy Mountain,* 1944, Hirshhorn Museum and Sculpture Garden, Washington, D.C.; *John Brown Going to His Hanging,* 1942, The Pennsylvania Academy of the Fine Arts, Philadelphia

Porter, James A., 1905-1971, painter. *Woman Holding a Jug,* 1930, Fisk University, Nashville, Tennessee

Powers, Harriet, 1837-1911, quilter. *Bible Quilt,* c. 1895-1898, Museum of Fine Arts, Boston, Massachusetts

Prophet, Nancy Elizabeth, 1890, sculptor. *Congolais,* 1931, Whitney Museum of American Art, New York City

Saar, Allison, 1956, sculptor. *Terra Firma,* 1991, Santa Barbara Museum of Art, Santa Barbara, California

Saar, Betye, 1926, sculptor. *The Liberation of Aunt Jemimah,* 1972, University Art Museum, University of California, Berkeley

Saunders, Raymond, 1934, painter. *Jack Johnson,* 1971, The Pennsylvania Academy of Fine Arts, Philadelphia

Savage, Augusta, 1892-1962, sculptor. *Gamin,* 1929, Howard University Gallery of Art, Washington, D.C.

Scott, William Edouard, 1884-1964, painter. *When the Tide Is Out,* c. 1931, Harmon Foundation Collection, the National Archives

Searles, Charles, 1937, painter. *Dancer Series,* 1976, Collection of Dr. and Mrs. Maurice Clifford, Philadelphia

Stout, Renee, 1958, sculptor. *Fetish #1,* 1988, Dallas Museum of Art, Dallas, Texas

Tanner, Henry Ossawa, 1859-1937, painter. *Banjo Lesson,* 1893, Hampton University Museum Collection, Hampton, Virginia; *The Thankful Poor,* 1894, Collection of Dr. William and Dr. Camille Cosby

Thomas, Alma W., 1896-1978, painter. *Light Blue Nursery,* National Museum of American Art, Washington, D.C.; *Elysian Fields,* 1973, National Museum of American Art, Washington, D.C.; *Three Red Hats,* 1964, Collection of Mrs. J.E. Spingarn

White, Charles, 1918-1979, painter. *Take My Mother Home,* 1957, Collection of Dr. Richard Simms, Harbor City, California

Wilson, Ed, 1925-1996, sculptor. *Jazz Musicians,* 1982-1984, Douglass High School, Baltimore, Maryland

Wilson, Ellis, 1899-1977, painter. *Field Workers,* date unknown, National Museum of American Art, Washington, D.C.; *Haitian Funeral Procession,* c. 1950s, Amistad Research Center, Tulane University, New Orleans

Wilson, Fred, 1954, sculptor. *Guarded Men,* 1991, Whitney Museum of American Art, New York City

Woodruff, Hale, 1900-1980, painter. *Golden State Life Insurance Murals,* 1948-1949, Los Angeles, California; *Poor Man's Cotton,* 1934, Newark Museum, New Jersey

List 8-10. African American Art Collections

African American Museum (Dallas, Texas)

The African American Museum in Philadelphia (Philadelphia, Pennsylvania)

Afro-American Historical and Cultural Museum (Philadelphia, Pennsylvania)

Amistad Research Center, Tulane University (New Orleans, Louisiana)

Bennett College (Greensboro, North Carolina)

Black Heritage Museum (Miami, Florida)

DuSable Museum of African American History (Chicago, Illinois)

Fisk University (Nashville, Tennessee)

Great Plains Black Museum (Omaha, Nebraska)

Hampton University (Hampton, Virginia)

Howard University (Washington, D.C.)

Joseph Hirschhorn Museum, Smithsonian Institution (Washington, D.C.)

Morgan State University (Baltimore, Maryland)

Museum for African Art (New York, New York)

Museum of African American Art (Tampa, Florida)

Museum of African American Art (Los Angeles)

Museum of African American History (Detroit, Michigan)

National Museum of African Art, Smithsonian Institution (Washington, D.C.)

San Francisco African American Historical and Cultural Society (San Francisco, California)

Schomburg Center for Research in Black Culture (New York, New York)

The Studio Museum in Harlem (New York, New York)

Talladega College (Talladega, Alabama)

Will T. Murphy African American Museum (Tuscaloosa, Alabama)

MUSIC

The music lists, from popular to classical, show a range of past and present performers in their main area of accomplishments.

List 8-11. Popular Singers

Pearl Bailey (1918-1990)	jazz, comedienne
Anita Baker (1958-)	jazz, rhythm and blues
Josephine "Jo" Baker (1906-1975)	blues, jazz
Shirley Bassey (1937-)	pop
Harry Belafonte (1922-)	calypso, pop
George Benson (1943-)	jazz, rhythm and blues
Chuck Berry (1926-)	rhythm and blues, rock & roll
Brandy (1979-)	pop
Toni Braxton (1967-)	pop, rhythm and blues
James Brown (1928-)	rock & roll
Diahann Carroll (1935-)	pop
Ray Charles (1930-)	rhythm and blues, jazz
Nat "King" Cole (1917-1965)	pop
Natalie Cole (1950-)	pop
Sam Cooke (1935-1964)	soul, pop
Sammy Davis, Jr. (1925-1990)	pop
Antoine "Fats" Domino (1928-)	rock & roll
Billy Eckstine (Mr. "B") (1914-)	jazz, be-bop, pop
Kenneth "Babyface" Edmonds (1959-)	rhythm and blues
Lola Falana (1943-)	rhythm and blues
Ella Fitzgerald (1918-1996)	jazz
Roberta Flack (1940-)	jazz, rhythm and blues
Aretha Franklin (1942-)	soul, rhythm and blues
Marvin Gaye (1939-1984)	pop, rhythm and blues
Adelaide Hall (1901-1993)	jazz, rhythm and blues, pop
Isaac Hayes (1942-)	soul, rhythm and blues
Lauryn Hill (1976-)	pop, rhythm and blues
Billie Holiday ("Lady Day") (1915-1959)	rhythm and blues

Mahalia Jackson

Lena Horne (1917-)	jazz
Whitney Houston (1963-)	pop, gospel
Phyllis Hyman (1977-1995)	soul, rhythm and blues
Ice-T (Tracy Marrow) (1958-)	rap, hip hop
Mahalia Jackson (1911-1972)	gospel
Michael Jackson (1958-)	pop
Al Jarreau (1940-)	rhythm and blues, jazz
Salena Jones (Joan Shaw) (1944-)	rhythm and blues, jazz, pop
R. Kelly (Robert) (1969-)	rap, rhythm and blues
Eartha Kitt (1928-)	pop
Gladys Knight (1944-)	pop, rock & roll
Huddie Ledbetter (1888-1949)	singer, songwriter
Johnny Mathis (1933-)	ballads, pop
Clyde L. McPhatter (1931-1972)	rhythm and blues; rock & rock pioneer

Carmen McRae (1922-)	jazz, pop
Florence Mills (1895-1927)	rhythm and blues, jazz; comedienne
Abbie Mitchell (1895-1960)	pop, concert
Melba Moore (Melba Hill) (1945-)	pop, rhythm and blues
Odetta (Holmes-Felious) (1930-)	pop, concert
Charley Pride (1938-)	country western
"Ma" Rainey (Gertrude Malissa Nix Pridgett) (1886-1939)	blues; "Mother of the Blues"
Lou Rawls (1935-)	soul, rhythm and blues
Otis Redding (1941-1989)	soul, rock & roll
Della Reese (1932-)	gospel, pop
Little Richard (1932-)	rock & roll
Lionel Richie (1949-)	pop, ballads
Paul Robeson (1898-1976)	concert singer (bass-baritone), actor
Diana Ross (1944-)	rock & roll, pop
Nina Simone (1933-)	soul, rhythm and blues
Bessie Smith (1895-1937)	blues, jazz; "The Empress of the Blues"
Will Smith (of DJ Jazzy Jeff & The Fresh Prince) (1969-)	rap
Tina Turner (1939-)	rock & roll
Leslie Uggams (1943-)	pop
Sarah Vaughan (1924-1990)	jazz, pop
Dionne Warwick (1941-)	pop
Dinah Washington (1924-1963)	pop
Ethel Waters (1896-1977)	blues, jazz; "Sweet Mama Stringbean"
Mary Wells (1943-1992)	rock & roll
Joe Williams (1918-1999)	jazz, blues
Vanessa Williams (1963-)	pop, rhythm and blues
Jackie Wilson (1935-1984)	rock & roll
Nancy Wilson (1937-)	jazz
Stevie Wonder (1950-)	pop

List 8-12. Performing Groups: The Famous and the Obscure
(a selected list)

Archie Bell and the Drells

Ashford and Simpson

BackYard

Boyz to Men

The Capitols

The Chambers Brothers

The Chilites

Clyde McPhatter and the Dominoes

The Clovers

The Coasters

The Commodores

Debarge

The Delfonics

The Dells

Diana Ross and the Supremes

Dougie Fresh and The Get Fresh Crew

The Drifters

Earth, Wind, and Fire

The Four Tops

The Funkadelics

George Clinton and the P-Funk All-stars

Gladys Knight and the Pips

Harold Melvin and the Blue Notes

Hot Boyz

Ike and Tina Turner

The Impressions

The Isley Brothers

The Jackson Five

Jr. Walker and the All Stars

KC and Jo Jo

K.C. and the Sunshine Band

King Curtis and the Kingpins

Little Anthony and the Imperials

The Marvalettes

Martha Reeves and the Vandellas

The Midnighters

The Moonglows

North East Groovers

The O' Jays

Ohio Players

Parliament

Pattie Labelle and the Blue Bells

The Platters

The Ramsey Lewis Trio

Sam and Dave

Shep and the Lime Lights

The Shirelles

Silk

Sly and the Family Stone

Smoky Robinson and the Miracles

The Spinners

The Supremes

The Sweet Inspirations

The Temptations

Vanity

Will Smith and DJ Jazzy Jeff

The Young-Holt Unlimited

List 8-13. Instrumentalists, Band Leaders, Composers

Louis "Satchmo" Armstrong (1900-1971)	leading trumpeter in jazz history, bandleader
William James "Count" Basie, Jr. (1904-1984)	jazz pianist, bandleader
Sidney Bechet (1891-1959)	jazz clarinetist
Thomas "Blind Tom" Bethune (1849-1908)	pianist
James Herbert "Eubie" Blake (1883-1983)	ragtime pianist, composer of popular show tunes
James A. Bland (1854-1911)	popular composer, lyricist; wrote words and music to "Carry Me Back to Old Virginny" (1878)
Oscar Brown, Jr. (1926-)	singer, songwriter
Raymond Matthews "Ray" Brown (1926-)	jazz bassist
Cabel "Cab" Calloway III (1907-1994)	jazz bandleader, singer, composer
Ron Carter (1937-)	bassist, cellist
James Milton "Jimmy" Cleveland (1926-)	trombonist
Ornette Coleman (1930-)	jazz alto saxophonist, composer
John Coltrane (1926-1967)	leading saxophonist in jazz history, bandleader
Tadley Ewing "Tadd" Dameron (1917-1965)	jazz, be-bop pianist, arranger
Miles Dewey Davis, Jr. (1926-1991)	jazz trumpeter, bandleader
Edward Kennedy "Duke" Ellington (1899-1974)	pianist, bandleader, composer; a founder of big-band jazz, leading to swing
Herschel Evans (1909-1939)	jazz tenor saxophonist
Erroll Garner (1921-1977)	jazz pianist, composer; developed unique style of stride-piano playing
John Birks "Dizzy" Gillespie (1917-1993)	jazz trumpeter; leader of revolutionary be-bop style of jazz
Lionel Hampton (c. 1913-)	jazz vibraphonist, bandleader
W.C. (William Christopher) Handy (1873-1958)	blues composer, musician; founder of Black Swan Phonograph Corporation
James Henry "Jimmy" Harrison (1900-1931)	jazz trombonist

Coleman "Bean" Hawkins (1904-1969)	tenor saxophonist
(James) Fletcher Hamilton "Smack" Henderson, Jr. (1898-1952)	pianist, arranger, bandleader; pioneer of large jazz orchestras
James Marshall "Jimi" Hendrix (1942-1970)	hard rock guitarist, singer
Earl "Fatha" Hines (1903-1983)	jazz pianist, bandleader
Milton Milt "Bags" Jackson (1923-1999)	jazz vibraharpist, singer, pianist, guitarist
Ahmad Jamal (1930-)	jazz pianist, composer
Francis "Frank" Johnson (1792-1844)	trumpeter, bandleader, composer
J. Rosamond Johnson (1873-1954)	pianist, composer
James P. "Jimmy" Johnson (1894-1955)	jazz pianist, composer
Robert Johnson (1911-1938)	blues singer, songwriter, guitarist; "King of the Delta Blues"
Quincy Jones, Jr. (1933-)	jazz trumpet player, bandleader, arranger, composer
Scott Joplin (1868-1917)	pianist, composer; "King of Ragtime"
Riley B. "B.B." King (1925-)	guitarist, singer
James Melvin "Jimmie" Lunceford (1902-1947)	jazz, swing bandleader

Robert Johnson

Charles McPhearson (1939-)	alto saxophonist
Branford Marsalis (1960-)	saxophonist
Wynton Marsalis (1962-)	trumpeter
Charles Mingus (1922-1979)	"hard-bop" jazz bassist, bandleader, composer
Thelonius Monk (1917-1982)	jazz, be-bop pianist, composer; major influence on modern jazz
Charles F. "Buddy" Montgomery (1930-)	jazz pianist, vibraphonist
John Leslie "Wes" Montgomery (1925-1968)	jazz guitarist
Jelly Roll Morton (Ferdinand Joseph LeMcnthe) (1885-1941)	pianist, composer; pioneered use of prearranged, semiorchestrated effects in jazz band performances
Joe "King" Oliver (1885-1938)	cornetist, bandleader, composer
Charlie "Byrd" Parker (1920-1955)	jazz alto saxophonist
Don Redman (1900-1964)	saxophonist, arranger, bandleader; one of founders of big band jazz, leading to swing
James Andrew "Jimmy" Rushing (1902-1972)	singer, arranger, composer
Maxwell "Max" Roach (1924-)	jazz drummer; quintet leader
Arthur James "Zutty" Singleton (1898-1975)	jazz drummer
Noble Sissle (1899-1975)	bandleader, vocalist, lyricist; teamed with Eubie Blake
Valaida Snow (1903-1956)	trumpet stylist, singer, arranger, founder of all-girl orchestra
Art Tatum (1909-1956)	jazz pianist; unique stylist
Thomas Wright "Fats" Waller (1904-1943)	pianist, organist, vocalist, composer
Muddy Waters (McKinley Morganfield) (1915-1983)	blues singer, guitarist, bandleader, songwriter
William Henry "Chick" Webb (1902-1939)	bass drummer, bandleader
Mary Lou Williams (Mary Elfrieda Winn) (1910-1981)	ragtime, jazz, swing, be-bop pianist, composer
Howlin' Wolf (Chester Arthur Burnett) (1910-1976)	blues singer, harmonica and guitar player
Lester Williams "Prez" Young (1909-1959)	tenor saxophonist, clarinetist

List 8-14. Choreographers and Dancers

Alvin Ailey (1931-1991)	modern dancer, choreographer, founder of Alvin Ailey American Dance Theater, 1958
Debbie Allen (1950-)	dancer, actress, singer, director
Josephine Baker (1906-1975)	entertainer, dancer, singer, actress
Clayton "Pegleg" Bates (1907-1998)	tap dancer
John Bubbles (1902-1986)	dancer, singer, introduced the "cramp roll" to dance
Janet Collins (1917-)	ballet dancer
Dance Theater of Harlem (1969)	dance troupe
Sammy Davis, Jr. (1925-1990)	tap dancer, singer, actor
Carmen de Lavallade (1931-)	dancer, choreographer
Katherine Dunham (1910-)	ballet dancer, choreographer, founder of Katherine Dunham Dance Troupe
Georgia Minstrels (1865)	minstrel troupe; led primarily by Billy Kersands, (c. 1840-c. 1915)
Gregory Hines (1946-)	tap dancer, actor
Geoffrey Holder (1930-)	dancer, actor, choreographer, director, painter
Judith Jamison (1941-)	ballet dancer, choreographer, artistic director of Alvin Ailey American Dance Theater
Florence Mills (1895-1927)	entertainer, dancer, singer
Arthur Mitchell (1934-)	dancer, choreographer
Fayard Nicholas (1914-)	dancer, brother to Harold Nicholas
Harold Nicholas (1921-2000)	dancer, choreographer, comedian, singer; with brother Fayard, a unique dance style combining elements of jazz, tap, ballet, acrobatics
Pearl Primus (1919-1994)	dancer, choreographer
Luther "Bojangles" Robinson (1878-1949)	tap dancer, introduced a new style to tap by dancing on the balls of the feet
Ben Vereen (1946-)	tap dancer, actor, singer

List 8-15. Opera Singers

Adele Addison (1925-)	soprano
Roberta Alexander (1949-)	soprano
Betty Lou Allen (1930-)	mezzo-soprano; educator
Marian Anderson (1902-1993)	contralto
Martina Arroyo (1939-)	soprano
Priscilla Baskerville (no date)	lyric soprano
Kathleen Battle (1948-)	soprano
Gwendolyn Bradley (1952-)	soprano
Grace Bumbrey (1937-)	mezzo-soprano
Steven Cole (no date)	tenor
Vinson Cole (1950-)	tenor
Philip Creech (1950-)	tenor
Osceola Davis (no date)	soprano
Mattiwilda Dobbs (1925-)	coloratura soprano
R. Todd Duncan (1903-)	baritone, actor
Simon Lamont Estes (1938-)	bass-baritone
Elizabeth Greenfield ("Black Swan") (1809-1876)	soprano
Denyce Graves (1964-)	mezzo-soprano
Reri Grist (1932-)	coloratura soprano
Hilda Harris (c. 1930)	mezzo-soprano
Roland Hayes (1887-1977)	tenor
Barbara Hendricks (1948-)	mezzo-soprano
Ben Holt (1956-1990)	baritone
Isole Jones (no date)	mezzo-soprano
Dorothy Leigh Maynor (1910-)	soprano
Robert McFerrin (1921-)	baritone, educator

Myra Merritt (1949-)	soprano
Leona Mitchell (1949-)	soprano
Jessye Norman (1945-)	soprano
Leontyne Price (1927-)	lyric soprano
Florence Quivar (1944-)	mezzo-soprano
George Shirley (1934-)	tenor
Andrew Smith (1941-)	baritone
Arthur Thompson (1942-)	baritone
Shirley Verrett (1933-)	mezzo-soprano
William Warfield (1920-)	baritone

List 8-16. Classical Instrumentalists, Conductors, and Composers

Thomas Jefferson Anderson (1928-)	composer, educator
Walter Anderson (1915-)	organist, composer, educator
David Nathaniel Baker, Jr. (1931-)	composer, educator
William C. Banfield (1961-)	composer, educator
Thomas Green Bethune (1849-1909)	pianist
Margaret Allison Bonds (1913-1972)	composer, pianist
Henry Thacker "Harry" Burleigh (1866-1949)	composer, arranger, singer
Frances Elaine Cole (1937-1983)	violinist
Samuel Coleridge-Taylor (1875-1912)	composer
Will Marion Cook (1869-1944)	violinist, composer, conductor; also composed a ragtime operetta
Charles L. "Doc" Cooke (1891-1958)	composer, conductor, arranger
Roque Cordero (1917-)	composer, educator
Arthur Cunningham (1928-)	pianist, composer
Anthony Davis (1951-)	pianist, composer
William Levi Dawson (1897-1990)	composer, conductor
Noel De Costa (1929-)	composer
James Anderson DePriest (1936-)	conductor, nephew of contralto Marian Anderson
Chevalier de Saint-Georges (1739-1799)	composer
R. Nathaniel Dett (1882-1943)	composer
Carl Rossini Diton (1886-1962)	pianist, composer, educator
Dean Dixon (1915-1976)	conductor
Lucille Dixon (Robertson) (1923-)	bassist
Shirley DuBois (1906-1977)	composer
Rudolph Dunbar (1917-1988)	composer, clarinetist
James Reese Europe (1881-1919)	conductor, musical director
Paul Douglas Freeman (1935-)	conductor
Louis Moreau Gottschalk (1829-1869)	composer, pianist
Emma Azalia Hackley (1867-1922)	singer, educator, choral director
Helen Eugenia Hagen (1891-1964)	pianist, composer
Margaret Rosezarion Harris (1943-)	pianist, conductor, composer

Hazel Harrison (1883-1969)	pianist
Gail Hightower (1946-)	bassoonist
Natalie Hinderas (1927-1987)	concert pianist
Ann Stevens Hobson (1943-)	harpist
Isaiah Allen Jackson III (1945-)	conductor
Eva Jessye (1895-1992)	choral conductor, composer
Hall Johnson (1887-1970)	violinist, founder and leader of Hall Johnson Choir
John Rosamond Johnson (1873-1954)	composer
Elayne Jones (1928-)	timpanist
Ulysses Kay (1917-)	composer, educator
Tania Justina Leon (1944-)	composer, conductor
Henry Lewis (1932-1996)	conductor, bassist
Lena Johnson McLin (1928-)	composer, conductor, educator
Dorothy Antoinette Handy Miller (1930-)	flutist
Carman Leroy Moore (1936-)	composer, educator
Dorothy Rudd Moore (1940-)	composer, singer
Kermit Diton Moore (1929-)	cellist, composer, conductor
Undine Smith Moore (1904-1989)	conductor
Michael DeVard Morgan (1957-)	conductor
Coleridge-Taylor Perkinson (1932-)	composer
Julia Perry (1924-1979)	composer, conductor
Evelyn LaRue Pittman (1910-1992)	choral director, composer
Karl Hampton Porter (1939-)	bassoonist, conductor, educator
Awadagin Pratt (1966-)	pianist, violinist
Florence Price (1888-1953)	composer, pianist
Kay George Roberts (1950-)	violinist, conductor
Philippa Schuyler (1932-1969)	composer, pianist
Calvin Simmons (1950-1982)	pianist, conductor
Alvin Singleton (1940-)	composer
Hale Smith (1925-)	composer, educator
William Grant Still (1895-1978)	classical and jazz composer, musician, arranger (known as "Dean of African American Composers")

Howard Swanson (1909-1978)	composer
William Henry Bennett Vodery (1885-1951)	conductor, composer, arranger
George Walker (1922-)	pianist, educator
Andre Watts (1946-)	pianist
Felix Fowler Weir (1884-1978)	violinist
Clarence Cameron White (1880-1960)	composer, violinist
Olly W. Wilson (1937-)	composer, educator
John Work (1901-1968)	composer, educator

LITERATURE

Although most of the writers listed here work in more than one genre, they have been placed in one list only; however, each name entry includes areas of accomplishments and titles of a few representative works.

List 8-17. Poets

Maya Angelou (1928-) poet, autobiographer, playwright, actress; *Just Give Me a Cool Drink of Water 'fore I Diiie* (1971); *Oh Pray My Wings Are Gonna Fit Me Well* (1975); *I Shall Not Be Moved* (1990); *Wouldn't Take Nothing for My Journey Now* (essays, 1993)

Amiri Baraka (LeRoi Jones) (1934-) poet, playwright, novelist; leader in Black Arts Movement; *Preface to a Twenty Volume Suicide Note* (1961); *Funk Love: New Poems, 1984-1994* (1996); *Obie for Dutchman* (play, 1964)

Gwendolyn Brooks (1917-) poet; 1950 Pulitzer Prize for *Annie Allen; A Street in Bronzeville* (1945); *Aloneness* (1971); *Primer for Blacks* (1980)

Sterling A. Brown (1901-1989) poet, educator, helped establish African American literary criticism; *Southern Road* (1932); *Collected Poems* (1980)

Lucille Clifton (1936-) poet, educator; *Good Times* (1969); *Two-Headed Woman* (1976)

Charlie Cobb (1944-) poet; *Furrows* (1967); *Everywhere Is Ours* (1971)

Countee Cullen (1903-1946) poet of the Harlem Renaissance; *Ballad of the Brown Girl* (1928); *On These I Stand* (1947)

Gwendolyn Brooks

Rita Dove (1952-) poet; won 1987 Pulitzer Prize for *Thomas and Beulah* (1985); Poet Laureate, 1993-95

Paul Laurence Dunbar (1872-1906) poet, novelist, short story writer; *Lyrics of a Lowly Life* (volume of poetry, 1896)

James Emanuel (1921-) poet, educator; *Treehouse* (1968); *A Poet's Mind* (1983)

Mari Evans (1923-) poet, writer, educator; *I Am the Black Woman* (1973); *Nightstar 1973-1978* (1981); *A Dark and Splendid Mass* (1992)

Nikki Giovanni (1943-) poet; *Re: Creation* (1970); *Black Feeling, Black Talk* (1968); *Blues for All the Changes* (1999)

Madhubuti Haki (Don L. Lee) (1942-) poet, publisher and editor of *Third World Press* (Chicago); *Think Black* (1967); *Don't Cry, Scream* (1969)

Jupiter Hammon (c. 1720-1800) poet, slave; "Poem to Miss Phillis Wheatley" (1778)

Lorraine Hansberry (1930-1965) playwright, poet, essayist; New York Drama Critics' Award for *A Raisin in the Sun* (1959)

Robert Hayden (1913-1980) poet, professor, playwright, editor; *Heartshape in the Dust* (1940); "Ballad of Remembrance" (won grand prize for poetry at First World Festival of Negro Arts in Dakar, Senegal, 1966); appointed as Consultant in Poetry to Library of Congress (precursor to Poet Laureate)

Langston Hughes (1902-1967) poet, playwright, novelist, short story writer, major influence in Harlem Renaissance; *The Weary Blues* (1926); *The Dream Keeper* (1932); *Freedom's Plow* (1943); *Mulatto* (play, 1935)

Georgia Douglas Johnson (1886-1966) poet, playwright of Harlem Renaissance; *The Heart of a Woman* (1918); *Share My World* (1962)

James Weldon Johnson (1871-1938) poet, lyricist, playwright, lawyer; *God's Trombones* (1927)

June Jordan (1936-) poet, novelist, playwright, essayist; *Things That I Do in the Dark* (1977); *Haruko/Love Poems* (1994)

Etheridge Knight (1931-1991) poet; *Poems from Prison* (1968)

Claude McKay (1891-1948) poet, novelist; *Songs of Jamaica* (1911); *Harlem Shadows* (1922)

Sonia Sanchez (1934-) poet, playwright, educator; *Does Your House Have Lions?* (poetry, 1997); *The Bronx Is Next* (play)

Derek Walcott (1930-) poet, playwright, essayist, educator; 1992 Nobel Prize in Literature; *Omeros* (1990); *Tiepolo's Hounds* (2000)

Marilyn Nelson Waniek (1946-) poet, educator; *For the Body* (1978); *The Fields of Praise* (1997)

Phillis Wheatley (c. 1753-1784) *Poems on Various Subjects, Religious and Moral; Memoirs and Poems of Phillis Wheatley*

List 8-18. Playwrights

Ed Bullins (1935-) playwright, scholar, leader in Black Arts Movement; New York Drama Critics Award and Obie for *The Taking of Miss Janie;* other Obies for *The Fabulous Miss Marie* and *In New England Winter*

Alice Childress (1920-1994) playwright; novelist, actress, director; *Trouble in Mind* (play, 1956); *Wedding Band* (play, 1966)

Lonne Elder III (1927-1996) playwright, *Ceremonies in Dark Old Men* (1969)

Charles Fuller (1939-) playwright; 1982 Pulitzer Prize and New York Drama Critics Award for *A Soldier's Play* (1982), adapted to film, *A Soldier's Story* (1984)

Charles Gordone (1929-1999) playwright; 1970 Pulitzer Prize for *No Place to Be Somebody*

Angelina W. Grimke (1880-1958) playwright, poet of Harlem Renaissance; *Rachel,* (play, 1916)

Adrienne Kennedy (Adrienne Lita Hawkins) (1931-) playwright; Obie for *Funnyhouse of a Negro; An Evening with Dead Essex* (1973)

Larry Neal (1937-1981) playwright, essayist, anthologist, scholar; leader in *Black Arts Movement; The Glorious Monster in the Bell of the Horn*

Willis Richardson (1889-1977) playwright; *The Chip Woman's Fortune* (1923); *The King's Dilemma* (1920); *Negro History in Thirteen Plays* (1935)

Ntozake Shange (Paulette Williams) (1947-) playwright, novelist, poet, educator; Tony Award for choreopoem, *For Colored Girls Who Have Considered Suicide When the Rainbow Is Enuf* (1976); *Betsey Brown* (novel, 1985)

Anna Deveare Smith (1950-) playwright, actor, educator; *Fires in the Mirror* (1992); Tony Award and Obie for *Twilight* (1993)

Douglas Turner Ward (1930-) playwright; co-founder (with Robert Hooks and Gerald S. Krone) and artistic director of the Negro Ensemble Company, New York City (1976); *Happy Ending/Day of Absence* (1965)

August Wilson (1945-) playwright; 1984 New York Drama Critics' Circle Award for *Ma Rainey's Black Bottom;* 1987 Pulitzer Prize and Tony Award for *Fences;* 1990 Pulitzer Prize for *The Piano Lesson*

George C. Wolfe (1954-) playwright; artistic director for the Public Theatre in New York City; *The Colored Museum* (1986); Tony Award for best direction of his dance musical, *Bring in Da Noise, Bring in Da Funk* (1996)

Marvin X (Marvin Jackmon/El Muhajir) (1944-) playwright, poet, essayist; *Flowers for the Trashman* (play)

List 8-19. Fiction Writers

James Baldwin (1924-1987) novelist, essayist, playwright, nonfiction writer; *Go Tell It on the Mountain* (novel, 1953); *The Fire Next Time* (essays, 1962); *Blues for Mr. Charlie* (play, 1964); *The Amen Corner* (play, 1964)

Toni Cade Bambara (1939-1995) novelist, short story writer; *The Salt Eaters* (1980); *Gorilla, My Love* (short stories, 1972)

Arna Bontemps (1902-1973) novelist and poet of the Harlem Renaissance; *Black Thunder* (1935); *Dreams at Dusk* (1939); *Personals* (poetry, 1964)

Connie Briscoe (1952-) novelist; *Big Girls Don't Cry* (1997); *A Long Way From Home* (1999)

William Wells Brown (1815-1884) novelist, playwright; *Narrative of William Wells Brown, a Fugitive Slave, Written by Himself* (1842); *The Escape* (play, 1858)

Octavia E. Butler (1947-) science fiction writer; *Kindred* (1979); *Parable of the Sower* (1993)

Bebe Moore Campbell (1950-) novelist, journalist; *Sweet Summer* (1990); *Brothers and Sisters* (1994)

Charles Waddell Chesnutt (1858-1932) novelist, short story writer, essayist; *The House Behind the Cedars; Conjure Woman and Other Tales* (1899)

John Henrick Clarke (1915-1998) writer, scholar, historian, educator; "The Boy Who Painted Christ Black" (short story, 1940); *Black American Short Stories* (1992)

Eric Jerome Dickey (no date) novelist; *Sister, Sister* (1996); *Cheaters* (1999)

Ralph Ellison (1914-1994) novelist, essayist; *The Invisible Man* (1952); *Shadow and Act* (essays, 1964)

Jessie Redmon Fauset (1882-1961) novelist, poet of Harlem Renaissance; *Plum Bun* (1929); *The Chinaberry Tree* (1931)

Leon Forrest (1937-1997) novelist, essayist; *Two Wings to Veil My Face* (1983); *Divine Days* (1992)

Ernest J. Gaines (1933-) novelist; *Autobiography of Miss Jane Pittman* (1972); *A Lesson Before Dying* (1994)

Alex Haley (1921-1992) novelist, biographer; 1976 Pulitzer Prize for *Autobiography of Malcolm X* (1965); *Roots* (1976)

Frances E. W. Harper (1825-1911) novelist, poet; *Minnie's Sacrifice* (1867); *Trial and Triumph* (1888)

E. Lynn Harris (1955-) novelist; *And This Too Shall Pass* (1997); *Just As I Am* (1996, ABA Novel of the Year)

Chester Himes (1909-1984) novelist, short story writer; *If He Hollers, Let Him Go* (1945); *Cotton Comes to Harlem* (1965)

Zora Neale Hurston (1891-1960) novelist; *Jonah's Gourd Vine* (1934); *Their Eyes Were Watching God* (1937)

Charles Johnson (1948-) novelist, short story writer, essayist, cartoonist, educator; *Faith and the Good Thing* (1974); *Middle Passage* (1990)

Audre Lorde (1934-1992) novelist, poet, educator; *The First Cities* (1968); *A Burst of Light* (1988)

Clarence Major (1936-) novelist, poet, short story writer; nonfiction; *Such Was the Season* (1987); *Dirty Bird Blues* (1996)

Paule Marshall (1929-) novelist, educator; *Praisesong for the Widow* (1983); *Daughters* (1992)

Terry McMillan (1951-) novelist; *Waiting to Exhale* (1992); *How Stella Got Her Groove Back* (1996)

Zora
Neale
Hurston

James Alan McPherson (1943-) short story writer; Pulitzer Prize for *Elbow Room* (1977)

Toni Morrison (1931-) novelist; *The Bluest Eye* (1970); 1988 Pulitzer Prize for Fiction for *Beloved* (1987); 1993 Nobel Prize for Literature

Walter Mosley (1952-) crime novelist; *Devil in a Blue Dress* (1990); *Gone Fishin'* (1997)

Willard Motley (1912-1965) novelist; *Knock on Any Door*

Walter Dean Myers (1937-) novelist; *The Young Landlords* (1979); *A Place Called Heartbreak* (1993)

Barbara Neely (1941-) crime novelist, short story writer; *Blanche on the Lam* (1992); *Blanche Passes Go* (2000)

Gloria Naylor Page (1950-) novelist; *The Women of Brewster Place* (1982); *Bailey's Café* (1992)

Ann Petry (1908-1997) novelist, short story writer; *The Street* (1946); *The Narrows* (1953)

Ishmael Reed (1938-) novelist, poet, essayist; *Mumbo Jumbo* (1973); *Japanese by Spring* (1993); *Airing Dirty Laundry* (essays, 1993)

Jean Toomer (1894-1967) novelist, poet; *Cane* (an acclaimed experimental novel of the Harlem Renaissance, 1923)

Brent Wade (1960-) novelist; *Company Man* (1992)

Alice Walker (1944-) novelist, poet, essayist, educator; 1983 Pulitzer Prize and National Book Award for *The Color Purple* (1982); *By the Light of My Father's Smile* (1998)

Dorothy West (1907-1998) novelist; *The Living Is Easy* (1948); *The Wedding* (1995)

John Edgar Wideman (1941-) novelist, short story writer, educator; *Sent for You Yesterday* (1983); *The Cattle Killing* (1996)

Alice Walker

John A. Williams (1925-) novelist; *The Man Who Cried I Am* (1967); *Jacobs Ladder* (1987)

Richard Wright (1908-1960) novelist; *Native Sun* (1940); *Black Boy* (1945)

Frank Yerby (1916-1991) novelist; *The Foxes of Harrow* (1976)

List 8-20. Books Written By or About African Americans

The following nonfiction books, by or about Africans or African Americans, are listed in alphabetical order.

The African-American Health Book: A Prescription for Improvement—Valerie Aleena (nonfiction)

The African-American Holiday of Kwanzaa—Maulana Karenga (nonfiction)

Am I the Last Virgin? Ten African-American Reflections on Sex and Love—Tara Roberts (nonfiction)

The Anti-Apartheid Reader—David Mermelstein (nonfiction)

Autobiography—Angela Davis (autobiography)

The Autobiography of Malcolm X—Alex Haley (biography)

The Autobiography of Miss Jane Pittman—Ernest Gaines (biographical novel)

Barbara Jordan: Congresswoman—Linda Carlson Johnson (biography)

Being and Race: Black Writing Since 1970—Charles Johnson (nonfiction)

Black Dance in America—James Haskins (nonfiction)

Black in Selma: The Uncommon Life of J. L. Chestnutt, Jr.—J. L. Chestnutt (autobiography)

Black Like Me—John Howard Griffin (nonfiction)

Black Looks: Race and Representation—bell hooks (nonfiction)

Black Music in America: A History Through Its People—James Haskins (nonfiction)

Black Odyssey—Nathan Irvin Huggins (nonfiction)

Black Profiles in Courage: A Legacy of African-American Achievement—Kareem Abdul-Jabbar (biography)

Black Theater in America—James Haskins (nonfiction)

Black Women Writers (1950-1980): A Critical Evaluation—Mari Evans (nonfiction)

Blues People—Imamu Amiri Baraka (nonfiction)

Booker T. Washington: The Making of a Black Leader, 1856-1901—Louis R. Harlan (biography)

Booker T. Washington

Booker T. Washington: The Wizard of Tuskegee, 1901-1915—Louis R. Harlan (biography)

Breaking the Chains: African-American Slave Resistance—William Loren Katz (nonfiction)

Brothers and Keepers—John Edgar Wideman (nonfiction)

The Crisis of the Negro Intellectual—Harold Cruse (non-fiction)

Crusade for Justice: The Autobiography of Ida B. Wells—Ida B. Wells-Barnett (autobiography)

Diary of a Harlem Schoolteacher—James Haskins (nonfiction)

Maya Angelou

Duke Ellington—James Lincoln Collier (biography)

The Flip Side of Soul: Letters to My Son—Bob Teague (nonfiction)

Freedom Road—Howard Fast (nonfiction)

Freedom Train—Dorothy Sterling (biography of Harriet Tubman)

From Slavery to Freedom—John Hope Franklin (nonfiction)

George Washington Carver—Linda O. McMurry (biography)

Great Slave Narratives—Arna Bontemps (biography)

I Know Why the Caged Bird Sings—Maya Angelou (autobiography)

In My Place—Charlayne Hunter-Gault (biography)

Invented Lives: Narratives of Black Women 1860-1960—Mary Helen Washington (biography)

Jocelyn Elders, M.D.: From Sharecropper's Daughter to Surgeon General—Jocelyn M. Elders (autobiography)

Judith Jamison: Aspects of a Dancer—Olga Maynard (biography)

Jump Ship to Freedom—James L. and Christopher Collier (nonfiction)

Kareem—Kareem Abdul-Jabbar and Mignon McCarthy (autobiography)

The Life of Langston Hughes: I Dream a World, 1941-1967—Arnold Rampersad (biography)

The Life of Langston Hughes: I, Too, Sing America, 1902-1941—Arnold Rampersad (biography)

Louis Armstrong: An American Genius—James Lincoln Collier (biography)

Manchild in the Promised Land—Claude Brown (biography)

Mary McLeod Bethune: Voice of Black Hope—Milton Meltzer (biography)

The Me Nobody Knows—Steven M. Joseph, editor (nonfiction)

The Mis-Education of the Negro—Carter G. Woodson (nonfiction)

Mutiny on the Amistad—Howard Jones (nonfiction)

Narrative of the Life of Frederick Douglass: An American Slave—Frederick Douglass (autobiography)

The New Negro—Alain Locke (nonfiction)

Oprah Winfrey: The Real Story—George Mair (biography)

Parting the Waters: America in the King Years—Taylor Branch (nonfiction)

Paul Robeson: The Life and Times of a Free Black—Virginia Hamilton (biography)

Prince Among Slaves—Terry Alford (nonfiction)

The Promised Land: The Great Black Migration and How It Changed America—Nicholas Leman (nonfiction)

Race: How Blacks and Whites Think and Feel About the American Obsession—Studs Terkel (nonfiction)

Race Matters—Cornel West (nonfiction)

Roots—Alex Haley (biography)

Skin Deep: Women Writing on Color, Culture and Identity—Elena Featherston (nonfiction)

Soaring Above Setbacks: The Autobiography of Janet Harmon Bragg, African Aviator—Janet Harmon Bragg (autobiography)

Sorrow's Kitchen: The Life and Folklore of Zora Neale Hurston—Mary E. Lyons (biography)

Soul on Ice—Eldridge Cleaver (autobiography)

The Souls of Black Folk—W.E.B. Du Bois (nonfiction)

South African Dispatches: Letters to My Countrymen—Donald Wood (nonfiction)

Spike Lee and the African-American Filmmakers: A Choice of Colors—Maurice Jones (biography)

W.E.B. Du Bois

Stop the Violence: Overcoming Self-Destruction—Nelson George, editor (nonfiction)

The Story of Booker T. Washington—Patricia McKissack (biography)

The Story of Ruby Bridges—Robert Coles (biography)

The Substance of Things Hoped For: A Memoir of African-American Faith—Samuel D. Proctor (biography)

Tapping the Power Within: A Path to Self-Empowerment for Black Women—Iyanla Vanzant (nonfiction)

Thank You, Jackie Robinson—Barbara Cohen (biography)

Martin Luther King, Jr.

There Are No Children Here: The Story of Two Boys Growing Up in the Other America—Alex Kotlowitz (nonfiction)

Thirteen Ways of Looking at a Black Man—Louis Henry Gates (nonfiction)

To Be Young, Gifted and Black—Lorraine Hansberry (essay/nonfiction)

Up from Slavery—Booker T. Washington (nonfiction)

Voices in the Mirror: An Autobiography—Gordon Parks (autobiography)

Wade in the Water: Great Moments in Black History—Lerone Bennett, Jr. (nonfiction)

Walter Dean Myers—Diane Patrick-Wexler (biography)

When and Where I Enter: The Impact of Black Women on Race and Sex in America—Paula J. Giddings (nonfiction)

Why We Can't Wait—Martin Luther King, Jr. (nonfiction)

The Words of Martin Luther King, Jr.—Coretta Scott King, compiler (nonfiction)

World's Great Men of Color—John Henrick Clarke (nonfiction)

Yes I Can—Sammy Davis, Jr. (autobiography)

List 8-21. Children and Young Adult Literature

Informational Books

Amos Fortune (1950), Elizabeth Yates

Railroad to Freedom (1932), Hildegarde H. Swift

The Story of the Negro (1950), Arna Bontemps

Your Most Humble Servant (1949), Shirley Graham Dubois

Folklore

Black Folk Tales (1969), Julius Lester

John Henry and American Legend (1960), Ezra Jack Keats

John Henry and the Double-Joint Steam Drill (1945), Irving Shapiro

John Henry and His Hammer (1950), Harold Felton

Poetry

Bronzeville Boys and Girls (1956), Gwendolyn Brooks

A Crocodile Has Me by the Leg (1967), Leonard Doob

How God Fix Jonah, Every Man Heart Down, A Road Down in the Sea (1970), Lorenz Graham

North Star Shining (1947), Hildegarde Swift

The Voice of Children (1970), June Jordon

Who Looked at Me? (1969), June Jordon

Gwendolyn Brooks

Fiction

Bimby (1968), Peter Burchard

The Drinking Gourd (1970), F.N. Monjo

The Friendship (1988), Mildred D. Taylor

Let the Circle Be Unbroken (1981), Mildred D. Taylor

Sad Faced Boy (1937), Arna Bontemps

The Time-Ago Tales of Jobdu (1960), Virginia Hamilton

Tituba of Salem Village (1964), Ann Petry

RADIO AND TELEVISION

List 8-22. Chronology of Early African American Radio

1921—Miles Hardy started Pioneer Radio Club, New York City, for teaching radio and electronics to African Americans

1922—Roland Carrington started "Banneker Radio Club" in Baltimore, for instruction in broadcasting

1922—"Shuffle Along" was first live radio performance (Boston) of a Broadway musical with original cast (led by Eubie Blake and Noble Sissle)

1922-1930—African American disk jockeys, precursors to today's disk jockeys, gained popularity

1923—Duke Ellington performed at station WDT, New York; by late 1920s, would be one of first to have a network radio show of his own

1924—Harry Burleigh sang on station WJZ, New York, during a performance of St. George's Episcopal Church choir

1930s—black audience exclusive programs—African American businesspeople bought hour blocks of time for their own programming from large city stations

1948—WDIA, Memphis, Tennessee was first radio station with an all African American format

1949—WERD, in Atlanta, Georgia was first African American owned radio station, put on the air by Jesse Blayton, Sr.

1954—National Negro Network—African American oriented programming service

8-23. Radio Pioneers

Radio played an important role in spreading the achievements of African Americans during the Harlem Renaissance, beginning in the early 1920s, and after World War II, when many left a southern way of life for urban areas in the north. Disk jockeys helped with the transition—they played familiar music and gave tips on how to function as northern city dwellers.

Profile of an Early Pioneer, Jack L. Cooper

- Credited with being the first African American announcer in the early 1920s; started with WCAP, Washington, D.C. (a segregated station)

- By late 1920s, with WSBC in Chicago featuring his own variety show, "The All Colored Hour," with guests in comedy, radio plays, and music

- Began a "disc jockey" show before the term became popular; introduced style of talking in rhythm with music and using rhyming slang, a style emulated by many and possibly precursor of rap format

Other Radio Pioneers

William T. "Hoss" Allen - WHIN, Gallatin; WLAC, Nashville

Edward J. "Eddie" Castleberry - WEDR & WJLD, Birmingham; WMBM, Miami; WCIN, Cincinnati; WABQ, Cleveland; WVKO, Columbus; WHAT, Philadelphia; WEBB, Baltimore

"Sir Johnny O" Compton - WOV, New York; WWIN, Baltimore

Moses Lindberg "Luck" Cordell - WHFC & WCFL, Chicago; WGRY, Gary; WGES, Chicago; WYRR & WYON, Chicago

Larry Dean Faulkner - WERD, Atlanta; WCHB, Detroit; WCIN, Cincinnati; KSAN, San Francisco; WCHB & WJLB, Detroit; WEBB, WINN, WLIF & WITH, Baltimore; WEAA-FM, Baltimore (Morgan State University)

Jack Gibson - WERD, Atlanta; WCIN, Cincinnati

"Joltin Joe" Howard - KNUZ & KYOK, Houston; WAKE & WERD, Atlanta; WJLB, Detroit

Maurice "Hot Red" Hubert, Jr. - WDIA-AM, Memphis; WITH-AM, Baltimore

Tom Joyner - WMRA, Montgomery; WLOK, Memphis; KKDA, Dallas; WJPC & WGCI-FM, Chicago; WHUR, Washington

Eddie O'Jay - WABQ, Cleveland; WUFO, Buffalo; WLIB, New York

Donnie Simpson - WPGC, Washington

Norman W. Spaulding - WFJL; WNIB; WGN; WIND; WGES; WAAF

Richard Stams - WGES, WHFC; WOPA, WEAW, Chicago

8-24. Spotlight: ED BRADLEY

➤ Born 1941 in Philadelphia, Pennsylvania, the son of Gladys and Edward R. Bradley

➤ Earned a bachelor's degree in education, 1964, Cheyney State College in Pennsylvania

➤ Began a career in broadcast journalism, 1963, at radio station WDAS in Philadelphia as disk jockey and news reporter

➤ Joined WCBS radio in New York, 1967, and CBS television news, 1971, as reporter in the Paris bureau

➤ Held international posts in Paris and then Saigon, where he covered the Vietnam War until 1974, then began reporting from Washington, D.C.

➤ In addition to duties as CBS White House correspondent, became principal correspondent on *CBS Reports* news program, 1978

➤ Anchor of *CBS Sunday Night News,* 1976-1981

➤ Joined the CBS Sunday night news show *60 Minutes,* 1981, for which he received a number of awards in journalism

➤ 1983: Won Emmys for "Lena" (interview with Lena Horne) and "In the Belly of the Beast" (interview with John Henry Abbott)

➤ 1991: Received the Alfred I. DuPont-Columbia University Silver Baton; another Emmy for "Made in China" (Chinese forced labor camps)

➤ 1992: Host of "Street Stories" on *CBS News*

➤ 1996: Received the Robert F. Kennedy Journalism Award grand prize for "In the Killing Fields of America," *CBS Reports'* documentary on violence in the United States

➤ Other awards:

—George Foster Peabody Broadcasting Award
—George Polk Award
—National Collegiate Athletic Association Anniversary Award

8-25. Spotlight: BRYANT GUMBEL

➤ Born 1948, New Orleans, Louisiana, son of Rhea LeCesne and Richard Dunbar Gumbel; raised in Chicago

➤ Graduated from Bates College in Maine, 1970, with a major in Russian history

➤ Began sportswriting career for *Black Sports* magazine, 1971, first as freelancer, then as staff; became editor-in-chief within eight months

➤ Began television broadcasting as weekend sportscaster for KNBC-TV in Los Angeles, 1972

➤ KNBC-TV sports director, 1976-1981

➤ Emmys, 1976 and 1978, for pregame hosting for sports events

➤ Father of two children, Bradley Christopher and Jillian Beth

➤ Co-anchor with Jane Pauley on the *Today* show, 1981 to 1996; first black host during the show's history; anchored the 1992 presidential election coverage and 1988 Olympic Summer Games in Seoul, Korea

➤ 1984: Received Edward R. Murrow Award for Outstanding Foreign Affairs Work for his *Today* show broadcasts from Soviet Union and a George Peabody Award for reporting in Vietnam

➤ 1986: Created teen magazine show, *Mainstreet;* voted as best morning television interviewer by over 1,000 journalists

➤ Host of HBO's "Real Sports with Bryant Gumbel"

➤ 1993: Award for broadcasts from sub-Saharan Africa by TransAfrica, UNICEF, the National Association of Black Journalists

➤ Signed a five-year contract with CBS, 1997, for a primetime news magazine show, *Public Eye,* entertainment specials, and a production company co-ownership

➤ 1999: Trumpet Award from Turner Broadcasting System

➤ Other awards: Frederick D. Patterson Award, the highest award issued by the United Negro College Fund; three NAACP Image Awards; Martin Luther King Award from the Congress of Racial Equality

➤ Serves on the United Negro College Fund Board, the United Way of New York City, Bates College, and Xavier University

➤ Celebrity sponsor of golf tournament to support the work of the United Negro College Fund

➤ Host, CBS's "Early Show," 1999

PLAYS AND MOVIES

List 8-26. Broadway Plays with African American Themes

Within These Gates (1919)

All God's Chillun (1920)

The Emperor Jones (1920)

The Chip Woman's Fortune (1923)

Purlie Victorius (1950)

Take a Giant Step (1950)

A Raisin in the Sun (1959)

Ceremonies in Dark Old Men (1959)

The Dutchman (1963)

No Place to Be Somebody (1969)

Putney Swope (1969)

Black Girl (1971)

Don't Bother Me I Can't Cope (1971)

Sty of the Blind Pig (1971)

For Colored Girls Who Considered Suicide When the Rainbow Is Enuf (1976)

Fences (1987)

The Piano Lesson (1990)

List 8-27. Movies with African American Themes

A Soldier's Story (1984)

Purple Rain (1984)

She's Gotta Have It (1986)

Mo' Better Blues (1988)

Do the Right Thing (1989)

Glory (1990)

Boyz n the Hood (1991)

Daughters of the Dust (1991)

Jungle Fever (1991)

Malcolm X (1992)

Waiting to Exhale (1996)

Get on the Bus (1997)

How Stella Got Her Groove Back (1997)

Beloved (1998)

List 8-28. Filmmakers

Julie Dash	*Daughters of the Dust* (1991)
Bill Duke	*Rage in Harlem* (1991); *Deep Cover* (1992)
Spike Lee	*Do the Right Thing* (1989); *Four Little Girls: Bombing of the 16th Street Baptist Church, Birmingham, Alabama (1998)*
Oscar Micheaux	*Within Our Gates* (1919); *The Homesteader* (1919); *The Exile* (1931)
Gordon Parks, Sr.	*The Learning Tree* (1969); *Shaft* (1971)
Marty Rich	*Straight Out of Brooklyn* (1991)
John Singleton	*Boyz n the Hood* (1991)
Robert Townsend	*Hollywood Shuffle* (1987); *The Five Heartbeats* (1991); and *Meteor Man* (1993)
Mario Van Peebles	*New Jack City* (1991)

ACTORS AND ACTRESSES

List 8-29. TV and Film Appearances
(a selected list)

- **John Amos**—TV: "Good Times" (late 1970s); FILM: *Let's Do It Again* (1975), *American Flyer* (1985)

- **Eddie "Rochester" Anderson**—TV: "The Jack Benny Show" (1950s); FILM: *Man About Town* (1939), *Gone With the Wind* (1939), *The Sailor Takes a Wife* (1946)

- **Margaret Avery**—*Magnum Force,* (1973), *The Color Purple* (1985)

- **Pearl Bailey**—*St. Louis Blues* (1958), *Porgy and Bess* (1959), *Hello Dolly* (1967), *The Fox and the Hawk* (1981)

- **Angela Bassett**—*Waiting to Exhale* (1996), *How Stella Got Her Groove Back* (1997)

- **Harry Belafonte**—*Uptown Saturday Night* (1974), *Beat Street* (1984)

- **Jim Brown**—*The Split* (1968), *Take a Hard Ride* (1975)

- **Diahann Carroll**—TV: "Julia" (1968-1971); FILM: *Carmen Jones* (1954), *Porgy and Bess* (1959)

- **Nell Carter**—*Jesus Christ Superstar, The Musical* (1971), *Ain't Misbehavin'* (1978), *Modern Problems* (1981)

- **Olivia Cole**—TV: "Roots" (1977); FILM: *The Onion Field* (1979)

- **Gary Coleman**—TV: "Different Strokes" (1978-1986); FILM: *On the Right Track* (1981), *Jimmy the Kidd* (1982)

- **Bill Cosby**—TV: several series (1984-present); FILM: *Uptown Saturday Night* (1974), *Bill Cosby Himself* (1983)

- **Dorothy Dandridge**—*Ebony Parade* (1947), *Tarzan's Peril* (1951), *Carmen Jones* (1954), *Porgy and Bess* (1959)

- **Ossie Davis**—*No Way Out* (1950), directed *Cotton Comes to Harlem* (1970), *Gordon's War* (1973), *Harry and Son* (1984)

- **Sammy Davis, Jr.**—*Pepe* (1960), *Johnny Cool* (1963), *Sweet Charity* (1969)

- **Ruby Dee**—*The Jackie Robinson Story* (1950), *No Way Out* (1950), *Cat People* (1982)

- **Stepin Fetchit**—*One More Spring* (1935), *Zenobia* (1939)

- **Redd Foxx**—TV: "Sanford and Son" (early 1980s), "The Redd Foxx Show" (1986); FILM: Cotton Comes to Harlem (1970)

- **Al Freeman**—*The Rebel Breed* (1960), *The Detective* (1968), *A Fable* (1971), directed and acted in *A Fable* (1971), *Countdown at Kusini* (1976)

- **Morgan Freeman**—*Driving Miss Daisy* (1989), *Glory* (1989), *The Power of One* (1992), *The Shawshank Redemption* (1994)

- **Marla Gibbs**—TV: "The Jeffersons" (1975-1985); FILM: *Preacher Man* (1973), *Black Belt Jones* (1974)

- **Danny Glover**—*The Color Purple* (1985), *Lethal Weapon* movie and sequels (1987-1998)

- **Whoopi Goldberg**—*The Color Purple* (1985), *Jumpin' Jack Flash* (1986), *Sister Act I and II* (1990, 1992)

- **Louis Gossett, Jr.**—TV: "The Young Rebels" (late 1960s), "Roots" (1977); FILM: *The Landlord* (1970), *An Officer and a Gentleman* (1982)

- **Robert Guillaume**—TV: "Benson" (1988); FILM: *Wanted Dead or Alive* (1987)

- **Sherman Hemsley**—"The Jeffersons" (1975-1985)

- **Gregory Hines**—*White Nights* (1985), *Running Scared* (1986)

- **Lena Horne**—*Panama Hattie* (1942), *Stormy Weather* (1943), *Till the Clouds Roll By* (1946)

- **Whitney Houston**—*The Bodyguard* (1992), *Waiting to Exhale* (1996), *The Preacher's Wife* (1997)

- **Samuel L. Jackson**—*A Time to Kill* (1996), *The Negotiator* (1998), *Shaft* (2000)

- **James Earl Jones**—TV: "Jesus of Nazareth" (1979), "Paul Robeson" (1979); FILM: *End of the Road* (1970), voice of Darth Vader in *Star Wars* trilogy (1977, 1980, 1983), *Gardens of Stone* (1987)

- **Hattie McDaniel**—*Gone With the Wind* (1939), *Never Say Goodbye* (1946), *The Flame* (1948)

- **Butterfly McQueen**—*Gone With the Wind* (1939), *Killer Diller* (1948), *Mosquito Coast* (1986)

- **Juanita Moore**—*Imitation of Life* (1959), *Abby* (1974), *The Singing Nun* (1996)

- **Eddie Murphy**—*Beverly Hills Cop I, II, and III* (1984, 1987, 1994), *Golden Child* (1986), *48 Hours* (1988), *The Nutty Professor* (1995, 2000), *Dr. Dolittle* (1998)

- **Clarence Muse**—*Way Down South* (1939), *Porgy and Bess* (1959), *The Black Stallion* (1979)

- **Gordon Parks, Jr.**—*Superfly* (1972), *Thomasine and Bushrod* (1974)

- **Gordon Parks, Sr.**—*The Learning Tree* (1969), *Shaft* (1971), *The Super Cops* (1974)

- **Brock Peters**—*Porgy and Bess* (1959), *To Kill a Mockingbird* (1962), *Black Girl* (1972)

- **Sidney Poitier**—*No Way Out* (1950), *The Defiant Ones* (1958), *Porgy and Bess* (1959), *Guess Who's Coming to Dinner?* (1967), *In the Heat of the Night* (1967)

- **Richard Pryor**—*Uptown Saturday Night* (1974), *Which Way Is Up?* (1977), *Critical Condition* (1987)

- **Phylicia Rashad**—TV: several Bill Cosby series (1984-2000); *Uncle Tom's Cabin* (1987)

- **Paul Robeson**—*Body and Soul* (1926), *Show Boat* (1936), *King Solomon's Mine* (1937), *Native Land* (1942)

- **Esther Rolle**—TV: "Good Times" (late 1970s); FILM: *I Know Why the Caged Bird Sings* (1979), *Driving Miss Daisy* (1989), *A Raisin in the Sun* (1989)

- **Harold Rollins**—*Ragtime* (1981), *A Soldier's Story* (1984)

- **Diana Ross**—*Lady Sings the Blues* (1975)

- **Richard Roundtree**—*Shaft* (1971), *Embassy* (1972), *Diamonds* (1975)

- **Isabel Sanford**—TV: "Sandford and Son" (early 1970s), "Love Boat" (1980); FILM: *Love at First Bite* (1975)

- **Will Smith**—TV: "Fresh Prince of Bel-Air" (1990-1996); FILM: *Independence Day* (1997), *Men in Black* (1998), *Wild, Wild, West* (1999)

- **Wesley Snipes**—*Mo Better Blues* (1990), *Jungle Fever* (1991)

- **Mr. T.**—TV: "The A Team" (1983-1987); FILM: *Rocky 3* (1982), *D.C. Cab* (1983)
- **Billie "Buckwheat" Thomas**—*Our Gang* (1934-1944)
- **Cicely Tyson**—*Sounder* (1972), *The Autobiography of Miss Jane Pittman* (1974)
- **Leslie Uggams**—TV: "Sing Along With Mitch" (early 1960s); FILM: *Two Weeks in Another Town* (1962), *Skyjacked* (1972), *Black Girl* (1972)
- **Jimmie Walker**—"Good Times" (1974-1979)
- **Denzel Washington**—*A Soldier's Story* (1984), *Glory* (1989), *Malcolm X* (1992), *The Hurricane* (1999)
- **Ethel Waters**—*Gift of Gab* (1934), *The Sound and the Fury* (1959)
- **Billy Dee Williams**—TV: "Ocean of Fire" (1986); FILM: *Lady Sings the Blues* (1972), *The Return of the Jedi* (1983)
- **Flip Wilson**—TV: "The Flip Wilson Show" (1970-1975); FILM: *Uptown Saturday Night* (1974)
- **Paul Winfield**—TV: "Mission Impossible" (1968); FILM: *Sounder* (1972), *Gordon's War* (1973)
- **Oprah Winfrey**—TV: "The Oprah Winfrey Show" (1994-present); FILM: *The Color Purple* (1985), *Native Son* (1986), *Beloved* (1999)
- **Alfre Woodard**—TV: "Hill Street Blues" (1982-1983); FILM: *Guess Who's Coming to Dinner?* (1967), *Cross Creek* (1983), *Down in the Delta* (1998)

List 8-30. Academy Award® and Emmy® Nominations and Recipients

- **Margaret Avery**—*The Color Purple* (1985), nominated for Academy Award for Best Supporting Actress
- **Olivia Cole**—"Roots" (1977), won an Emmy as Best Supporting Actress in a Drama Series
- **Morgan Freeman**—*Driving Miss Daisy* (1989) and *The Shawshank Redemption* (1994), nominated twice for Academy Award for Best Actor
- **Whoopi Goldberg**—*The Color Purple* (1985), nominated for Academy Award for Best Actress
- **Cuba Gooding, Jr.**—*Jerry McGuire* (1997), won Academy Award for Best Supporting Actor
- **Louis Gossett, Jr.**—*An Officer and a Gentleman* (1982), won Academy Award for Best Supporting Actor
- **Hattie McDaniel**—*Gone With the Wind* (1939), won Academy Award for Best Supporting Actress (first African American woman to win award)

- **Juanita Moore**—*Imitation of Life* (1959), nominated for Academy Award for Best Supporting Actress

- **Sidney Poitier**—*Lilies of the Field* (1963), won Academy Award for Best Supporting Actor (first African American man to win award)

- **Esther Rolle**—"The Summer of My German Soldier" (1978), won Emmy for Best Supporting Actress in a Limited Series or Special

- **Harold Rollins, Jr.**—*Ragtime* (1981), nominated for Academy Award for Best Supporting Actor

- **Cicely Tyson**—*Sounder* (1974), won Academy Award for Best Actress; "The Autobiography of Miss Jane Pittman" (1974), won Emmy for Best Actress in a Special Series

- **Denzel Washington**—*Glory* (1989), won Academy Award for Best Supporting Actor

- **Paul Winfield**—*Sounder* (1972), nominated for Academy Award for Best Actor

- **Oprah Winfrey**—*The Color Purple* (1985), nominated for Academy Award for Best Supporting Actress

- **Alfre Woodard**—*Cross Creek* (1983), nominated for Academy Award for Best Supporting Actress

List 8-31. TV Series

"The A Team" (1983-1987)

"Amen" (premiered September 1986)

"Amos 'n Andy" (1951-1953)

"Baby, I'm Back" (January 1978-August 1978)

"B.A.D. Cats" (January 1980-February 1980)

"Barefoot in the Park" (1970-1971)

"Baretta" (1975-1978)

"Barney Miller" (1975-1982)

"Battlestar Galactica" (1978-1980)

"Benson" (1979-1986)

"Beulah" (1950-1953)

"The Bill Cosby Show" (in various forms, 1984-2000)

"Cosby Kids" (1996-present)

"Different Strokes" (1978-1986)

"Fame" (1982-1983)

"The Flip Wilson Show" (1970-1975)

"Gimme a Break" (premiered October 1981)

"Good Times" (1974-1979)

"The Hughleys (1999-present)

"I Spy" (early 1960s)

"In Living Color" (1994-1997)

"The Insiders" (1985-1986)

"The Jeffersons" (1975-1985)

"Julia" (1968-1971)

"Living Single" (1995-1997)

"Melba" (premiered January 1984)

"The Mod Squad" (1968-1973)

"The Redd Foxx Show" (January 1986-April 1986)

"Room 222" (1970s)

"Sanford and Son" (early 1970s)

"Webster" (early 1980s)

List 8-32. TV Movies, Mini-Series, and Specials

"The Atlanta Child Murders" (1985)

"The Autobiography of Miss Jane Pittman" (1974)

"Backstairs at the White House" (1979)

"Brian's Song" (1971)

"Don't Look Back: The Story of Leroy Satchel Paige" (1981)

"Freedom Road" (1979)

"I Know Why the Caged Bird Sings" (1979)

"King" (1978)

"The Marva Collins Story" (1981)

"Ministrel Man" (1977)

"Motown 25: Yesterday, Today, Forever" (1983)

"Roots" (1977)

"Roots: The Next Generation" (1979)

"Scott Joplin: King of Ragtime" (1977)

"Sister, Sister" (1982)

"A Woman Called Moses" (1978)

List 8-33. Documentary Videos and Films

Black History: Lost, Stolen or Strayed

Black West

Eyes on the Prize (I and II)

Hoop Dreams

Jesse Jackson

Madam C.J. Walker

A Raisin in the Sun

Repercussions: A Celebration of African-American Music

Sojourner Truth

That's Black Entertainment

SPOTLIGHTS

List 8-34. Spotlight: OPRAH WINFREY

A successful businesswoman, TV talk show hostess, actress, studio chief, producer, and publisher, Oprah Winfrey is an extraordinary woman.

➤ Born January 29, 1954 in Kosciusko, Mississippi

➤ Exhibited talent as an orator by reciting the sermons of James Weldon Johnson when she was around four years old

➤ Taught to read by her grandmother, Oprah became and remains a voracious reader

➤ Surviving a rocky childhood, Oprah emerged as an excellent student and won a full scholarship to Tennessee State University, earning a Bachelor's degree in speech and drama in 1976

➤ At nineteen and still in college, Oprah became the first black woman to anchor the news on a television station in Nashville

➤ After graduation, she worked as a reporter and co-anchor for an ABC news affiliate in Baltimore, Maryland for one year and became the co-host of the Baltimore morning show *People Are Talking* where she remained for seven years

➤ Moved to Chicago in 1984 to become host of the television talk show *A.M. Chicago*

➤ *A.M. Chicago* was renamed *The Oprah Winfrey Show* in 1985 and syndicated in 1986

➤ Established Harpo Productions in 1986 to produce her show and other film projects

➤ Made the *Forbes* list as one of the wealthiest women in America

➤ Organized the Family for Better Lives Foundation and contributes millions of dollars to charities, with educational institutions receiving large grants

➤ Activist for children, she proposed a bill to create a national database of convicted child abusers; the "Oprah Bill" or the *National Child Protection Act* was signed into law in 1994 by President Bill Clinton

Film Credits

The Color Purple (1985)

Native Son (1986)

The Women of Brewster Place (1989) in which she costarred and produced

Beloved (1999)

Publications

Make the Connection: Ten Steps to a Better Body—and a Better Life (1996) with Bob Greene

O—a new woman's magazine launched in April, 2000

Awards

Golden Globe Award® and an Academy Award® nomination for *The Color Purple*

Inducted into the Television Academy Hall of Fame in 1996

Emmy's® Lifetime Achievement Award in 1998

Broadcaster of the Year Award by the International Radio and Television Society

List 8-35. Spotlight: SPIKE LEE

➤ Born 1957 as Shelton Jackson Lee in Atlanta, Georgia, the oldest of five children

➤ The Lee family moved to New York from Chicago in 1959 and settled in the predominantly African American Fort Green section of Brooklyn

➤ Graduated from Morehouse College in 1979 and obtained an internship at Columbia Pictures studio in Burbank, California

➤ Worked toward Master's Degree in filmmaking at New York University Institute of Film and Television, Tisch School of Arts

➤ Quote: "To come up with a script that could be done for as little money as possible, yet still be commercial."

➤ *She's Gotta Have It*, first movie by an independent African American filmmaker, awarded best new film by San Francisco Film Festival and Cannes Film Festival

➤ Movies include:

School Daze
Do the Right Thing
Mo' Better Blues
Jungle Fever
Malcolm X
Get on the Bus
Crooklyn

List 8-36. Spotlight: QUEEN LATIFAH

➤ Born 1970 as Dana Owens in East Orange, New Jersey

➤ Began performing in high school for the rap group Ladies Fresh

➤ Recorded a solo album in 1989, *All Hail the Queen*

➤ Other recordings include *Nature of a Sista'* featuring the single "Latifah Had It Up 2 Here," and "Black Reign"

➤ CEO of Flavor Unit Records and Management Company

➤ Runs rap artist management and entertainment companies

➤ Appearances on television and films include:

"Living Single"
"Fresh Prince of Bel-Air"
House Party II
Jungle Fever
The Bone Collector
Set It Off

➤ Autobiography, *Ladies First: Revelations of a Strong Woman*

➤ Produces and hosts a daily one-hour talk show, "The Queen Latifah Show"

PERFORMING ARTS ORGANIZATIONS AND FACILITIES

List 8-37. Performing Arts Organizations and Facilities

Opera Companies

Colored American Opera Company, Washington, D.C.

National Negro Opera Company, Pittsburgh, Pennsylvania

Sister M. Elise, Opera-South, Jackson, Mississippi

National Opera Ebony, Philadelphia, Pennsylvania

Theaters

Lou Bellamy's Penumbra Theatre, St. Paul, Minnesota

Jomandi Productions, Atlanta, Georgia

Black Repertory, St. Louis, Missouri

Freedom Theatre, Philadelphia, Pennsylvania

Crossroads Theatre, New Brunswick, New Jersey

Unions and Guilds

Actors Equity Association (AEA), 165 West 46th Street, New York, New York 10036

American Federation of Television and Radio Artists (AFTRA), 260 Madison Avenue, 7th Floor, New York, New York 10016

American Guild of Musical Artists (AGMA), 1727 Broadway, New York, New York 10019

American Guild of Variety Artists (AGVA), 184 Fifth Avenue, New York, New York 10010

Screen Actors Guild (SAG), 5757 Wilshire Boulevard, Los Angeles, California 90036

Samuel French's Theater and Film Bookshop, 7623 Sunset Boulevard, Hollywood, California 90046

The Theatre Arts Bookshop, 405 West 42nd Street, New York, New York 10036

Theatrebooks, 1600 Broadway, Room 1009, New York, New York 10019

TRADE PUBLICATIONS AND RESOURCE GUIDES

List 8-38. Trade Publications and Resource Guides

Auditions News, 6272 W. North Avenue, Chicago, Illinois 60639

Back Stage/The Performing Arts Weekly, Back Stage Publications, 330 West 42nd Street, New York, New York 10036

Back Stage West/The Performing Arts Weekly, Back Stage Publications, 5055 Wilshire Boulevard, Los Angeles, California 90036

Billboard, 1515 Broadway, New York, New York

Black Masks, P.O. Box 2, Riverdale Station, Bronx, New York 10471

Black Talent News, P.O. Box 7374, Culver City, California 90233-7374

Casting Call, 11222 Weddington Street, North Hollywood, California 91601

Harlem Cultural Council Newsletter, 215 West 125th Street, New York, New York 10027

Hollywood Reporter, 6715 Sunset Boulevard, Hollywood, California 90028

New York Casting and Survival Guide, Peter Gleen Publications, 17 East 48th Street, New York, New York 10017

Performink, 2632 N. Lincoln, Chicago, Illinois 60614

Ross Reports Television, Television Index, 40-29 27th Street, Long Island City, New York 11101

Summer Theatre Directory, edited by Jill Charles, Theatre Directories, American Theatre Works, Inc., P.O. Box 519, Dorset, Vermont 05251

Variety, Variety, Inc., 154 West 46th Street, New York, New York 10036

Section 9
SPORTS

SECTION 9

SPORTS

Physical competition and athletic ability were important components of African American culture. The conditions of slavery placed definite limits on the pursuit of sports as a leisure activity among slaves, but on Sundays and holidays many slaves enjoyed such activities as horseracing, boxing, cockfighting, ball-playing, and games.

The history of African American athletes in the United States is one of great encouragement, enthusiasm, and achievement. Until 1947, when Jackie Robinson joined the Brooklyn Dodgers and became the first African American major league baseball player, most college and professional sports were segregated or discriminated against African Americans. Once the color barrier was lifted, African American athletes became an integral part of the sports scene in the United States.

By the 1970s, black athletes represented one-quarter of the regulars in major league baseball, one-third of the regulars in professional football, and one-half of the regulars in professional basketball. Of all the team sports, football defied the Jim Crow influence the longest. Unlike baseball, football began as a college sport in the United States. Although African Americans were allowed to play on the teams of northern colleges, they were not well represented in professional football until the 1960s. Until the late 1990s, sports such as golf and racing had limited involvement of blacks.

Remnants of a segregated history in sports remain. Despite the success African Americans achieved as players, there is a paucity of African Americans in managerial and administrative positions. In Section 9, the African Americans who, in spite of barriers, made substantial achievements or had notable histories in the field of sports are listed.

AFRICAN AMERICANS IN SPORTS

List 9-1. Firsts in Sports

1805	Bill Richmond	prominent boxer in England
1859	Abraham M. Hewlitt	director, Physical Culture, Harvard University
1875	Oliver Lewis	won Kentucky Derby (horseracing)
1876	Nat Love	rodeo champion
1878	John Jackson	pitcher and outfielder for predominately white baseball team; also known as John "Bud" Fowler
1879	Frank Hart	set U.S. record for marathon walking; known as "O'Leary's Smoking Irishman"
1884	Moses Fleetwood	catcher for Toledo team of American Baseball Association
1884	Isaac Murphy	won Kentucky Derby—1884, 1890, and 1891
1885	Cuban Giants	salaried baseball team
1890	George Dixon	bantamweight boxing champion; known as "Little Chocolate"
1892	William H. Lewis	selected All-American 1892 and 1893 (college football)
1896	John Shippen	professional golfer
1898	Marshall "Major" Taylor	won major bicycle race
1901	Joe Walcott	welterweight boxing champion; known as "Jersey Joe"
1902	Joe Gans	lightweight boxing champion
1904	Charles Follis Wallace	professional football player; signed with Shelby Blues
1904	George C. Poage	first to represent U.S. in Olympic Games; hurdles
1905	William Craighead	captain of white college football team, Massachusetts State
1905	Bill Pickett	invented modern art of bulldogging
1908	John "Jack" Johnson	heavyweight boxing champion
1915	Joseph Trigg	varsity rowing team
1916	American Tennis Association	founded to promote tennis among African Americans
1916	Charlie Smoot	won Beverwyck Steeplechase—1916, 1926, and 1933
1916	Fritz Pollard	played in Rose Bowl game (college football)

1917	Tally Holmes	won men's title, American Tennis Association tournament
1917	Lucy Stone	won women's title, American Tennis Association tournament
1920s	Dewey Brown	member, Professional Golf Association (PGA); golf teacher and caddy
1923	Rojo Jack	auto racer
1923	The Rens	professional basketball team
1923	Robert J. Douglas	founder of the Rens
1924	William D. Hubbard	won Olympic gold medal in broad jump (track and field)
1926	Tiger Flowers	middleweight boxing champion
1932	Eddie Tolan	won Olympic gold medal (track)
1936	Jesse Owens	won four Olympic gold medals (track)
1937	Henry Armstrong	held three boxing championships and three world titles at same time; known as "Hammering Hank"
1939	The Rens	first team on record to win professional world's championship
1939	National Bowling Association	organized; held first tournament
1939	Wynston Brown	president, National Negro Bowling Association
1946	Marion Motley	admitted to major league professional sport (football); Cleveland Browns
1947	Jackie Robinson	joined Brooklyn Dodgers in National League (baseball)
1947	Larry Doby	joined Cleveland Indians in American League (baseball)
1947	Don Barksdale	selected for All-American basketball team
1948	Reginald Weir	admitted to U.S. Lawn Tennis Association
1950	Charles "Chuck" Cooper	drafted by National Basketball Association
1950	Earl Lloyd	played in National Basketball Association
1950	Arthur Dorrington	played in organized hockey
1951	John Davis	won eight consecutive world and Olympic championships; elected to Helms and Black Athletes Halls of Fame (weightlifting)
1953	Marcenia Lyle Alberga	played in Negro Baseball League, 1953-54; also known as Toni Stowe
1953	Willie Thrower	professional quarterback (football); Chicago Bears

1954	Berton Groves	entered Pikes Peak Hill Climb auto race
1956	Ann Gregory	played in integrated women's amateur championship
1956	Rafer Johnson	won high hurdles in Olympic decathlon (track and field)
1956	Althea Gibson	won women's singles title, French Open (tennis)
1957	Althea Gibson	won Wimbledon championship (tennis)
1957	Charles Sifford	won major professional golf tournament
1957	Jim Brown	participated in lacrosse's North-South games
1958	Ernie Banks	Most Valuable Player in National League (baseball); won two consecutive years (1958 and 1959)
1958	Willie Eldon O'Rhee	professional hockey player with National Hockey League
1959	Elgin G. Baylor	rookie to win All-State and Most Valuable Player awards (National Basketball Association)
1960	Fuller Gordy	professional bowler; played Professional Bowlers Assn. tour
1960	Wilma Rudolph	first woman to win three gold medals in Olympics (track)
1961	Ernest Davis	Heisman Trophy winner (college football)
1962	Wilt "The Stilt" Chamberlain	scored 100 points in a single game (basketball)
1962	Jackie Robinson	enshrined in Baseball Hall of Fame
1963	Buck Buchanon	player from a black college (Grambling) drafted by a professional football team; Kansas City
1963	Jim Brown	first NFL player to rush for more than one mile in one season (football)
1963	Elston Howard	Most Valuable Player in American League (baseball)
1965	Emlen Tunnell	coach in the National Football League
1966	Emmett Ashford	appointed umpire by major league (baseball)
1966	Bill Russell	player-coach for Boston Celtics and head coach in major league professional sports
1967	Emlen Tunnell	elected to the National Football Hall of Fame
1967	Renee Powell	joined Ladies Professional Golfers Association tour
1968	Marion Motley	inducted into Football Hall of Fame; helped desegregate football in the 1940s
1968	Althea Gibson	inducted into International Tennis Hall of Fame
1968	Arthur Ashe	won U.S. Open tennis championship
1970	Arthur Ashe	won Australian Open tennis championship

1970	Chris Dickerson	won Mr. America title (bodybuilding)
1971	Cheryl White	woman jockey (horseracing)
1971	Bill Pickett	elected to National Rodeo Cowboy Hall of Fame
1972	Wayne Embry	general manager in professional sport (basketball)
1972	Adelle Nutter	U.S. dart champion
1973	Wendy Hilliard	member, U.S. National Rhythmic Gymnastics Team
1974	Henry "Hank" Aaron	broke Babe Ruth's record career homeruns
1974	Althea Gibson	inducted into Black Hall of Fame (tennis)
1975	R. Lee Elder	qualified for Masters Championship (golf)
1975	Arthur Ashe	won Wimbledon and world championships (tennis)
1980	Sharon R. Jones	director, outreach activities, Oakland Athletics (baseball)
1981	Frank Robinson	manager in National League (baseball): only player to win Most Valuable Player Award in National and American Leagues
1981	Grant Fuhr	drafted player of the National Hockey League
1981	Dianne Durham	won U.S. gymnastics championship
1982	Charles Sampson	world rodeo champion
1984	Carl Lewis	won four Olympic gold medals (track)
1984	Lynette Woodard	first woman to become member of Harlem Globetrotters (basketball)
1985	Dwight "Doc" Gooden	won Cy Young Award (baseball)
1985	Arthur Ashe	inducted into International Tennis Hall of Fame
1986	Harriet Hamilton	athletic director, Southern Intercollegiate Athletic Conference
1988	Doug Williams	quarterback to win a Super Bowl (football)
1988	Florence Griffith-Joyner	set world record for 100- and 200-meter races (track); known as "Flo Jo"
1988	Charles Lakers	member, U.S. Olympic team (gymnastics)
1988	Debi Thomas	won silver medal in Winter Olympics (ice skating)
1988	Wendell Chestnut	member, men's All-American Squash Team, National Intercollegiate Squash Racquet Association
1989	Bill White	president, Professional Baseball Clubs, National League
1989	Eric Gregg	umpire, officiated World Series game (baseball)

1990	Elaine Weddington	assistant general manager, Boston Red Sox (baseball)
1990	Donna Creek	inducted into Woman's Sport Hall of Fame (horse riding); member of U.S. Equestrian Team
1991	Rickey Henderson	set record of steals, 939 bases in career (baseball)
1991	Eldrick "Tiger" Woods	youngest to win U.S. Junior Amateur championship; defended title in 1992 and 1993; only golfer to win three straight titles
1992	Jackie Joyner-Kersee	won Olympic gold medal in heptathlon and bronze medal in long jump
1992	Art Price and Marty Stephean	sailed in America's Cup
1992	Dominque Dawes	member of U.S. Olympic team to win bronze medal (gymnastics)
1992	Robert Pipkins	member of Olympic luge team; first in international competition
1992	Cito Gaston	manager to lead team to World Series Championship (baseball); Toronto Blue Jays
1992	John Merchant	served on executive committee of U.S. Golf Association
1992	Ron Simmons	heavyweight wrestling champion
1993	George Branham	professional bowling title
1994	Fredia Gibbs	world super lightweight kickboxing championship; known as "The Cheeta"
1995	Lenda Murray	won Ms. Olympia title (bodybuilding)
1997	Eldrick "Tiger" Woods	won Masters championship (golf)
1998	Venus Williams	winner, semifinals: U.S. Open in 1998 and 1999 (tennis)
1999	Briana Scurry	goalkeeper, winning the U.S. Women's Soccer Team's national championship
1999	Venus Williams	winner, Grand Slam Cup, quarterfinals of French Open; finalist in Sydney International; with sister, Serena, won women's doubles at U.S. Open (tennis)
1999	Serena Williams	winner, U.S. Open (tennis); with sister, Venus, won women's doubles at U.S. Open
1999	Eldrick "Tiger" Woods	won Professional Golfers Association championship
2000	Eldrick "Tiger" Woods	largest winning margin, major golf championship; largest winning margin, U.S. Open; lowest winning score in relation to par, U.S. Open; Winner, three major golf championships: U.S. Open, British Open, PGA

List 9-2. Notable Athletes

©2001 by Prentice Hall

1911	Jess Conley	rode in Kentucky Derby (horse racing)
1920s	Josh Gibson	played professional baseball with Homestead Grays; hit longest homerun ever documented—580 feet, 1937; earned nickname "the Babe Ruth of Negro Baseball"
1927	Harlem Globetrotters	organized in Chicago (basketball)
1935	Joseph Louis "Joe Louis" Barrow	boxer; known as "Brown Bomber"; lost only once in career
1936	Lula Hymes	Tuskegee University girls track team; high point winner of 1938 AAAU meet; won 100-meter dash and broad jump
1941	Eddie Robinson	coached at Grambling University; considered the "winningest" coach in college football history
1946	Sugar Ray Robinson	boxer; welterweight champion 1946-51; world middleweight champion 1957, 1958-1960
1947	Jackie Robinson	first to play in major league—Brooklyn Dodgers (baseball)
1948	Alice Coachman	member, U.S. Olympic Team; won gold medal in high jump; earned Olympiad champion crown
1948	Charley Fonville	captured world's record for shotput (track and field)
1948	Leroy "Satchell" Paige	pitcher in American League; first to pitch in a World Series game; inducted into Baseball Hall of Fame, 1971
1948	Mal Whitfield	won Olympic gold medal in 800-meter race (track)
1949	Ezzard Charles	heavyweight world boxing champion, 1949-51
1949	Don Newcombe	pitcher for Brooklyn Dodgers (baseball); won 20 games
1951	Roy Campanella	named National League's Most Valuable Player three times: 1951, 1953, and 1955
1951	Willie Mays	led New York Giants to pennant and World Series victories: 1951 and 1954 (baseball)
1951	"Jersey" Joe Walcott	heavyweight world boxing champion
1952	Sonny Liston	Golden Gloves heavyweight title; world heavyweight boxing champion, 1962
1952	Archie Moore	light heavyweight champion (boxing), 1952-1961
1952	Milt Campbell	finished second in decathlon in Helsinki Olympics; won decathlon, 1956

1953	Roosevelt Brown	named to Black College All-American Team; drafted by New York Giants, 1953; inducted into Football Hall of Fame, 1975
1956	Floyd Patterson	youngest person to win world heavyweight boxing title
1960s	Curt Flood	centerfielder for St. Louis Cardinals (baseball)
1960	David "Deacon" Jones	defensive end with Los Angeles Rams; five-time All-Pro team from 1965-69; inducted into Football Hall of Fame, 1980
1960	Walt Bellamy	played on U.S. Olympic basketball team
1960	Oscar "Big O" Robertson	led team in assists 1960-66 and 1968-69; Most Valuable Player, 1963-64; inducted into Basketball Hall of Fame, 1979
1961	Herb Adderly	signed with Green Bay Packers; held record for most touchdowns for National Football League
1962	Maury Wills	earned National League's Most Valuable Player award; stole 104 bases, batted .299, scored 130 runs (baseball)
1964	Richie Allen	voted Rookie of the Year, National League (baseball)
1964	Henry Carr	won 200-meter dash in Tokyo Olympics; played with New York Giants and Baltimore Colts (football)
1964	Bob Hayes	won 100-meter race and 400-meter relay in Toyko Olympics; joined Dallas Cowboys, 1965 (football)
1964	Wynomia Tyus	won 100-meter dash at Tokyo Olympics
1967	Earl "The Pearl" Monroe	drafted by Baltimore Bullets; joined New York Knicks, 1971; inducted into Basketball Hall of Fame, 1990
1967	Cazzie Russell	signed with New York Knicks; joined Golden State Warriors, 1967 (basketball)
1967	Nate Thurmond	signed with Golden State Warriors; led Warriors into finals, 1967; inducted into Basketball Hall of Fame, 1984
1967	Kareem Abdul-Jabbar	elected United Press International Player, 1967 and 1969; signed with Milwaukee Bucks, 1969; National Basketball Association scoring leader, 1971-73; Most Valuable Player, 1970-71, 1971-72, 1973-74
1967	Dave Bing	scoring leader for Detroit Pistons 1967-68; inducted into Basketball Hall of Fame, 1990

1968	George Foreman	won heavyweight Olympic gold medal; world heavyweight boxing title, 1973
1970	Willis Reed	joined New York Knicks; National Basketball Association Rookie of the Year, 1970; coach of New York Knicks, 1977; inducted into Basketball Hall of Fame, 1981
1971	Julius "Dr. J" Erving	signed by Virginia Squires (American Basketball Association); Most Valuable Player, 1981 and 1983, with Philadelphia 76ers; inducted into Basketball Hall of Fame, 1993
1976	Reginald "Reggie" Jackson	broke Babe Ruth's record of homeruns in World Series competition (baseball)
1979	Earvin "Magic" Johnson	joined Los Angeles Lakers; Most Valuable Player 1986-87 (first rookie), 1988-89, 1989-90; leader in assists, 1985-86, 1986-87 (basketball)
1979	Ray Charles "Sugar Ray" Leonard	welterweight champion, 1979-82; middleweight champion, 1987; lightweight champion, 1988 (boxing)
1980	Calvin Peete	most successful player on Professional Golf Tour
1983	Zina Garrison	Wimbledon finalist, 1990; ranked in Top 10 from 1983-90 (tennis)
1983	Michael Spinks	light heavyweight championship, 1983-85 (boxing)
1984	Edwin Moses	won gold medal at 1984 Olympics; won bronze medal at 1988 Olympic games (track—hurdles)
1985	Mike Tyson	heavyweight champion, 1985; consolidated heavyweight crown, 1987-90, 1996 (boxing)
1990	Evander Holyfield	heavyweight boxing champion, 1990-92, 1993-94, 1996-present
1991	Tommy "Hit Man" Hearns	light heavyweight boxing champion
1992	Gail Devers	won gold medals in 1992 and 1996 Olympic games; world champion 100-meter relay in 1993; won 100-meter hurdles, 1993, 1995; overcame Graves' disease in 1989-90 (track and field)
1992	Riddick Bowe	heavyweight boxing champion, 1992-93
1996	Malivai Washington	Wimbledon finalist (tennis)
1999	Leila Ali	female professional boxer (heavyweight); daughter of Muhammad Ali
1999	Jim Brown	Football Athlete of the Century
2000	Marlon St. John	first to ride in Kentucky Derby since the 1920s (horse racing)

FOOTBALL

List 9-3. Heisman Trophy Winners

1961	Ernie Davis, Syracuse University
1965	Mike Garrett, University of Southern California
1968	O. J. Simpson, University of Southern California
1975	Archie Griffin, Ohio State University
1976	Archie Griffin, Ohio State University
1977	Billy Simms, University of Oklahoma
1978	Tony Dorsett, University of Pittsburgh
1979	Earl Campbell, University of Texas
1980	Charles White, University of Southern California
1981	Marcus Allen, University of Southern California
1982	Herschel Walker, University of Georgia
1983	Mike Rozier, University of Nebraska
1985	Bo Jackson, Auburn University
1987	Tim Brown, University of Notre Dame
1988	Barry Sanders, Oklahoma State University
1991	Desmond Howard, University of Michigan
1993	Charlie Ward, Florida State University
1994	Rashaan Salaam, University of Colorado
1995	Eddie George, Ohio State University
1997	Charles Woodson, University of Michigan
1998	Ricky Williams, University of Texas
1999	Ron Dayne, University of Wisconsin

List 9-4. Notable Football College Coaches

- Eddie Robinson, Grambling
- Gideon Smith, Hampton University
- Harry R. Jefferson, Hampton University
- Henry A. Kean, Tennessee A & I

- Edward P. Hurt, Morgan State
- Talmadge I. Hill, Morgan State
- Earl Banks, Morgan State
- Nathaniel "Nat" Taylor, Morgan State
- Vernon E. "Skip" McCain, Maryland State
- B.T. Harvey, Morehouse
- Alonzo S. "Jake" Gaither, Florida A & M
- Cleve Abbott, Tuskegee
- John McLendon, Tennessee A & I
- Ernest Marshall, Howard
- George Johnson, Lincoln University at Oxford, Pennsylvania
- R.W.E. Jones, Grambling
- Fred T. "Pop" Long, Wiley
- W.J. Nicks, Prairie View A & M
- J.W. Barco, Virginia Union
- Tom Harris, Virginia Union
- John T. Williams, Kentucky State
- Robert "Bob" White, Kentucky State
- William Bell, North Carolina A & T

List 9-5. All-Time National Football League Leaders

Total yards gained:	Walter Payton	21,803
Total rushing yards:	Walter Payton	16,726
Touchdowns:	Jerry Rice	166
Total receptions:	Jerry Rice	1,057
Total receiving yards:	Jerry Rice	16,455
Quarterback sacks:	Reggie White	176.5

List 9-6. Spotlight: DEION SANDERS

➤ Born 1967 in Fort Myers, Florida

➤ Achieved fame as All-American defensive back at Florida State University

➤ Left Florida State in 1989 and pursued professional careers in baseball and football

➤ Drafted by Atlanta Falcons and played for the San Francisco 49ers and the Dallas Cowboys

➤ Selected as All-Pro seven times and named the top defensive player in 1994

➤ Won Super Bowls with San Francisco in 1994 and with Dallas Cowboys in 1995

➤ Baseball career; drafted and played with the New York Yankees and traded to the Atlanta Braves in 1991

➤ Played in two World Series with the Braves and played with the San Francisco Giants and Cincinnati Reds

➤ Known as "Prime Time" for flashy clothing and theatric gestures on the field

➤ Changed his image and rediscovered his Christian faith in 1998

➤ Signed by Washington Redskins, 2000

THE KENTUCKY DERBY

List 9-7. Winners of Kentucky Derby

Year	Name	Year	Name
1875	Oliver Lewis	1890	Isaac Murphy
1877	William "Billy" Walker	1892	Alonzo Clayton
1880	George Lewis	1895	James Perkins
1882	Babe Hurd	1896	Willie Sims
1884	Isaac Murphy	1898	Willie Sims
1885	Erskine Henderson	1901	Jimmie Winkfield
1887	Isaac Murphy	1902	Jimmie Winkfield

List 9-8. Spotlight: ISAAC MURPHY

➤ Born 1861 in Kentucky

➤ Known as one of the best jockeys of all time

➤ Obtained jockey apprentice license and began a career as an exercise rider at age 12

➤ Won first major victory aboard Lady Greenfield at Louisville in 1875

➤ Earned $10,000 per year by 1882, $25.00 per winning ride and $15.00 for every loss

➤ Rode Buchanan in 1884; rode Riley in 1890; and rode Kingsman in 1891

➤ Won six races by 1884 with four different horses, including the Kentucky Derby

➤ First jockey to win three Kentucky Derby's, a record that held until 1948

➤ Appears in the Hall of Fame by two famous race courses (Pimlico, Maryland, and Saratoga, New York)

➤ In 1891, *Louisville Times* wrote, "His integrity and honor are the pride of the Turf, and many of the best horsemen pronounce him the greatest jockey that ever mounted a horse."

➤ Died in 1896 of pneumonia at age thirty-five

BOXING

List 9-9. Notable Boxers

Muhammad Ali (Cassius Clay)	light heavyweight Olympic gold medal, 1960; world heavyweight title, 1964-1967, 1974-1978
Joseph Louis "Joe Louis" Barrow	"Brown Bomber"; world heavyweight title, 1930-1949
Ezzard Charles	world heavyweight champion, 1949-1951
George "Little Chocolate" Dixon	bantamweight boxing champion, 1890
Tiger Flowers	world middleweight champion, 1926
George Foreman	heavyweight Olympic gold medal, 1968; world heavyweight title, 1973-1974, 1994-1995
Joe Frazier	heavyweight Olympic gold medal, 1964; world heavyweight champion, 1968-1973
Joe Gans	world lightweight champion, 1902-1908
Evander Holyfield	world heavyweight champion, 1990-1992, 1993-1994, 1996-1997
John "Jack" Johnson	world heavyweight champion, 1908-1915
Ray Charles "Sugar Ray" Leonard	light welterweight Olympic gold medal, 1976; welterweight champion, 1979-1982; middleweight champion, 1987; lightweight champion, 1988
Sonny Liston	Golden Gloves heavyweight title, 1952; world heavyweight champion, 1962-64
Archie Moore	world light heavyweight champion, 1952-1961
Floyd Patterson	middleweight Olympic gold medal, 1952; world heavyweight champion, 1956-1959, 1960-1962
Sugar Ray Robinson	welterweight champion, 1946-1950; world middleweight champion, 1951-1952, 1955-1960
Leon Spinks	Olympic gold medal, 1976; world heavyweight champion, 1978
Michael Spinks	Olympic gold medal, 1976; world light heavyweight champion, 1981-1983, 1985-1987
Mike Tyson	world heavyweight champion, 1985; consolidated heavyweight crown, 1987-1990, 1996
Joe "Jersey Joe" Walcott	world heavyweight boxing champion, 1951-1952

List 9-10. Spotlight: MUHAMMAD ALI

➢ Born in 1942 as Cassius Clay in Louisville, Kentucky

➢ Pursued boxing as an adolescent

➢ Amateur record of 100-5

➢ Won light heavyweight gold medal in 1960 Olympics

➢ Turned pro after the Olympics

➢ Quick wit and confidence made him an instant media star

➢ Skillful in rhyming—"Float like a butterfly, sting like a bee"

➢ Spoke out readily about the social issues of the times

➢ Converted to Islam in 1963

➢ Won world heavyweight title in 1964

➢ Announced name change to Muhammad Ali after title bout

➢ Refused to submit to the draft; stripped of his title and banned from boxing (1968-69)

➢ Cleared by U.S. Supreme Court in 1970 and returned to boxing

➢ Lost bid to regain world heavyweight title from Joe Frazier in 1971

➢ Regained world heavyweight title in 1974; lost and regained title in 1978

➢ From 1960-1981, had 9 KO's (knockouts), 28 TKO's (technical knockouts), 18 WU's (won by unanimous decision), 1 WS (won by split decision), 2 LU's (lost by unanimous decision), and 2 LS's (lost by split decision)

➢ Retired in 1981 with pro record of 56-5-0

BASEBALL

List 9-11. Negro Leagues

In the late 1800s, a number of African Americans played in the minors. Some examples: John "Bud" Fowler pitched for the Lynn Live Oaks of the International League, 1878; and Welday and Moses "Fleetwood" Walker, brothers, moved from the minors, 1884, when their team joined the American Association, but the team folded after the season. Before 1890, all doors were closed to black players, and the history of the Negro Leagues began.

The following are the predominant leagues that were active from the 1920s to the integration of the major leagues. Teams sometimes lasted only a season or were bought and consolidated with other teams. Some of the best known are included here.

Note: The Negro National League and the Eastern Colored League folded during the Depression. Shortly after, the National and American Negro Leagues were formed under new ownership.

Leagues

1920-1931 Negro National League (formed by Rube Foster, pitcher and owner of Chicago Leland Giants)

Chicago American Giants
Dayton Marcos
Detroit Stars
Indianapolis ABCs
Kansas City Monarchs
St. Louis Giants

1923-1928 Eastern Colored League (formed by Ed Bolden)

Atlantic City Bacharach Giants
Baltimore Black Sox
Brooklyn Royal Giants
Lincoln Giants
New York Cuban All-Stars
Philadelphia Hilldales

1933-1948 Negro National League (formed by Gus Greenlee, nightclub owner/gambler)

Baltimore Elite Giants
Chicago American Giants
Columbus Blue Birds
Detroit Stars
Homestead Grays
Indianapolis ABCs, replaced by Baltimore Black Sox
Nashville Elite Giants
Newark Eagles
New York Black Yankees
Pittsburgh Crawfords

1929-1930 American Negro League (replaced Eastern Colored League when it folded in 1928, taking its teams)

1937-1960 Negro American League

Atlanta Black Crackers
Baltimore Elite Giants
Birmingham Black Barons
Indianapolis Clowns
Kansas City Monarchs
Memphis Red Sox

Negro League Players in Baseball Hall of Fame

Induction Year	Name, position, claim to fame
1962	Jackie Robinson, shortstop; first player to integrate major leagues
1969	Roy Campanella, catcher; top hitter
1971	Satchel Paige, pitcher; credited with 55 no hitters
1972	Josh Gibson, catcher; legendary hitter
1972	Walter "Buck" Leonard, firstbaseman; top hitter
1973	Monford "Monte" Irvin, outfielder; clutch hitter
1974	James "Cool Papa" Bell, outfielder; fastest base runner in Negro Leagues
1975	William "Judy" Johnson, thirdbaseman
1976	Oscar Charleston, centerfielder/firstbaseman; hard hitter
1977	Martin Dihigo, pitcher/infielder/outfielder
1977	John Henry "Pop" Lloyd, shortstop, powerful clutch hitter
1979	Willie Mays, centerfielder; top hitter
1981	Rube Foster, top pitcher; credited with being top manager of Negro Leagues; owner of Chicago Leland Giants
1982	Hank "Hammerin' Hank" Aaron, outfielder; champion homerun hitter
1987	Ray Dandridge, thirdbaseman; wide range and power
1995	Leon Day, complete player—pitcher, infielder, outfielder, consistent hitter
1996	Bill "Willie" Foster, fastball pitcher with Negro league's records
1998	Larry Doby, centerfielder; second African American to play in major leagues, first in American League
1998	"Bullet" Joe Rogan, fastball pitcher; leading hitter
2000	Norman "Turkey" Stearnes, centerfielder; power hitter

First Notable Negro League Players Signed by Major Leagues

Year Signed	Player, position	Negro League team	Signing team
1945	Jackie Robinson, shortstop	Kansas City Monarchs	Brooklyn Dodgers
1946	Roy Campanella, catcher	Baltimore Elite Giants	Brooklyn Dodgers
1947	Larry Doby, outfielder	Newark Eagles	Cleveland Indians
1948	Satchel Paige, pitcher	Pittsburgh Crawfords	Cleveland Indians
1949	Don Newcombe, pitcher	Newark Eagles	Brooklyn Dodgers
1949	Monte Irvin, outfielder	Newark Eagles	New York Giants
1950	Willie Mays, outfielder	Birmingham Black Barons	New York Giants
1952	Hank Aaron, outfielder	Indianapolis Clowns	Milwaukee Braves
1956	Buck O'Neill, firstbaseman (joined as scout, not player; became coach, 1962)	Kansas City Monarchs	Chicago Cubs

List 9-12. Highest Paid African Americans in Major League Baseball

Gary Sheffield—Los Angeles Dodgers

Albert Belle—Baltimore Orioles

Barry Bonds—San Francisco Giants

Ken Griffey, Jr.—Cincinnati Reds

Kenny Lorton—Cleveland Indians

Frank Thomas—Chicago White Sox

Mo Vaughn—Anaheim Angels

David Justice—Cleveland Indians

Fred McGriff—Tampa Bay Devil Rays

Barry Larkin—Cincinnati Reds

List 9-13. Major League Leaders

Homeruns:	Hank Aaron	755
Runs batted in:	Hank Aaron	2,297
Total bases:	Hank Aaron	6,856
Stolen bases:	Rickey Henderson	1,297
Saves:	Lee Smith	478

BASKETBALL

List 9-14. Top Ten Earners in NBA (1997-1998)

Michael Jordan—Chicago Bulls

Patrick Ewing—New York Knicks

Horace Grant—Seattle Supersonics

Shaquille O'Neal—Los Angeles Lakers

David Robinson—San Antonio Spurs

Alonzo Mourning—Miami Heat

Juwan Howard—Washington Wizards

Gary Payton—Seattle Supersonics

Dikembe Mutombo—Atlanta Hawks

Chris Webber—Sacramento Kings

List 9-15. All-Time National Basketball Association Leaders

Most points, career:	Kareem Abdul-Jabbar	38,387
Most points, season:	Wilt Chamberlain	4,029
Highest scoring average, career:	Michael Jordan	31.5
Highest scoring average, season:	Wilt Chamberlain	50.4
Most rebounds, career:	Wilt Chamberlain	23,924
Most rebounds, season:	Wilt Chamberlain	2,149

List 9-16. All-Time Top Scorers in NBA-ABA

Kareem Abdul-Jabbar—Bucks, Lakers

Wilt Chamberlain—Warriors, 76ers, Lakers

Julius Erving*—Nets, 76ers

Moses Malone*—Rockets, 76ers, Bullets, Hawks, Bucks, Spurs

Michael Jordan—Bulls

Karl Malone—Jazz

Elvin Hayes—Bullets

Oscar Robertson—Royals, Bucks

George Gervin*—Spurs

Dominique Wilkins—Hawks, Magic, Celtics

Alex English—Nuggets

Artis Gilmore*—Bulls, Spurs

Hakeem Olajuwan—Rockets

Robert Parish—Warriors, Celtics

Adrian Dantley—Lakers, Jazz

Elgin Baylor—Lakers

---

*NBA players with ABA experience

List 9-17. NBA's Greatest African American Players

Kareem Abdul-Jabbar—Bucks, Lakers

Nate Archibald—Celtics

Charles Barkley—76ers, Rockets

Elgin Baylor—Lakers

Dave Bing—Pistons

Wilt "The Stilt" Chamberlain—Warriors, 76ers, Lakers

Clyde Drexler—Rockets

Julius "Dr. J" Erving—Nets, 76ers

Patrick Ewing—Knicks

Walt Frazier—Knicks

George Gervin—Spurs

Elvin Hayes—Bullets

Magic Johnson—Lakers

Sam Jones—Celtics

Michael Jordan—Bulls

Karl Malone—Jazz

Moses Malone—Rockets, 76ers, Bullets, Hawks, Bucks, Spurs

Earl "The Pearl" Monroe—Bullets, Knicks

Hakeem Olajuwon—Rockets

Shaquille O'Neal—Magic, Lakers

Robert Parish—Warriors, Celtics

Scottie Pippen—Bulls, Rockets, Trailblazers

Willis Reed—Knicks

Oscar Robertson—Royals, Bucks

David Robinson—Spurs

Bill Russell—Celtics

Isiah Thomas—Pistons

Nate Thurmond—Warriors

Wes Unseld—Bullets

Lenny Wilkins—Hawks

James Worthy—Lakers

List 9-18. NBA Finals Most Valuable Players

1970	Willis Reed, New York Knicks
1971	Kareem Abdul-Jabbar, Milwaukee Bucks
1972	Wilt Chamberlain, Los Angeles Lakers
1973	Willis Reed, New York Knicks
1976	Jo Jo White, Boston Celtics
1978	Wes Unseld, Washington Bullets
1979	Dennis Johnson, Seattle Supersonics
1980	Magic Johnson, Los Angeles Lakers
1981	Cedric Maxwell, Boston Celtics
1982	Magic Johnson, Los Angeles Lakers
1983	Moses Malone, Philadelphia 76ers
1985	Kareem Abdul-Jabbar, Los Angeles Lakers
1987	Magic Johnson, Los Angeles Lakers
1988	James Worthy, Los Angeles Lakers
1989	Joe Dumars, Detroit Pistons
1990	Isiah Thomas, Detroit Pistons
1991	Michael Jordan, Chicago Bulls
1992	Michael Jordan, Chicago Bulls

1993	Michael Jordan, Chicago Bulls
1994	Hakeem Olajuwon, Houston Rockets
1995	Hakeem Olajuwon, Houston Rockets
1996	Michael Jordan, Chicago Bulls
1997	Michael Jordan, Chicago Bulls
1998	Michael Jordan, Chicago Bulls
1999	Tim Duncan, San Antonio Spurs
2000	Shaquille O'Neal, Los Angeles Lakers

List 9-19. Spotlight: MICHAEL JORDAN

➤ Born 1963 in Brooklyn, New York

➤ Attended the University of North Carolina

➤ As a rookie with the Chicago Bulls, named to the All-Star team during the 1985 season

➤ 1986, became the second NBA (National Basketball Association) player in history to score more than 3,000 points in a single year

➤ NBA's individual scoring champ from 1987 through 1991; also named the NBA's most valuable player at the end of the 1987-88 season

➤ 1991, led the Chicago Bulls to their first NBA Championship and was the league's most valuable player

➤ Led the Chicago Bulls to three consecutive NBA titles in 1991, 1992, 1993 and was voted MVP (Most Valuable Player) of the playoffs for those years

➤ Obtained an all-time scoring average of 32.2 points per game

➤ 1992, played for the United States Olympic Basketball team and won the gold medal in Barcelona, Spain

➤ 1993, retired from basketball to pursue a career in professional baseball

➤ 1995, returned from retirement with the Chicago Bulls

➤ Founder of the Michael Jordan Celebrity Golf Classic which raises money for the United Negro College Fund and dedicated to encouraging children and youth

➤ Owns a clothing store, Jordan/Silverberg; has clothing, athletic, and cologne lines

➤ Several books written about Michael: *Hang Time, Taking to the Air, For the Love of the Game, My Story, Michael Jordan Speaks, Rare Air*

TRACK AND FIELD

List 9-20. Track and Field Olympic Champions (Gold Medalists)

1924	Dehart Hubbard	Long jump
1936	Cornelius Johnson	High jump
1936	Ralph Metcalfe	400-meter relay
1936	Jesse Owens	100 and 200 meters; 400-meter relay; long jump
1936	Archie Williams	400 meters
1936	John Woodruff	800 meters
1948	Alice Coachman	High jump
1948	Harrison Dillard	100 meters
1948	Willie Steele	Long jump
1948	Mal Whitfield	800 meters
1952	Jerome Biffle	Long jump
1952	Andy Stanfield	200 meters
1952	Harrison Dillard	110-meter hurdles
1952	Mal Whitfield	800 meters
1956	Gregory Bell	Long jump
1956	Charles Dumas	High jump
1956	Charles Jenkins	400 meters
1956	Milton Campbell	Decathlon
1956	Lee Calhoun	110-meter hurdles
1956	Mildred McDaniel	High jump
1960	Ralph Boston	Long jump
1960	Lee Calhoun	110-meter hurdles
1960	Otis Davis	400 meters
1960	Rafer Johnson	Decathlon
1960	Wilma Rudolph	100 and 200 meters
1964	Bob Hayes	100 meters; 400-meter relay
1964	Wyomia Tyus	100 meters
1964	Henry Carr	200 meters
1964	Hayes Jones	110-meter hurdles
1964	Edith McGuire	200 meters
1968	Bob Beamon	Long jump
1968	Willie Davenport	110-meter hurdles
1968	Lee Evans	400 meters
1968	Jim Hines	100 meters

©2001 by Prentice Hall

1968	Tommie Smith	200 meters
1968	Wyomia Tyus	100 meters
1972	Vince Matthews	400 meters
1972	Rodney Milburn	110-meter hurdles
1972	Randy Williams	Long jump
1976	Edwin Moses	400-meter hurdles
1976	Arnie Robinson	Long jump
1984	Evelyn Ashford	100 meters
1984	Benita Brown	100-meter hurdles
1984	Valerie Brisco-Hooks	200 and 400 meters; 400-meter relay
1984	Roger Kingdom	110-meter hurdles
1984	Alonzo Babers	400 meters
1984	Edwin Moses	400-meter hurdles
1984	Al Joyner	Triple jump
1984	Carl Lewis	100 and 200 meters; long jump; 400-meter relay
1988	Steve Lewis	400 meters
1988	Andre Phillips	400-meter hurdles
1988	Florence Griffith-Joyner	100 and 200 meters; 400-meter relay
1988	Jackie Joyner-Kersee	Heptathlon; long jump
1988	Roger Kingdom	110-meter hurdles
1988	Mike Conley	Triple jump
1988	Carl Lewis	100 meters; long jump
1988	Joe Deloach	200 meters
1992	Gail Devers	100 meters
1992	Jackie Joyner-Kersee	Heptathlon
1992	Carl Lewis	Long jump; 400-meter relay
1992	Michael Marsh	200 meters
1992	Gwen Torrence	200 meters
1992	Quincy Watts	400 meters
1996	Derrick Adkins	400-meter hurdles
1996	Charles Austin	High jump
1996	Gail Devers	100 meters
1996	Kenny Harrison	Triple jump
1996	Carl Lewis	Long jump
1996	Michael Johnson	200 and 400 meters
1996	Dan O'Brien	Decathlon

List 9-21. Outstanding Performers in Track and Field

1939	John Borican	Holder of four world records from 600-yard to 1,000-yard runs and AAU pentathlon winner in 1938, 1939, and 1941
1956	Ira Murchison	100 meters world record—time: 10.1
1981	Wilye White	Long jump—five-time Olympian; national hall of fame
1991	Mike Powell	Long jump world record—distance: 29´4½″
1988-1999	Butch Reynolds	400 meters world record—time: 43.7
1994	Leroy Burrell	100 meters world record—time: 9.85
1997, 1999	Marion Jones	World champion—100 and 200 meters
1999	Maurice Green	World record holder, 100-meter dash—time: 9.79

List 9-22. Spotlight: FLORENCE GRIFFITH-JOYNER

➤ Born 1959 in Los Angeles, California

➤ One of eleven children whose father was an electrical technician and mother was a teacher

➤ Known as "Flo Jo" by fans and the media

➤ Began running at the age of seven

➤ Graduated from Jordan High School in Los Angeles, California

➤ A straight-A student, enrolled as a business major at Cal State Northbridge

➤ Received a scholarship to UCLA and graduated in 1983 with a degree in psychology

➤ Trained at UCLA with track coach Bob Kersee and earned her first medal at the 1984 Olympics in the 200-meter event

➤ Married Al Joyner on October 10, 1987

➤ Won three gold and one silver medals at the 1988 Summer Olympics, making her the first American woman to win four medals in a single Olympic year

➤ Held the world record in the 100- and 200-meter events

➤ Labeled as the "World's Fastest Woman"

➤ Began designing and modeling clothes and working with children, both through sports programs and a series of books

➤ Experienced heart seizure problems in 1996

➤ Trained for the 1996 Olympics in Atlanta for the 400-meter; however, an Achilles tendon injury halted her participation

➤ Athletic awards included:

Sullivan Award

U.S. Olympic Committee's Spokeswoman of the Year

Jesse Owens Outstanding Track and Field Sportswoman of the Year by *Track and Field* magazine

Distinguished Service Award from the United Negro College Fund

The Associated Press Female Athlete of the Year for 1988

Appointed co-chair of the President's Council on Physical Fitness and Sports, the first woman to hold this position

➤ Died of an apparent heart seizure in 1998 at the age of 38

List 9-23. Four-Minute Milers

1973	Reggie McAffee	3:57.8 (First black under four minutes, Durham, NC, May 12)
1973	Tommy Fulton	3:57.8 (Second under four minutes, Texas Southern University, May 25)
1974	Denis Fikes	3:55.0
1981	Sydney Maree	3:48.83
1995	Terrance Harrington	3:53.64 (Eugene, Oregon)
1997	Steve Holman	3:50.46

List 9-24. Notable Track Coaches

Dave Bethany	Texas Southern University
Lee Evans	National coach of Nigeria and Qatar
Dr. William Exum	Kentucky State University
Dick Hill	Florida A&M, Southern University
Eddie Hurt	Morgan State University
Nell Jackson	Tuskegee Institute, U.S. Women's coach 1956 Olympics
Brooks Johnson	Stanford University
Rob Johnson	Wabash College, U.S. relay coach 2000 Olympics

Bob Kersee	Head women's coach, UCLA
Russ Rogers	Ohio State, U.S. Olympic coach 1996
Wilber Ross	Winston-Salem University, Author of the book *The Hurdlers Bible*
John Smith	Sprint coach, UCLA
Ed Temple	Tennessee State University, U.S. sprint coach (women) 1960 Olympics
Fred Thompson	Atoms track club in Brooklyn, New York
Dr. Leroy T. Walker	North Carolina Central University, chairman of the U.S. Olympic Committee (USOC)
Hoover Wright	Prairie View A&M, U.S. Sprint coach 1972 Olympics
Stan Wright	Texas Southern University, U.S. sprint coach 1968 Olympics

List 9-25. Olympic Weightlifting Champions

1948-1952	John Davis	Heavyweight class—Olympic weightlifting champion—six times national and world weightlifting champion—undefeated from 1938-1953
1960	Jim Bradford	Heavyweight class—Silver medalist
1992	Mark Henry	Super heavyweight—National champion—Olympic team member
1992	Tim McRae	148-pound class—National champion five times
1995	Wes Barnett	238-pound class—1992 Olympic team member—Pan American Games champion—National champion four times—holds the American record in the snatch, clean and jerk, and total

List 9-26. Powerlifting Champions

1974	Franklin Riley	World powerlifting champion, 132-pound class
1980	Lamar Gant	Member, International Powerlifting Association Hall of Fame—World champion, 123-pound class
1989	Ausby Alexander	World powerlifting champion, 165-pound class
1995	Mark Henry	World powerlifting champion—Super heavy-weight class
1998	Gene Bell	World powerlifting champion, 181-pound class

List 9-27. Bodybuilding Champions (Male and Female)

Male

1967	Sergio Oliva	Mr. Olympia
1970	Chris Dickerson	First black AAU Mr. America
1973	Jim Morris	Mr. America
1977	Dave Johns	Mr. America
1978	Tony Pearson	Mr. America
1982	Chris Dickerson	Mr. Olympia
1984-1991	Lee Haney	Mr. Olympia
1998-2000	Ronnie Coleman	Mr. Olympia

Female

1980	Carla Dunlap	IFBB Ms. America
1983	Carla Dunlap	Ms. Olympia
1990-1995	Laura Creavalle	Ms. International
1991-1995	Lenda Murray	Ms. Olympia
1997, 1998	Yolanda Hughes	Ms. International

SPOTLIGHTS

List 9-28. Spotlight: TIGER WOODS

➢ Born December 30, 1975 in Cypress, California

➢ Special interests: basketball, fishing

➢ Putted against Bob Hope on "The Mike Douglas Show" at age 2

➢ Shot 48 for nine holes at age 3

➢ Featured in *Golf Digest* at age 5

➢ Nicknamed "Tiger" after a Vietnamese soldier, a friend of his father

➢ Attended Stanford University

➢ Won 1991, 1992, and 1993 U.S. Junior Amateur Championships

➢ Named top amateur player by *Golf Digest* and *Golfweek* in 1992, and *Golf World* in 1992 and 1993

➢ Became youngest winner of U.S. Amateur in 1994

➢ *Golf World's* "Man of the Year" in 1994

➢ Won 1996 NCAA Championship and named Collegiate Player of the Year

➢ Turned professional in 1996 at Greater Milwaukee Open

➢ Named PGA of America and Golf Writers Association of American players, 1997

➢ Concluded year with Associated Press naming his Masters tour top sports story of 1997

➢ First golfer (after 26 years) to be honored "AP Male" Athlete of the Year, 1997

➢ First player to win three consecutive U.S. amateur titles

➢ 1998 season highlights

    —Earned second international victory

    —Finished tied for 8th place in defense of Masters tournament title

    —Earned seventh victory with one-stroke win at Bell South Classic

    —Tied round 63 at TPC at Sugarloaf

    —Regained no. 1 spot on Official World Golf Ranking

    —Defeated Vijay Singh to win PGA Grand Slam Golf

    —Made first United States Presidents Cup Team

    —Defeated Greg Norman

➢ Named to Blackwell's Best Dressed List in 1998

➤ Found Tiger Woods Foundation, chaired by father, Earl

➤ Eighth athlete to be named Wheaties permanent representative

➤ Website: www.tigerwoods.com

➤ 2000 season highlights:

—Won U.S. Open

—Broke record for largest winning margin, major championship: 15 strokes

—Broke record for largest winning margin, U.S. Open: 15 strokes (previous record, 11 strokes, 1899)

—Broke record for lowest winning score in relation to par, U.S. Open: 12-under (previous record, 8-under)

—Broke largest 54-hole lead—10 strokes (previous record, 7 strokes, 1921)

—Broke largest 36-hole lead—6 strokes (previous record, 5 strokes, 1903)

—British Open champion at St. Andrews, Scotland

—PGA champion

—First player since Ben Hogan in 1953 to win three majors in one year

—First player to repeat as PGA titlist since 1937

List 9-29. Spotlight: MARSHALL W. "MAJOR" TAYLOR

➢ Born 1878 in Indianapolis, Indiana

➢ Son of a coachman

➢ Worked at a bicycle store part-time as a teen

➢ Became America's first African American U.S. National Cyclist Champion in 1899

➢ At sixteen, he worked in a factory owned by a former cyclist champion and competed in races in Canada, Europe, Australia, and New Zealand

➢ In 1899, established a new one-mile world record and won the world championship in Montreal

➢ First European tour in 1901, he competed in sixteen cities

➢ Won numerous championships and set several world records during his sixteen years of competition

➢ Captured two world records before retiring in 1910

➢ After retiring, he met President Theodore Roosevelt, who followed his career path

➢ Member of the Bicycle Hall of Fame

➢ Died in 1934

List 9-30. Spotlight: VENUS & SERENA WILLIAMS

➤ The Williams sisters, Venus born 1980 and Serena born 1981 in Lynnwood, California

➤ Both tennis prodigies in the mid-1990s

➤ Coached initially by their father, Richard Williams

➤ First professional coach, Richard Macci

➤ In 1997, Venus made her professional debut followed by her sister the next year

➤ Venus achieved fame in the finals of the U.S. Open, 1997

➤ Serena entered the top ten ranks in the spring of 1999

➤ The two played against one another in the finals of the 1999 Lipton Championships, with Venus winning the match

➤ Serena won the 1999 women's U.S. Open

➤ Venus and Serena won the 1999 women's U.S. Open and French Open Doubles

➤ Venus won her first Grand Slam at Wimbledon in 2000, the first black women's singles champion since Althea Gibson in 1957-1958

➤ Venus and Serena won the Doubles Championship at Wimbledon in 2000—the first sisters to do so

List 9-31. Spotlight: DOMINIQUE DAWES

➤ Born November 20, 1976 in Silver Spring, Maryland

➤ Began gymnastics in 1983

➤ Favors all gymnastic apparatus

➤ Four-time World Championship Team Member in the 1992 Seoul Olympics, helping the team to win a bronze medal

➤ Named USA Gymnastic Athlete of the Year in 1993

➤ Won a Gold medal in the 1994 Coca-Cola National Championship in the all-around and all four event finals in the uneven bars, beam, floor, and vault events; first to do so since 1969

➤ Finalist for the Sullivan Award and named Sportsperson of the Year by USA Gymnastics in 1994

➤ 1995 recipient of the Arch McDonald Award presented by the Touchdown Club of Washington, D.C.

➤ Awarded the 1995 McDonald's "Balancing It All" Award and won the Henry P. Iba Citizen Athlete Award

➤ Entered Stanford University in 1995

➤ Appeared in the Broadway show "Grease" in 1996

➤ Selected for the 2000 United States Olympic team

SPORTS ON FILM

List 9-32. Sports on Film

- *Clay vs. Liston*
- *Harlem Globetrotters: Six Decades of Magic*
- *The History of Great Black Baseball Players*
- *Jackie Robinson*
- *Magic Johnson: Put Magic in Your Game*
- *Jesse Owens Returns to Berlin*
- *Michael Jordan's Playground*
- *Michael Jordan: Come Fly with Me*
- *Muhammad Ali*
- *Muhammad Ali vs. Zora*
- *Ringside with Mike Tyson*
- *Sugar Ray Leonard*
- *Sugar Ray Robinson: Pound for Pound*

Section 10

THE MILITARY

Black Americans in Defense of Our Nation

DEPARTMENT OF DEFENSE

Office of the Deputy Assistant Secretary of Defense for Civilian Personnel Policy/Equal Opportunity

SECTION 10

THE MILITARY

African Americans have a military history that dates back to the seventeenth century. Military service, since the Revolutionary War, was significant in bestowing the highest claim to American citizenship on individuals who served. In the case of African Americans who defended the nation, the privilege of citizenship was an exception. Blacks were underutilized as soldiers during the Revolutionary War, the War of 1812, the Spanish-American War, and the Civil War. Legislation prevented their full involvement and, when allowed, specified differential treatment, i.e., lower pay and fewer provisions.

African Americans joined military forces willingly, often to escape segregation or to lend support to the North in ending slavery. Although questions of courage and valor of black soldiers persisted, African Americans saw action and served with distinction in every American War.

In recent years, a new impression of African Americans in the military evolved. By the 1990s, African Americans provided vital services and expertise for the military. General Colin Powell headed the Joint Chiefs of Staff as the first African American to hold such a title. African American men and women were represented in peacekeeping missions in the Persian Gulf, Somalia, Haiti, Bosnia, and Kuwait for the Army, Navy, Air Force, Marine Corps, and Coast Guard.

Despite early distinguished military service, African Americans continued to experience racial, political, and segregation issues. Section 10 highlights some of the contributions made by African American men and women.

MILITARY HISTORY

List 10-1. Chronology of Military History

African Americans had few opportunities to participate in the social and political issues in America. Through the colonial militia, African Americans became defenders of the English colonies. When the colonial militia dropped in numbers or troops were confronted with a military situation, African Americans were accepted into military service. The colonial militia became the first American institution to admit African Americans.

1652	Massachusetts law requires African Americans to train and serve in the colonial militia. Four years later, the law is reversed, banning all "Negroes and Indians" from the militia.
1689	King William's War begins. One of the first casualties in Massachusetts is an African American killed at Falmouth.
1695	Massachusetts exempts all African Americans from military training but allows them to use arms and ammunition in case of emergency.
1746	New Jersey raises a troop of 500 free African Americans and Native Americans to fight the French in Canada.
1753	James Robinson is awarded a medal for bravery at the Battle of Yorktown.
1770	Crispus Attucks is killed by British soldiers during the Boston Massacre, one of the precipitating events of the American Revolution.
1774	The Committees of Safety organize Minutemen companies, which enlist African American volunteers.
1775	The Earle of Dunmore's Ethiopian Regiment is made up of slave soldiers who are promised their freedom in exchange for fighting on the British side.
1776	African Americans are able to enlist in the Continental Army.
1778	African American unit, First Rhode Island Regiment, fights in the American Revolution.
1783	Oliver Cromwell receives "Badge of Merit" for six years of service.
1792	The Enlistment Act excludes blacks from serving in the national militia.
1792	Congress passes a law that only white males may enroll in militias during peacetime.
1798	U.S. Navy issues restrictions against enlisting African Americans on men-of-war (warships) and in the Marine Corps.
1812	Africans Americans account for one-sixth of the seamen in the Navy during the War of 1812; uses African Americans as cooks and seamen.

1812	Army and Marine Corps exclude blacks. Navy uses African Americans as cooks and seamen.
1814	"Battalion of Free Men of Color" is organized.
1837	John Horse, commander of the Seminole Indians, helps defeat U.S. troops at the Battle of Okeechobee in Florida.
1840	Committee for the Participation of Negroes in National Defense is formed.
1861	African Americans are rejected at beginning of Civil War. Confederates are first to accept blacks as soldiers.
1861	Tennessee becomes the first state to pass a law for the enlistment of African American soldiers.
1862	First armed and uniformed African American regiment in the Civil War is known as the "South Carolina Volunteer Regiment."
1862	First African American artillery regiment is organized in Rhode Island.
1862	First Civil War battle of African Americans is fought by the 79th Colored Infantry from Kansas in a battle at Island Mound, Missouri.
1863	The Bureau of Colored Troops is established.
1864	Congress passes the Army Appropriation Bill that declares African American troops should receive the same pay as other soldiers.
1864	Lieutenant Colonel Alexander T. Augusta, an Army surgeon with the U.S. Colored Troops, receives $7.00 a month in pay, the same as an enlisted man.
1865	The Freedman's Bureau, established within the War Department, provides food, clothing, shelter, fuel, medical assistance, and economic help to former slaves.
1865	Confederate troops are mustered into service for the southern cause.
1865	Harriet Tubman becomes a spy and scout for the Union Army.
1866	Two African American Cavalries made up of Civil War veterans are organized to serve in the West.
1867	First all-black units in the regular Army approved by Congress include the 9th and 10th Cavalry Regiments, later known as "Buffalo Soldiers."
1869	Four African American infantry regiments were formed, adding a total of 12,500 soldiers.
1880	The Pea Island, North Carolina lifesaving station is the first and only all-black Coast Guard facility.
1916	Charles Young, highest ranking U.S. Army Lieutenant Colonel, commands a squadron in Mexico.
1917	During World War I, over 300,000 African Americans serve in the armed forces; 1,400 are commissioned officers.

1917	Emmett J. Scott is appointed special assistant to the Secretary of War to maintain morale among African Americans, both civilian and military.
1917	Fort Dodge near Des Moines, Iowa provides training for African Americans in WWI.
1918	The 369th Infantry is the first Allied unit to reach the Rhine. The regiment is awarded the Croix de Guerre award for heroism.
1938	African Americans are among the American forces fighting on the Republican side of the Spanish Civil War.
1939	U.S. Army enlists 3,640 African American men.
1940	A. Phillip Randolph, president of the Brotherhood of Sleeping Car Porters and the NAACP's executive secretary, meets with President Franklin Roosevelt to consider new approaches to blacks in the military.
1941	The only training facility for African American airmen in WWII is at Tuskegee, Alabama. The 99th Pursuit Squadron, first black Fighter Squadron.
1941	Over 100 African American military officers are locked in the stockade at Frecman Field, Indiana after entering a white's-only officers' club.
1942	African American women are eligible to join the Women's Army Auxiliary Corps (WAC).
1943	The USS *Mason* destroyer has a predominantly African American crew and one African American officer.
1943	The 99th Pursuit Squadron performs its first combat mission by attacking axis forces on the Italian island of Pantelleria.
1944	The 92nd Division of the U.S. Army is first unit sent into combat duty in Europe.
1944	The 761st Tank Battalion is first armored unit in combat.
1944	The U.S. Navy removes restrictions for African Americans to serve at sea. African Americans are allowed to join the Marine Corps and the Coast Guard.
1944	Women's Naval Corps (WAVES) permits African American women to enter.
1945	The Army Nurse corps admits African American nurses.
1946	Number of African American U.S. Army military officers: 1 general; 7 colonels; 818 second lieutenants.
1946	Committee on Equality of Treatment and Opportunity in the Armed Services is established; eliminates segregation and discrimination within the military.
1950	The 24th Regiment spearheads the first victory in the Korean War.
1953	The Department of Defense orders racial desegregation of all schools on military bases and in veterans hospitals.

1968   Clifford L. Sims, U.S. Army, dies while saving the lives of his men near Hue, Vietnam.

1968   The reenlistment rate for African Americans in the U.S. Army increases.

1970   The number of African American troops killed in Vietnam decreases from 1969.

1972   The USS *Jesse L. Brown* is first U.S. navy ship named for an African American naval officer.

1974   Fifty African American sailors decline to report for duty on the USS *Midway*, claiming racial discrimination and mistreatment.

1976   The U.S. Army provides a college scholarship program to African Americans participating in ROTC.

1979   American Civil Liberties Union files suit against the U.S. Navy for using quota system against African American recruitment.

1981   The U.S. Air Force Academy in Colorado Springs abandons its policy of not accepting applications with a genetic predisposition to sickle cell anemia.

1981   The Veterans Administration reports that the unemployment rate among African American veterans of the Vietnam War is five times as high as the unemployment rate among white veterans.

1982   The NAACP reports that Patsy Moore, an equal employment officer, wore a Ku Klux Klan costume during visits to four U.S. Army Engineers offices in Europe.

1984   Jesse Jackson negotiates the release of U.S. Navy Lieutenant Robert O. Goodman from a Syrian prison.

1986   Over 400,000 African Americans serve in the U.S. Armed Forces.

1988   The U.S. Navy issues a report citing "widespread but subtle bias against African American and Hispanic sailors and other minorities in its rank."

1991   Twenty-eight African Americans die in the Persian Gulf War.

1992   First significant deployment of African American troops to an African country.

1993   General Colin Powell retires as chairman of the Joint Chiefs of Staff.

1993   James Morgan, last Buffalo Soldier, dies at age 100.

1996   African American women are 6.5 percent of enlisted personnel in the armed services. There are 4,200 African American women officers (13.7 percent of all officers).

1996   Paul Reason is nominated as Four-Star Admiral in U.S. Navy.

1996   Daniel James III is appointed Adjutant General, Texas National Guard.

1998   Thirteen African American women are graduated from the U.S. Military Academy at West Point.

IN BATTLE

List 10-2. First African Americans to Participate in Battles

Buffalo Soldiers

Emanuel Stance (earned the Medal of Honor in 1870)

Battalion of Free Men of Color

Second Lieutenant Isidore Honore (U.S. State Militia)

Revolutionary War

George Gire (Massachusetts, fought in the French and Indian War; he was the first example in American history of a free African American fighting for the British colonies, 1754-1763)

Crispus Attucks, an escaped slave, was killed in the Boston Massacre (1770)

Peter Salem (a private in Captain Simon Edgel's Company; was a military hero of the War of Independence)

War of 1812

Major Jeffrey (fought in the battle for American liberty and was awarded the title of "Major" by President Andrew Jackson)

Pompey (an African American soldier in Andrew Jackson's Army; created the cottonbag fort and designed its construction)

Civil War

Nicholas Biddle (wounded in 1861)

James Stone (fought with Union forces during 1862)

James Harvey Carney (earned the Medal of Honor, 1863, 54th Massachusetts Colored Infantry)

Robert Smalls (only African American to attain the rank of Captain in the Navy, 1863)

Robert Blake (awarded the Naval Medal of Honor aboard the USS *Marblehead,* 1864)

World War I

Charles Young (only African American to earn the rank of Lieutenant Colonel during the war, 1916)

Corporal Freddie Stowers (recommended in 1918 for the Medal of Honor; earned it in 1991)

Charles H. Gavin (physician, commissioned during the war)

Henry Johnson and Needham Roberts (received the Croix de Guerre for their heroic stand against a German raiding expedition)

World War II

General Benjamin Oliver Davis, Sr. (served in 8th U.S. Volunteers Army Infantry, 1940)

Dorie Miller (honored with Navy Cross)

Samuel L. Gravely, Jr. (commissioned an officer in the Navy, 1944)

Korean War

Jesse Leroy Brown (pilot in Naval Reserve, 1950)

William Henry Thompson (earned the Medal of Honor, 24th Infantry Regiment, 1951)

General Benjamin Oliver Davis, Jr. (first to command an Air Force base)

Vietnam War

Milton L. Olive III (received the Medal of Honor as Private First Class, 503rd Infantry, 1965)

James Anderson, Jr. (Marine, received the Medal of Honor, 1967)

Daniel H. "Chappie" James, Jr. (promoted to Four-Star General in the U.S. Air Force, 1967; promoted to Brigadier General in 1970)

Colin Powell (won the Bronze Star for his persistence and devotion to duty)

Colin Powell

The Persian Gulf War

General Colin Powell (served as chairman of the Joint Chiefs of Staff, 1989-1993)

WOMEN IN THE MILITARY

List 10-3. First African American Women in the Military

1782	Deborah Gannett, aka "Robert Shurtliff," disguises herself as a male soldier and serves for 17 months in the Continental Army
1902	Susan Kent Taylor, publishes Civil War memoirs, providing only written record of activity of black volunteer nurses
1941	Eva Jones Dulan, nurse, commissioned in the U.S. Army
1942	Margaret Barnes Jones, Major, U.S. Army, serves during World War II
1943	Harriet M. West, Major, Women's Army Corps (WAC)
1943	Margaret Charity, First Sergeant
1944	Nancy C. Leftenant, nurse, regular Army
1944	Lieutenant Harriet I. Pickens and Ensign Frances Wills, commissioned in the WAVES
1945	Phyllis Mae Daily, nurse, U.S. Navy
1949	Annie L. Grimes, Marine officer, Chief Warrant Officer
1949	Annie E. Graham (September 8, 1949) and Ann E. Lamb (September 9, 1949) first to enlist in the U.S. Marine Corps
1963	Colonel Irene Trowell-Harris, nurse, Air National Guard
1968	Ruth A. Lucas, Colonel, U.S. Air Force
1970	Margaret E. Bailey, Colonel, Army Nurse Corps
1972	Mildred C. Kelly, Sergeant Major, WAC
1974	Jill Brown, pilot, U.S. Navy
1975	Lieutenant Donna Davis, doctor, U.S. Navy Medicine Corp
1976	Clara Leach Adams-Ender, graduated from the U.S. Army Command and General Staff College
1977	Hazel W. Johnson, General, Army Nurse Corps
1979	Second Lieutenant Marcella Hayes, pilot, U.S. Army
1979	Hazel W. Johnson, Brigadier General, Army Nurse Corps
1980	Janie L. Mines, graduate, Naval Academy
1985	Sherian Grace Cadoria, Brigadier General, regular army
1988	Clara L. Adams-Ender, Army Nurse Corps officer appointed as Director of Personnel for the Surgeon General of the Army

1990   Marcelite J. Harris, Brigadier General, U.S. Air Force

1992   Doris Daniels, Lieutenant Colonel, U.S. Marines

1999   Marcelite J. Harris, Major General, U.S. Air Force

List 10-4. Nurses in World War I

- Lillian F. Ball
- Marion H. Brown
- Sophia A. Hill
- Nancy J. Minnis
- Clara Rollins
- Lillian E. Spears
- Aileen B. Cole Stewart
- Clara J. West

SPECIFIC MILITARY BRANCHES

List 10-5. Firsts in Specific Military Branches

National Guard

1869   Robert Brown Elliott, Commanding General of South Carolina National Guard

ND*   Vertner W. Tandy, officer in New York National Guard

U.S. Air Force

1954   Benjamin Oliver Davis, Jr., General, commander of an air base

1975   Daniel H. Chappie James, Jr., Four-Star General

1979   Marcella Hayes, Second Lieutenant, pilot

1990   Marcelite J. Harris, female Brigadier General

1999   Daryl Jones, nominee for Air Force Secretary at Pentagon

U.S. Army

1861   James Stone, fought with Union forces during Civil War

1869   Henry McNeal Turner, U.S. Army chaplain and commissioned Army officer

1870   James Wester Smith, admitted to U.S. Military Academy at West Point

*ND = no date

Sherian Grace Cadoria

1877	Henry Ossian Flipper, graduated from U.S. Military Academy at West Point
1906	Allen Ellensworth, held rank of Lt. Colonel
1940	Benjamin O. Davis, Sr., General
1961	Fred Moore, guard at the Tomb of the Unknown Soldier in Arlington National Cemetery
1965	Milton L. Olive III, Medal of Honor winner during Vietnam War
1977	Clifford L. Alexander, Secretary of Army
1979	Hazel Winifred Johnson, flag officer, Brigadier General, Chief of Army Nurse Corps
1979	Vincent K. Brooks, chaplain and brigade commander at West Point; "First Captain" of the Corps of Cadets, the highest position for student leaders
1982	Roscoe Robinson, Four-Star General
1985	Sherian Grace Cadoria, Brigadier General in regular Army
1987	Colin Powell, National Security Advisor

U.S. Coast Guard

1865	Michael Augustine Healy, appointed to Coast Guard; Captain in 1883; demoted in 1896; rank restored in 1902; retired in 1903 at age 44
1966	Merle J. Smith, Jr., graduated from Coast Guard Academy

1998   Erroll M. Brown, appointed Admiral, first African American USCG flag officer

1999   USCG commissioned a 282-foot cutter, formerly the USS *Edenton,* honoring Alex Haley, a former mess attendant and chief journalist as well as the author of *Roots* (July 6, 1999)

U.S. Marines

1944   James E. Johnson, warrant officer

1945   Frederick C. Branch, officer

1950   William K. Jenkins, first officer to lead Marines in combat

1952   Frank E. Peterson, Jr., pilot, won Marine Corps wings

1954   Edgar R. Huff, infantry battalion sergeant major

1969   Hurdle L. Maxwell, officer in command of infantry battalion

1979   Frank Peterson, first active General

ND   Charles Shaw, drill instructor at Paris Island Recruit Depot

1999   Alford L. McMichael, Sergeant Major

U.S. Navy

1849   Wesley Brown, graduate of U.S. Naval Academy at Annapolis

1863   Robert Smalls, attained rank of captain during Civil War

1872   James Henry Conyers, appointed to U.S. Naval Academy at Annapolis, Maryland

1898   Robert Penn, seaman during Spanish-American War awarded Naval Medal of Honor

1945   Phyllis Mae Dailey, nurse

1949   Jesse Leroy Brown, naval aviator

1971   Samuel L. Gravely, Rear Admiral, served on combat ship, USS *PC-1264;* first to reach the rank of Rear Admiral in the Navy

1974   Vivian McFadden, chaplain

1980   Janie L. Mines, student at U.S. Naval Academy at Annapolis

1999   Sergeant Major Alford L. McMichael, 14th Sergeant Major of the Marine Corps and the first African American to achieve this rank

MEDAL-OF-HONOR RECIPIENTS

List 10-6. Soldiers

Civil War

Private William H. Barnes (April 6, 1865)

First Sergeant Powhatan Beaty (April 1, 1865)

First Sergeant James H. Bronson (April 6, 1865)

Sergeant William H. Carney (May 23, 1900)

Sergeant Decatur Dorsey (November 8, 1865)

Sergeant Major Christian A. Fleetwood (April 6, 1865)

Private James Gardiner (April 6, 1865)

Sergeant James H. Harris (February 18, 1874)

Sergeant Major Thomas R. Hawkins (February 8, 1870)

Sergeant Alfred B. Hilton (April 6, 1865)

Sergeant Major Milton M. Holland (April 6, 1865)

Corporal Miles James (April 6, 1865)

First Sergeant Alexander Kelly (April 6, 1865)

First Sergeant Robert Pinn (April 6, 1865)

First Sergeant Edward Ratcliff (April 6, 1865)

Private Charles Veal (April 6, 1865)

Indian Campaigns*

Sergeant Thomas Boyne (January 6, 1882)

Sergeant Benjamin Brown (February 19, 1890)

Sergeant John Denny (November 27, 1894)

Private Pompey Factor (May 28, 1875)

Corporal Clinton Greaves (June 26, 1879)

Sergeant Henry Johnson (September 22, 1890)

Sergeant George Jordan (May 7, 1890)

Corporal Isaiah Mays (February 19, 1890)

Sergeant William McBreyar (May 15, 1890)

*See also List 10-7.

©2001 by Prentice Hall

Private Adam Paine (October 13, 1875)

Trumpeter Isaac Payne (May 28, 1875)

Sergeant Thomas Shaw (December 7, 1890)

Sergeant Emanuel Stance (June 28, 1870)

Private Augustus Walley** (October 1, 1890)

Sergeant John Ward (May 28, 1875)

First Sergeant Moses Williams (November 12, 1896)

Corporal William O. Wilson (September 17, 1891)

Sergeant Brent Woods (July 12, 1894)

Navy Medals of Honor

Landsman Aaron Anderson (June 22, 1865)

Ship's Cook Daniel Atkins (May 20, 1898)

Landsman Robert Blake (April 16, 1864)

Landsman William H. Brown (August 5, 1864)

Landsman Wilson Brown (December 31, 1864)

Landsman John Lawson (December 31, 1864)

Seaman Joseph B. Noil (December 31, 1873)

Seaman Joachim Pease (December 31, 1864)

Seaman Robert Penn (December 14, 1898)

Spanish-American War*

Sergeant Major Edward L. Baker (July 3, 1902)

Sergeant Dennis Bell (June 23, 1899)

Private Fritz Lee (June 23, 1899)

Sergeant William H. Thompkins (June 23, 1899)

Private George H. Wanton (June 23, 1899)

World War I (Awarded posthumously)

Corporal Freddie Stowers (April 24, 1991)

**Walley lost stripes several times during his career. He was a Private when he applied for the Medal of Honor but had regained rank when he received it.

World War II (Awarded posthumously)

Second Lieutenant Vernon Joseph Baker*** (January 13, 1997)

Staff Sergeant Edward Allen Carter, Jr. (January 13, 1997)

First Lieutenant John Robert Fox (January 13, 1997)

Private First Class Willy F. James, Jr. (January 13, 1997)

Staff Sergeant Ruben Rivers (January 13, 1997)

Major Charles L. Thomas (January 13, 1997)

Private George Watson (January 13, 1997)

Korean War

Sergeant Cornelius H. Charlton (March 12, 1952)

Private First Class William Thompson (June 21, 1951)

Vietnam War

Sergeant First Class Webster Anderson (October 15, 1967)

Private First Class James A. Anderson, Jr. (February 28, 1967)

Sergeant First Class Eugene Ashley (February 7, 1968)

Private First Class Oscar Austin (February 23, 1969)

Sergeant First Class William M. Bryant (March 24, 1969)

Sergeant Rodney M. Davis (September 6, 1967)

Private First Class Robert H. Jenkins (March 5, 1969)

Specialist Lawrence Joel (March 9, 1967)

Specialist First Class Dwight H. Johnson (November 19, 1968)

Private First Class Ralph K. Johnson (March 5, 1968)

Private First Class Garfield M. Langhorn (January 15, 1969)

Platoon Sergeant Matthew Leonard (February 28, 1967)

Sergeant Donald R. Long (February 8, 1968)

Private First Class Milton L. Olive III (April 26, 1966)

Captain Riley R. Pitts (October 31, 1967)

Lt. Colonel Charles C. Rogers (November 1, 1968)

First Lieutenant Rupert L. Saergent (March 15, 1967)

Specialist First Class Clarence E. Sasser (January 10, 1968)

Staff Sergeant Clifford C. Sims (February 21, 1968)

First Lieutenant John E. Warren (January 14, 1969)

***Only surviving recipient

List 10-7. Buffalo Soldiers

Name, Rank, and Unit	Campaign or Action
Baker, Edward L., Jr. Sergeant Major, 10th Calvary	Spanish-American War, 1898
Bell, Dennis Private, H Troop/10th Calvary	Spanish-American War, 1898
Boyne, Thomas Sergeant, C Troop/9th Calvary	Victorio Campaign, 1879
Brown, Benjamin Sergeant, C Troop/24th Infantry	Paymaster Escort, 1889
Denny, John Private, C Troop/9th Calvary	Victorio Campaign, 1879
Factor, Pompey Private, 24th Infantry	Staked Plains Expedition, 1875
Greaves, Clinton Corporal, C Troop/9th Calvary	Apache Campaign, 1877
Johnson, Henry Private, K Troop/10th Calvary	Ute Campaign, 1879
Jordan, George Sergeant, K Troop/9th Calvary	Victorio Campaign, 1880
Lee, Fritz Private, M Troop/10 Calvary	Spanish-American War, 1898
Mays, Isaiah Corporal, B Troop/24th Infantry	Paymaster Escort, 1889
McBryar, William Sergeant, K Troop/10th Calvary	Apache Campaign, 1890
Paine, Adam Private, 24th Infantry	Comanche Campaign, 1874
Payne, Isaac Trumpeter, 24th Infantry	Staked Plains Expedition, 1875
Shaw, Thomas Sergeant, K Troop/10th Calvary	Apache Campaign, 1881
Stance, Emanuel Sergeant, F Troop/9th Cavalry	Texas Raid, 1870
Thompkins, William H. Corporal, A Troop/10th Cavalry	Spanish-American War, 1898
Walley, Augustus Sergeant, E Troop/10th Cavalry	Apache Campaign, 1881

©2001 by Prentice Hall

Name, Rank, and Unit	Campaign or Action
Wanton, George H. Private, M Troop/10th Cavalry	Spanish-American War, 1898
Ward, John Sergeant, 24th Infantry	Staked Plains Expedition, 1875
Williams, Moses First Sergeant, I Troop/9th Cavalry	Apache Campaign, 1881
Wilson, William O. Corporal, I Troop/9th Cavalry	Pine Ridge Campaign, 1890
Woods, Brent Sergeant, B Troop/9th Cavalry	Apache Campaign, 1881

Note: Buffalo Soldiers may also be found on List 10-6.

MILITARY OFFICERS

List 10-8. U.S. Air Force Flag and General Officers

General Benjamin O. Davis, Jr.

General Daniel "Chappie" James, Jr.

General Lester L. Lyles

General Lloyd W. "Fig" Newton

General Bernard P. Randolph

Lieutenant General William E. Brown, Jr.

Lieutenant General Russell C. Davis

Lieutenant General Albert J. Edmonds

Lieutenant General Winston D. Powers

Major General Rufus L. Billups

Major General Claude M. Bolton, Jr.

Major General Thomas E. Clifford

Major General Archer L. Durham

Major General Albert Edmonds

Major General Titus C. Hall

Major General Marcelite J. Harris

Major General John D. Hopper, Jr.

Major General John F. Phillips

Major General Lucius Theus

Major General John H. Voorhees

Brigadier General Frank J. Anderson, Jr.

Brigadier General James T. Boddie, Jr.

Brigadier General Elmer T. Brooks

Brigadier General Alonzo L. Ferguson

Brigadier General David M. Hall

Brigadier General Avon C. James

Brigadier General Walter I. James

Brigadier General Charles B. Jiggets

Brigadier General Raymond V. McMillan

Brigadier General Norris W. Overton

Brigadier General Leonard M. Randolph, Jr.

Brigadier General Horace L. Russell

Brigadier General Mary L. Saunders

Brigadier General William E. Stevens

Brigadier General Francis X. Taylor

List 10-9. Army Officers-Nonactive Duty

	Appointed to BG*	Retirement
General Colin L. Powell	1979	1993
General Johnnie E. Wilson	1989	1999
Lieutenant General Julius Wesley Becton, Jr.	1972	1983
Lieutenant General Marvin D. Brailsford	1985	1992
Lieutenant General Andrew Phillip Chambers	1978	1989
Lieutenant General Henry Doctor	1977	1989
Lieutenant General Samuel E. Ebbesen	1997	1988
Lieutenant General Robert E. Gray	1990	1997
Lieutenant General Arthur James Gregg	1972	1981
Lieutenant General James Reginal Hall, Jr.	1980	1991
Lieutenant General Edward Honor	1979	1989
Lieutenant General James Franklin McCall	1980	1991
Lieutenant General Emmett Paige, Jr.	1976	1988
Lieutenant General Roscoe Robinson, Jr. (deceased)	1973	1985
Lieutenant General Alonzo E. Short	1986	1994
Lieutenant General Calvin A.H. Waller (deceased)	1984	1991
Major General Robert Bradshaw Adams	1980	1986
Major General Wallace C. Arnold	1985	1995
Major General Harry William Brooks, Jr.	1972	1976
Major General John M. Brown	1979	1988
Major General Charles D. Bussey	1982	1989
Major General Eugene P. Cromartie	1982	1990
Major General Jerry Ralph Curry	1975	1984
Major General Frederic Ellis Davison	1968	1974

---

* BG = Brigadier General

	Appointed to BG	**Retirement**
Major General Arthur T. Dean	1992	1998
Major General Olive Williams Dillard	1972	1980
Major General Robert Clarence Gaskill	1975	1981
Major General Fred A. Gordon	1985	1996
Major General Kenneth D. Gray	1991	1997
Major General Edward Greer	1972	1976
Major General James Franklin Hamlet	1971	1981
Major General Ernest J. Harrell	1988	1995
Major General Charles A. Hines	1985	1992
Major General Arthur Holmes, Jr.	1983	1987
Major General Charles E. Honore	1983	1990
Major General James R. Klugh	1983	1990
Major General Fredric H. Leigh	1990	1993
Major General Alfonso E. Lenhardt	1990	1997
Major General Frank L. Miller, Jr.	1990	1996
Major General James W. Monroe	1991	1998
Major General Julius Parker, Jr.	1980	1989
Major General Thomas L. Prather, Jr.	1989	1995
Major General Hugh Granville Robinson	1978	1983
Major General Charles Calvin Rogers (deceased)	1973	1983
Major General Jackson E. Rozier (deceased)	1981	1990
Major General Fred Clifton Sheffey	1973	1980
Major General Isaac D. Smith	1981	1989
Major General John H. Stanford (deceased)	1984	1991
Major General Charles E. Williams	1984	1989
Major General Harvey Dean Williams	1977	1982
Major General Matthew A. Zimmerman	1989	1994
Brigadier General Clara L. Adams-Ender	1987	1993
Brigadier General Leo Austin Brooks	1978	1984
Brigadier General Dallas Coverdale Brown, Jr.	1978	1984
Brigadier General Harold E. Burch	1991	1995
Brigadier General Melvin L. Byrd	1986	1991
Brigadier General Alfred Jackal Cade	1975	1978

	Appointed to BG	**Retirement**
Brigadier General Sherian Grace Cadoria	1985	
Brigadier General Roscoe Conklin Cartwright (deceased)	1971	1974
Brigadier General Benjamin O. Davis, Sr. (deceased)	1940	1948
Brigadier General Donald J. Delandro	1981	1985
Brigadier General Johnie Forte, Jr.	1979	1987
Brigadier General Robert A. Harleston	1986	1989
Brigadier General Julius F. Johnson	1989	1993
Brigadier General Walter F. Johnson III	1985	1988
Brigadier General Jude W. P. Patin	1989	1992
Brigadier General George Baker Price	1974	1978
Brigadier General Donald L. Scott	1988	1991
Brigadier General George Macon Shupfer, Jr.	1972	1975
Brigadier General Vernon C. Spaulding, Jr.	1993	1996
Brigadier General Robert L. Stephens, Jr.	1989	1993
Brigadier General Guthrie Lewis Turner, Jr.	1980	1983
Brigadier General John M. Watkins, Jr.	1991	1995

List 10-10. Navy and Marine Corps Flag and General Officers

Navy

Vice Admiral Samuel L. Gravely, Jr.

Rear Admiral Gerald E. Thomas

Rear Admiral Lawrence C. Chambers

Rear Admiral L. A. Walker

Rear Admiral Benjamin Thurman Hacker

Marine Corps

Major General Winston D. Powers

Brigadier General Frank E. Petersen, Jr.

List 10-11. Navy Captains

Officer	Ship
Commander Edward Barfield	USS *Comstock*
Commander Edward Lewis Brownlee	USS *John Paul Jones*
Commander Randy Clark	USS *Harpers Ferry*
Commander Albert Curry	USS *Pensacola*
Commander D.C. Curtis	*Desron Fourteen*
Commander Michelle Howard	USS *Rushmore*
Commander Samuel Charles-Henry Howard	USS *Raven*
Commander Vince Ifill	*Beach Master One*
Commander Bernard Jackson	USS *McFill*
Commander Derek B. Kemp	USS *John Young*
Captain Willie C. Marsh	*Philbron Five*
Commander Joseph Carl Peterson, Jr.	USS *Caron*
Captain Vince Smith	Commander at Naval Station
Captain Joe N. Stafford	USS *Supply*
Commander Ronald Thomas	USS *Anchorage*
Commander James E. Wise	USS *McCain*
Commander Orin Wayne Young	USS *Stark*

List 10-12. National Guard Generals (Late 1800s)

Major General Robert B. Elliott, Commanding General
National Guard of the State of South Carolina (1870)

Brigadier General Samuel J. Lee, Chief of Staff
National Guard of the State of South Carolina (1870)

Brevat Brigadier General William Beverly Nash
National Guard of the State of South Carolina (1873)

Brigadier General H.W. Purvis, Adjutant and Inspector General
National Guard of the State of South Carolina (1873)

Brigadier General Joseph Hayne Rainey, Judge Advocate General
National Guard of the State of South Carolina (1873)

Major General Prince R. Rivers, Commanding General, Third Division
National Guard of the State of South Carolina (1873)

Major General Robert Smalls
National Guard of the State of South Carolina (1873)

Brigadier General William J. Whipper, Second Brigade, Second Division
Guard of the State of South Carolina (1873)

Brigadier General T. Morris, Fourth Brigade
National Guard of the State of Louisiana (1873-1874)

List 10-13. Air National Guard General Officers

Brigadier General Cornelius O. Baker
Pennsylvania Army National Guard

Brigadier General Carl E. Briscoe
New Jersey Army National Guard

Major General Cunningham C. Bryant
District of Columbia National Guard

Brigadier General Louis Duckett
New York Army National Guard

Brigadier General Calvin G. Franklin
California Army National Guard

Brigadier General Edward S. Frye
New Jersey Army National Guard

Brigadier General Edward O. Goardin
Massachusetts Army National Guard

Brigadier General Chauncey M. Hooper
New York Army National Guard

Brigadier General Richard Lee Jones
Illinois Army National Guard

Brigadier General Raymond Watkins
Illinois Army National Guard

List 10-14. Army and Air Force Reserves General Officers

Major General Benjamin Lacy Hunton, USAR

Major General John Q.T. King

Brigadier General William C. Banton, USAFR

Brigadier General Albert Bryant, USAR

Colonel (Brigadier General upon mobilization) Vance Coleman, USAR

List 10-15. Active Duty Generals and Admirals in All Branches

Army

Lieutenant General Joe N. Ballard, Chief of Engineers/Commanding General, Army Corps of Engineers, Washington, D.C.

Lieutenant General Larry R. Ellis, Deputy Chief of Staff for Operations and Plans, U.S. Army, Washington, D.C.

Lieutenant General Larry R. Jordan, Deputy Commanding General, U.S. Army Europe and 7th Army

Lieutenant General Billy K. Solomon, Director for Logistics and Security Assistance, J-4/J-7, U.S. Central Command, MacDill Air Force Base, Florida

Major General Reginald G. Clemmons, Deputy Commanding General, V Corps, U.S. Army Europe and 7th Army

Major General James E. Donald, Deputy Commanding General/Chief of Staff, U.S. Army Pacific, Fort Shafter, Hawaii

Major General Robert A. Harding, Director for Operations, Defense Intelligence, Arlington, Virginia

Major General Russel L. Honore, Vice Director for Operations, J-3, The Joint Staff, Washington, D.C.

Major General Milton Hunter, Director of Military Programs, Army Corps of Engineers, Washington, D.C.

Major General Alan D. Johnson, Deputy Commanding General, First U.S. Army (North)/Commanding General, Fort George G. Meade, Maryland

Major General Robert L. Nabors, Commanding General, U.S. Army Communications-Electronics Command, Fort Monmouth, New Jersey

Major General Hawthorne L. Proctor, Commanding General/Commandant, U.S. Army Quartermaster Center and School, Fort Lee, Virginia

Major General Gregory A. Rountree, Director of Operations, Allied Forces Central Europe

Major General William H. Russ, Commanding General, U.S. Army Signal Command, Fort Huachuca, Arizona

Major General William E. Ward, Commanding General, 25th Infantry Division (Light), Schofield Barracks, Hawaii

Major General Ralph G. Wooten, Commanding General, U.S. Army Chemical and Military Police Centers, Fort McClellan, Alabama

Brigadier General Dorian T. Anderson, Commanding General, Joint Task Force 6, Fort Bliss, Texas

Brigadier General Eddie Cain, Joint Program Manager, Biological Defense, Falls Church, Virginia

Brigadier General Jonathan H. Cofer, Commander, Joint Rear Area Coordinator, U.S. Central Command, MacDill Air Force Base, Florida

Brigadier General Billy R. Cooper, Deputy Commanding General, U.S. Army Recruiting Command (East), Fort Knox, Kentucky

Brigadier General Craig D. Hackett, Director, Requirements, Office of the Deputy Chief of Staff for Operations and Plans, U.S. Army, Washington, D.C.

Brigadier General David H. Hicks, Deputy Chief of Chaplains, U.S. Army, Washington, D.C.

Brigadier General Mack C. Hill, Commanding General, Madigan Army Medical Center/Northwest Health Service Support Activity, Tacoma, Washington

Brigadier General Michael D. Rochelle, Senior Military Assistant to the Deputy Secretary of Defense, Office of the Secretary of Defense, Washington, D.C.

Brigadier General Bettye H. Simmons, Commanding General, U.S. Army Center for Health Promotion and Preventive Medicine, Aberdeen Proving Ground, Maryland

Brigadier General Earl M. Simms, Commanding General, U.S. Army Soldier Support Institute, Fort Jackson, South Carolina

Air Force

General Lester L. Lyles, Commander, Air Force Material Command, Wright-Patterson Air Force Base, Ohio

Lieutenant General Russell C. Davis, Chief, National Guard Bureau, Arlington, Virginia

Major General Claude M. Bolton, Jr., Program Executive Officer for Fighter and Bomber Programs, Office of the Assistant Secretary of the Air Force for Acquisitions, Headquarters, Washington, D.C.

Major General John D. Hopper, Commander of 21st Air Force, Headquarters at McGuire Air Force Base, New Jersey

Major General Leonard M. Randolph, Jr., Deputy Surgeon General, Headquarters U.S. Air Force, Bolling Air Force Base, Washington, D.C.

Brigadier General Frank J. Anderson, Jr., Commandant, Defense Systems Management College, Fort Belvoir, Virginia

Brigadier General Walter I. Jones, Vice Commander, Air Force Communications and Information Center and Director, Global Combat Support System—Air Force Requirements Integration, the Pentagon, Washington, D.C.

Brigadier General Mary L. Saunders, Commander, Defense Supply Center, Defense Logistics Agency, Columbus, Ohio

Brigadier General Francis X. Taylor, Commander, Headquarters Air Force Office of Special Investigations, Andrews Air Force Base, Maryland

Navy

Rear Admiral (Lower Half) Barry C. Black, Deputy Chief of Chaplains/Deputy Director of Religious Ministries, Washington, D.C.

Rear Admiral (Upper Half) David L. Brewer III, Vice Chief of Naval Education and Training, Pensacola, Florida

Rear Admiral (Lower Half) Lillian E. Fishburne, Director, Information Transfer Division, Washington, D.C.

Rear Admiral (Lower Half) James A. Johnson, Medical Officer to the Marine Corps, Washington, D.C.

Rear Admiral (Lower Half) Gene R. Kendall, Director, Commander in Chief Liaison Division, Washington, D.C.

Rear Admiral (Lower Half) Willie C. March, Deputy Director, Expeditionary Warfare, Washington, D.C.

Vice Admiral Edward Moore, Jr., Commander, Naval Surface Force, U.S. Pacific Fleet, San Diego, California

Rear Admiral (Upper Half) Larry L. Poe, Defense Attache, France, Defense Intelligence Agency

Rear Admiral (Lower Half) (Selectee) Vinson E. Smith, Head, Plans, Policy, and Programming, Washington, D.C.

Rear Admiral (Lower Half) (Selectee) Anthony L. Winns, Chief, Policy Division, J5, Joint Staff, Washington, D.C.

Marine Corps

Major General Charles F. Bolden, Jr., Deputy Commander, U.S. Forces, Japan/Yokoto Air Base, Japan

Major General Arnold Fields, Director, Marine Corps Staff

Major General Clifford L. Stanley, Commanding General, Marine Corps Air Ground Combat Center, Twentynine Palms

Major General, USMC Reserve Leo V. Williams III, Vice Director, Joint Experimentation (J-9)

Brigadier General (Select) Walter E. Gaskin, Commanding General, Training Command, Quantico

Brigadier General Johnny R. Thomas, Assistant Deputy Chief of Staff, Programs and Resources, Headquarters Marine Corps

Brigadier General Cornell A. Wilson, Jr., Deputy Commander, MARFORCENT, Hawaii

U.S. Coast Guard

Rear Admiral Erroll M. Brown, Commander, Maintenance and Logistics Command, Atlantic, Norfolk, Virginia

SPOTLIGHTS

List 10-16. Spotlight: COLIN POWELL

➤ Born 1937 in Harlem, New York, the son of Jamaican immigrants

➤ Grew up in the South Bronx in multi-ethnic community

➤ Graduated from Morris High School in 1954 and received a Bachelor of Arts degree in geology from the City College of New York in 1958

➤ Enrolled in the college's Reserve Officer's Training Corps (ROTC); attained the top rank of Corps of Cadet Colonel

➤ Commissioned as second lieutenant in the U.S. Army

➤ 1960—First assignment for the U.S. Army was in West Germany

➤ Served two tours of duty in South Vietnam as an advisor to South Vietnamese troops

➤ Received two Purple Hearts, Bronze Star, Soldier's Medal, and Legion of Merit

➤ 1971—Completed M.B.A. at George Washington University in Washington, D.C.

➤ Awarded White House Fellowship from 1972 to 1973 and worked for Frank Carlucci, then Deputy Director of the Office of Management and Budget under Casper Weinberger

➤ Commanded a battalion in South Korea and served as staff officer at the Pentagon

➤ 1976—Completed National War College

➤ 1987—National Security Advisor

➤ 1989—Appointed by President George Bush as Chairman of the Joint Chiefs of Staff

➤ Retired in 1993

➤ Active in volunteer movements, charities, and organizations

➤ Chairman of the President's Summit for America's Future and serves as chairman for America's Promise-Alliance for Youth

List 10-17. Spotlight: CLARA L. ADAMS-ENDER

➤ Born in Wake County, North Carolina

➤ Graduated from high school at age 16 and from the School of Nursing at North Carolina Agricultural and Technical State University

➤ 1961—Joined U.S. Army Nursing Corps and received a second lieutenant's commission

➤ Earned a reputation for achievement and leadership

➤ Accomplishments:

—1976, earned Masters of Military Arts and Science Degree, U.S. Army Staff College in Leavenworth, Kansas

—1982, first Nursing Corps officer to graduate from U.S. Army War College

—1986, chief of nursing at Walter Reed Army Medical Center, the largest health-care facility in the armed forces

—1987, eighteenth Chief of the Army Nursing Corps

—1991, appointed Deputy Commanding Officer for the Military District of Washington, and commanding general at Fort Belvoir

➤ Retired in 1993

MILITARY VESSELS

List 10-18. Military Vessels Named for African American Individuals or Institutions

- USS *Leonard R. Harmon*
- USS *Booker T. Washington*
- USS *George Washington Carver*
- USS *Frederick Douglass*
- USS *John Merrick*
- USS *Robert Vann*
- USS *Paul Laurence Dunbar*
- USS *James Weldon Johnson*
- USS *John Hope*
- USS *John H. Murphy*
- USS *Toussaint L'Ouverture*
- USS *Robert S. Abbott*
- USS *Harriet Tubman*

- USS *Edward A. Savoy*
- USS *Bert Williams*
- USS *James Kyron Walker*
- USS *Robert J. Banks*
- USS *William Cox*
- USS *George A. Lawson*
- USS *Dorie Miller*
- USS *Jesse L. Brown*
- USS *Fisk Victory*
- USS *Tuskegee Victory*
- USS *Howard Victory*
- USS *Lane Victory*

MILITARY FILMS

List 10-19. Soldiers in Films, Documentaries, and Semi-Documentaries

All Wars

The Black Soldier (1978)

World War I

Doing Their Bit (1918)

The Heroic Black Soldiers of the War (1918)

Our Colored Fighters (1918)

The Unknown Soldier Speaks (1919)

World War II

     At Their Side (1944)

     Fighting Americans (1943)

     Fighting Liberators Hailed (1944)

     From Whence Cometh My Help (1949)

     Men of Color to Arms (1943)

     Negro Troops in Clark's Army Rout Nazis in Italian Front (1944)

     One Tenth of Our Nation (1940)

     The Call of Duty (1946)

     The Negro Soldier (1944)

     This Is the Army (1943)

     Sergeant Joe Louis on Tour (1943)

     Wings for This Man (1944)

     Team Work (1944)

Korean War

     Army Ends Segregation: Korea (1957)

     The Navy Steward (1953)

Vietnam War

     The Black G.I. (1970)

     No Vietnamese Ever Called Me Nigger (1968)

     The Twentieth Century: Integration in the Military (1966)

     The Vietnam War: Black and White (1967)

List 10-20. Feature Films

Civil War

     Sergeant Rutledge (1960), with Woody Strodes

     Soul Soldier (1970), with Rafer Johnson

     Glory (1989), with Denzel Washington and Morgan Freeman

Spanish-American War

> *The Trooper of Troop K* (1916), with Noble Johnson

World Wars

> *Spying the Spy* (1917), with Sam Robinson
>
> *Battaan* (1934), with Kenneth Spencer
>
> *Home of the Brave* (1949), with James M. Johnson
>
> *Paisan* (1946), with Dots M. Johnson
>
> *Red Ball Express* (1952), with Sidney Poitier
>
> *The Story of a Three-Day Pan* (1967), with Harry Baird
>
> *Live in Peace* (1946), with John Kitzmiller
>
> *Without Pity* (1948), with John Kitzmiller
>
> *A Soldier's Story* (1984), with Howard Rollins and Adolph Caesar

Vietnam War

> *The Anderson Platoon* (1967), with Joseph Anderson

VETERANS' ORGANIZATIONS

List 10-21. Veterans' Organizations

American Veterans Committee
6309 Bannockburn Drive
Bethesda, Maryland 20817

Black Revolutionary War Patriots
Foundation
1612 K Street, NW, Suite 1104
Washington, D.C. 20006

Black Veterans for Social Justice
686 Fulton Street
Brooklyn, New York 11217

National Association for Black Veterans
3929 N. Humboldt Boulevard
Milwaukee, Wisconsin 53212

Organization of African American
Veterans
P.O. Box 873
Ft. Huachuca, Arizona 85613

369th Veterans Association
369th Regiment Armory
One 369th Plaza
New York, New York 10037

Tuskegee Airmen, Inc.
65 Cadillac Square, #3200
Detroit, Michigan 48226

MILITARY PUBLICATIONS

List 10-22. Books

Amos, Preston E. *Above and Beyond in the West: Black Medal of Honor Winners,* 1870-1890. Washington, DC: Potomac and Corral, 1974.

Carroll, John M. *The Black Military Experience in the American West.* New York: Liveright, 1971.

Curtis, Mary. *The Black Soldier, or The Colored Boys of the United States Army.* Washington, D.C.: Murray Bros., 1918.

Fletcher, Marvin E. *The Black Soldier and Officer in the United States Army, 1891-1917.* Columbia: University of Missouri Press, 1974.

Foner, Jack D., *The United States Soldier between Two Wars: Army Life and Reforms, 1865-1898.* New York: Humanities Press, 1970.

Fowler, Arlen L. *The Black Infantry in the West, 1869-1891.* Westport, CT: Greenwood Publishing Corp., 1971.

Haynes, Robert V. *A Night of Violence: The Houston Riot of 1917.* Baton Rouge: Louisiana State University Press, 1976.

Higginson, Thomas W. *Army Life in a Black Regiment.* New York: Penguin, 1869; reprint 1997.

Leckie, William H. *The Buffalo Soldiers: A Narrative of the Negro Cavalry in the West.* Norman: University of Oklahoma Press, 1967.

Lee, Irwin H. *Negro Medal of Honor Men.* New York: Dodd, Mead, 1967.

Lynk, Miles V. *The Black Troopers, or the Daring Heroism of the Negro Soldiers in the Spanish-American War.* Jackson, TN: Lynk Publishing Co., 1899.

Moore, Brenda L. *To Serve My Country, To Serve My Race.* New York: New York University Press, 1996.

Schubert, Frank N. *Buffalo Soldiers, Braves, and the Brass: The Story of Fort Robinson, Nebraska.* Shippensburg, PA: White Mane Publishing Co., 1993.

Stallard, Patricia Y. *Glittering Misery: Dependents of the Indian Fighting Army.* Fort Collins, CO: Old Army Press, 1978.

Weaver, John D. *The Brownsville Raid.* New York: W.W. Norton and Co., 1973.

List 10-23. Periodicals

- *Army and Navy Journal*
- *Army and Navy Register*
- *Army Digest*
- *Cavalry Journal*
- *Colored American Magazine*
- *Crisis*
- *The Independent*
- *Infantry Journal*
- *Leslie's Weekly*
- *9th and 10th Cavalry Association Bulletin*
- *The Voice of the Negro*
- *Winners of the West*

Section 11

MISCELLANEA

THE WESTERN FRONTIER

LANDMARKS

POSTAGE STAMPS HONORING AFRICAN AMERICANS

INTERNET SITES

SPINGARN MEDALS

LITTLE-KNOWN FACTS

ORGANIZATIONS THAT HATE

NEWSPAPERS

KWANZAA

SECTION 11

MISCELLANEA

African Americans have had a myriad of experiences since their ancestors first arrived on American soil. We have tried to identify and include major events, people, and issues of historical significance in the first ten sections of this book. There are some areas, however, that fall outside typical categories, but provide breadth to the understanding of African American experiences. Those items are placed together here in Section 11.

THE WESTERN FRONTIER

List 11-1. Trailblazers of the American West

- During the settling of the West, primarily between 1865 and 1895, many of the trailblazers, settlers, and cowboys were African American. Estimates vary by territory from at least one in seven to one in four and even higher.

- African American families, reportedly half a million people, headed westward in wagons and created towns along the way, filling all jobs from shop owners to teachers and doctors.

- James P. Beckwourth, 1798-c.1867, scout, trapper, and guide; discovered a pass—"Beckwourth Pass"—through the Sierra Nevada mountain range for wagon trains to pass through.

- One of the first gold discoveries in Colorado was made by mine owner Henry Parker.

- Bonga township in Cass County, Minnesota, was named after trapper and fur trader, George Bonga.

- York, a slave with the Lewis and Clark Expedition, acted as interpreter with Indian tribes and was freed by Clark after the journey.

- Some of the first millionaires in the West were African Americans who owned a great deal of the land as well as many leading businesses.

- Jean Baptiste Pointe Du Sable's trading post at the mouth of the Chicago River eventually grew into the city of Chicago.

- Trailblazer George Washington was the founder of Centralia, Washington.

- Black American West Museum and Heritage Center, Denver, Colorado, was founded by Paul Stewart, who began the "Paul Stewart Collection" of artifacts, memorabilia, and history in 1971. See http://www.BAWMHC@aol.com

List 11-2. Cowboys and Pioneers

An integral part of American western history, black cowboys and pioneers often were hired out as ranch or trail hands and became bronco busters, ropers, trail cooks, stagecoach drivers, and sharpshooters. Some reached the status of foreman or trail boss and started places of their own.

1830s

- Mary Fields
- James Kelly

1840s

- Lewis Callahan
- Bose Ikard
- John Taylor
- "Bronco" James Willis

1850s

- Isom Dart
- Ben Hodges
- Britton Johnson
- Willie Kennard
- Nat Love
- George McJunkin
- Bronco Sam
- John Ware

1860s

- Edward Cheatum
- George Dalton
- Matthew "Bones" Hooks
- Dan Sauls, Sr.
- Samuel Steward
- James Arthur Walker
- Daniel Webster "80 John Wallace"

Nat Love

1870s

- Thomas Bass
- Dennis and Horace Brown
- William Moses Dabney
- Dan Diamond, Sr.
- Crawford Goldsby "Cherokee Bill"
- Harvey Grooves
- Eli Lenzy
- Todd and Richard Phillips

- Bill Pickett
- Robert Rentie
- Charles J. Rhone

1880s

- Phillip Briggs
- Simon and Emmett Collins
- James O. DePriest
- Charlie Glass
- John B. Hayes
- Walter Jackson
- Mose Reeder
- Dr. Haskell J. Shoeboot
- Noelle R. Smith, Sr.
- Jessie Stahhl
- William Talton, Sr.
- James Monroe Thomas

1890s

- Charley Brown
- Jess Crumbly
- Lawrence Jackson
- Robert J. Lindsay
- Albert Mast, Jr.
- B. Mingo
- Charles W. Rothwell
- Tracy Thompson
- Monroe Tinkshell

1900-1910

- Bill Bailey
- Ben Boyer family
- Carl E. Clark

- Dan Diamond, Jr.
- Charles Fox
- Joseph Giles, Jr.
- Ogden Gray
- Frank Greenway
- James Robinson
- Steele family
- William G. "Bill" Steep

1911-1920

- John W. Bell, Sr.
- John Henry Harris
- Orlando Jones
- Willie "Smokey" Lornes
- Tillie and Halverton Mosely
- Alonzo Pettie

1921-1961

- Floyd Adkism
- Elmer D. Anderson
- Tommy "Tango" Anderson
- Fred Brown
- Lewis Daniels, Jr.
- Myrtis Dightman
- Dennis Jenkins
- Thryl Latting
- Henry Lewis
- Charles Lockett
- Marvel Rogers
- Charles Sampson
- Assa Simon
- Steve Wyckoff

Most Famous

Isom Dart	cattle herd driver, wild horse buster, started own herd in Colorado; killed by paid man-hunter, Tom Horn
Mary Fields "Stagecoach Mary"	stagecoach driver, mail carrier, gunfighter in Montana territory, late 1800s
Ben Hodges	fast-talking Dodge City con man, forger, card cheat, rustler
Nat Love "Deadwood Dick"	claimed to have won this title in an 1876 South Dakota roping contest
Bill Pickett	a "sweat and dirt cowhand" and rodeo bull-dogger (steer wrestler) credited with inventing the sport of bulldogging (watched bulldogs bite steers' lips to take them down; effectively used the same technique)
Jesse Stahhl	in an early 1900s Oregon rodeo, made a spectacular bronco-busting ride but was awarded second place in a discriminatory decision by the judges; protested by completing the next ride facing backwards, carrying a suitcase

Bill Pickett

List 11-3. Rodeo Facts

1971	Bill Pickett (1870-1932)	inducted into National Rodeo Hall of Fame
1979	Jesse Stahhl (1883-1938)	inducted into National Rodeo Hall of Fame
1984	Bill Pickett Invitational Rodeo "the only national touring Black rodeo company"	founded by Lu Vason, who attended his first rodeo in Cheyenne in 1977 and saw no black riders there; see http://www.billpickettrodeo.com
1999	Fred Whitfield (1967)	first to become all-around rodeo champion; also four-time World Calf Roping Champion

LANDMARKS

List 11-4. African American Landmarks

Alabama

Africa Town (Mobile [Plateau])

Birmingham Civil Rights Institute (520 Sixteenth Street North, Birmingham)

Carrollton Courthouse (U.S. 82 and Alabama 17, Carrollton)

Civil Rights Memorial (Washington Street, Montgomery)

Dexter Avenue-King Memorial Baptist Church (454 Dexter Avenue, Montgomery)

Edmund Pettis Bridge (U.S. 80, Selma)

Sixteenth Street Baptist Church (16th Street and 6th Avenue North, Birmingham)

Arkansas

Central High School (Little Rock)

California

Beckwourth Pass (Beckwourth)

California Afro-American Museum (600 State Drive, Los Angeles)

Ebony Museum of Art (1034 14th Street, Oakland)

Colorado

Black American West Museum and Heritage Center (Denver)

Connecticut

First Church of Christ (The Amistad Trials) (75 Main Street, Farmington)

Paul Robeson Residence (1221 Enfield Street, Enfield)

Delaware

Richard Allen Marker (Lockerman and Federal Streets, Dover)

Washington, D.C.

African American Civil War Memorial (Shaw Neighborhood)

Anacostia Museum (1901 Fort Place SE)

Carter G. Woodson House (1538 9th Street NW)

Charlotte Forten Grimke House (1608 R Street NW)

Emancipation Statue/Lincoln Park (East Capitol Street)

Frederick Douglass House (1411 W Street SE)

Mary McLeod Bethune Memorial (1318 Vermont Avenue)

National Museum of African Art (950 Independence Avenue SW)

Florida

American Beach (Amelia Island, Jacksonville)

Black Archives History and Research Foundation (Miami)

Kingsley Plantation (Fort George Island, Jacksonville)

Olustree State Historic Site (Olustree)

Georgia

APEX Museum (135 Auburn Avenue, Atlanta)

Atlanta Life Insurance Headquarters (148 Auburn Avenue, Atlanta)

First African Baptist Church (Black Baptist Historical Museum) (23 Montgomery Street, Savannah)

First Bryan Baptist Church (Rev. George Liele Memorial) (565 West Bryan Street, Savannah)

Harriet Tubman Historical and Cultural Museum (340 Walnut Street, Macon)

Martin Luther King, Jr. National Historic Site (Auburn Avenue, Atlanta)

Illinois

Daniel Hale Williams House (445 East 42nd Street, Chicago)

Du Sable Museum of African American History and Art (Clark Street, Chicago)

Ida B. Wells Barnett House (3624 South Martin Luther King Jr. Drive, Chicago)

Jean Baptiste Pointe Du Sable Homesite (401 North Michigan Avenue, Chicago)

Oscar Stanton DePriest House (4536-4538 Martin Luther King, Jr. Drive, Chicago)

Indiana

Freetown Village of the Indiana State Museum (202 North Alabama Street, Indianapolis)

Levi Coffin House (North Main Street, Fountain City)

Madame C. J. Walker Urban Life Center (617 Indiana, Indianapolis)

Underground Railroad Marker (U.S. Route 41, Bloomingdale)

Kansas

George Washington Carver Homestead (Route K-96, Ness County, Beeler)

John Brown Memorial State Park (10th and Main Streets, Osawatomie)

Kentucky

Josiah Henson Trail (U.S. 60, Owensboro)

Kentucky Derby Museum (Churchill Downs, Louisville)

Old Slave Market (U.S. 68, Washington)

Louisiana

Amistad Research Center (6823 St. Charles Avenue, New Orleans)

Louis Armstrong Park (Rampart Street, New Orleans)

Preservation Hall (726 St. Peter Street, New Orleans)

U.S. Mint Museum (Jazz collection) (Esplanade at Decatur Street, New Orleans)

Yucca (Melrose) Plantation (Route 119, Melrose)

Maryland

Antietam National Battlefield (Sharpsburg)

Banneker-Douglass Museum (84 Franklin Street, Annapolis)

Eubie Blake Cultural Center (409 North Charles Street, Baltimore)

Frederick Douglass Monument (Morgan State University, Baltimore)

Harriet Tubman Birthplace (Maryland 397, Bucktown)

Matthew Henson Memorial (Maryland State House, Annapolis)

Massachusetts

Abiel Smith School/African-American National Historic Site (46 Joy Street, Boston)

African Baptist Church (York and Pleasant Streets, Nantucket)

African Meeting House (8 Smiths Court, Boston)

Boston Massacre Site (State Street, Boston)

Colonel Robert Gould Shaw Memorial (Beacon and Park Streets, Boston)

Crispus Attucks Monument (The Boston Common, Boston)

Granary Burial Ground (Tremont Street, Boston)

Jan Ernst Matzeliger Statue (Pine Grove Cemetery, Lynn)

Paul Cuffe Memorial (938 Main Road, Friends Church, Central Village)

W.E.B. Du Bois Homesite (Route 23, Great Barrington)

William Monroe Trotter House (97 Sawyer Avenue, Suffolk County)

Michigan

Dr. Ossian Sweet Memorial (Frank Murphy Hall of Justice, Detroit)

Joe Louis Memorials (The Fist, Woodward and Jefferson Avenues; The Hamilton sculpture, Cobo Convention Center, Detroit)

Motown Museum (2648 West Grand Boulevard, Detroit)

Museum of African American History (Frederick Douglass Street, Detroit)

National Museum of Tuskegee Airmen (6325 Jefferson, Detroit)

Ralph Bunche Homesite Memorial (5685 West Fort, Detroit)

Sojourner Truth Memorial (Oakhill Cemetery, Battle Creek)

Mississippi

Black Confederate Memorial (Canton)

Booker-Thomas Museum (Lexington)

Delta Blues Museum (Clarksdale)

Isiah Thornton Montgomery House (West Main Street, Mound Bayou)

Smith Robertson Museum (528 Bloom Street, Jackson)

Missouri

Black Archives of Mid-America (2033 Vine Street, Kansas City)

George Washington Carver National Monument (U.S. Route 71, Diamond)

Old Courthouse/Dred Scott Case (North 4th and Market Streets, St. Louis)

Scott Joplin House (2685-A Delmar Avenue, St. Louis)

New Jersey

Afro-American Historical Museum (1841 Kennedy Memorial Boulevard, Jersey City)

First Black Voter's Memorial (St. Peter's Church, Perth Amboy)

Paul Robeson Center of Rutgers University (Central Avenue, Newark)

New York

Abyssinian Baptist Church (132 West 138th Street, New York City)

Apollo Theater (West 125th Street, New York City)

Black Fashion Museum (155 West 126th Street, New York City)

Emancipation Proclamation (N.Y. State Library, Albany)

Harlem (New York City)

Harriet Tubman House (180 South Street, Auburn)

Louis Armstrong House (3456 107th Street, New York City)

Madame C. J. Walker House (Irvington)

Schomburg Center for Research in Black Culture (515 Malcolm X Boulevard, New York City)

North Carolina

African Heritage Museum/North Carolina A&T State University (East Market Street, Greensboro)

North Carolina Mutual Life Insurance Company (114-116 West Parish Street, Durham)

Pea Island Coast Guard Station, N.C. Aquarium (U.S. 54, Roanoke Island)

Ohio

African American Museum (1765 Crawford Road, Cleveland)

Harriet Beecher Stow House (2950 Gilbert Avenue, Cincinnati)

John Brown Monument (Akron)

John Mercer Langston House (207 East College Street, Oberlin)

John Rankin House and Museum (Ripley)

National Afro-American Museum and Cultural Center/Wilberforce University (Brush Row Road, Wilberforce)

Paul Lawrence Dunbar House (219 North Summit Street, Dayton)

Sojourner Truth Monument (37 North High Street, Akron)

Oklahoma

101 Ranch (Wild Bill Pickett) (Ponca City on U.S. 177; Grave site, White Eagle Monument)

Boley Historic District (Black Rodeo) (U.S. 62, Boley)

Pennsylvania

Afro-American Historical and Cultural Museum (7th and Arch Streets, Philadelphia)

All-Wars Memorial to Black Soldiers (Landsdowne Drive, Philadelphia)

Henry O. Tanner House (2903 West Diamond Street, Philadelphia)

St. George's Methodist Church (235 North Fourth Street, Philadelphia)

Rhode Island

Black Regiment Memorial (Portsmouth)

Rhode Island Black Heritage Society (1 Hilton Street, Providence)

South Carolina

Avery Research Center for African-American History and Culture (College of Charleston, Charleston)

Denmark Vesey House (56 Bull Street, Charleston)

Robert Smalls House (511 Prince Street, Beaufort)

Stono River Slave Rebellion Historic Site (Rantowles)

Tennessee

Afro-American Museum (730 Martin Luther King, Jr. Boulevard, Chattanooga)

Alex Haley House (Haley Avenue, Henning)

Beck Cultural Exchange Center (1927 Dandridge Avenue, Knoxville)

James Weldon Johnson House (911 18th Avenue, Nashville)

Lorraine Motel (406 Mulberry Street, Memphis)

Virginia

Benjamin Banneker Boundary Stone (18th and Van Buren Streets, Arlington)

Black Civil War Veterans' Memorial (Princess Anne Road, Elmwood Cemetery, Norfolk)

Booker T. Washington National Monument (22 miles southeast of Roanoke)

Jamestown Settlement (Adjacent to Colonial National Historical Park, Jamestown)

Maggie Lena Walker House (110-A East Leigh Street, Richmond)

National Battlefield Park (Petersburg)

Prestwould Plantation (Clarksville)

Robert Rousseau Moton House (Capahosic)

Washington

Douglass-Truth Library (2300 East Yesler Way, Seattle)

West Virginia

Harpers Ferry National Historic Park (Harpers Ferry)

Wisconsin

Wisconsin Historical Society (816 State Street, Madison)

POSTAGE STAMPS HONORING
AFRICAN AMERICANS

List 11-5. Persons

Year	Person	Year	Person
1940	Booker T. Washington	1983	Scott Joplin
1948	George Washington Carver	1983	Jackie Robinson
1967	Frederick Douglass	1984	Carter G. Woodson
1968	John Trumbull	1984	Roberto Clemente
1969	W. C. Handy	1985	Mary McLeod Bethune
1973	Henry O. Tanner	1986	Matthew Henson
1975	Paul Laurence Dunbar	1986	Sojourner Truth
1978	Harriet Tubman	1986	Duke Ellington
1979	Martin Luther King, Jr.	1987	Jean Baptiste Pointe Du Sable
1980	Benjamin Banneker	1988	James Weldon Johnson
1981	Dr. Charles R. Drew	1989	A. Philip Randolph
1981	Whitney Moore Young	1990	Ida B. Wells
1982	Ralph Bunche	1990	Jesse Owens

Patricia Roberts Harris

1991	Jan E. Matzeliger	1995	John Coltrane
1992	W.E.B. Du Bois	1995	Thelonious Monk
1993	Joe Louis	1995	Charlie Parker
1993	Percy Lavon Julian	1995	Jelly Roll Morton
1993	Otis Redding	1995	Clyde McPhatter
1993	Dinah Washington	1995	Charles Mingus
1994	Robert Johnson	1995	James Johnson
1994	Bill Pickett	1995	Bessie Colman
1994	Jim Beckwourth	1995	James Herbert "Eubie" Blake
1994	Bessie Smith	1995	Louis Armstrong
1994	Howlin' Wolf	1995	Erroll Garner
1994	Nat King Cole	1995	Salem Poor
1994	Jimmy Rushing	1996	Count Basie
1994	Dr. Allison Davis	1996	Ernest E. Just
1994	Muddy Waters	1997	Benjamin O. Davis
1994	Ethel Waters	1998	Mahalia Jackson
1994	Billie Holiday	1998	Madame C. J. Walker
1994	"Ma" Rainey	1999	Malcolm X
1995	Coleman Hawkins	2000	Patricia Roberts Harris

List 11-6. Events

Year	Event
1940	Thirteenth Amendment
1963	Emancipation Proclamation
1973	*Porgy and Bess*
1995	Civil War (includes stamps of Frederick Douglass and Harriet Tubman)
1997	Kwanzaa
1998	Celebrating the Century (includes stamps of W.E.B. Du Bois and George Washington Carver)

List 11-7. Groups

Year	Groups
Various Years	Olympic Sports and Games
1998	Buffalo Soldiers
1998	Gospel Singers (includes stamps of Mahalia Jackson, Clara Ward, Sister Rosetta Tharpe, and Roberta Martin)

INTERNET SITES

List 11-8. African American Internet Sites

- African American Web Conn (http://www.aawc.com/aawc.html)
- African Fashion Site (http://www.anet-chi.com/-midwest)
- Afro-American Newspaper (http://afroam.org)
- Black Enterprise (http://blackenterprise.com)
- Black Collegian Online (http://www.black-collegian.com)
- Black Facts Online (http://www.blackfacts.com)
- Black In America (http://www.4bia.com)
- Black Literary (http://www.mosaicbooks.com)
- Black Mind (http://www.blackmind.com)
- Black Tech Guide (http://www.theconduit.com)
- Black Urban Prof (http://www.buppie.com)
- BlackWorld (http://www. Blackworld.com)
- Ebony Core (http://www.ebonycore.com)
- Ebony Magazine (http://ebonymag.com)
- Essence Magazine (http://www.essence.com)
- Everything Black (http://www.everythingblack.com)
- Funkjazz Kafe (http://wwwfunkjazzkafe.com)
- Hip Hop Online (http://www.sohh.com)
- Jazz Central (http://www.jazzcentralstation.com)
- Jazz Roots (http://www.jdscomm.com)
- Keep It Real Online (http://www.keepitreal.com)
- National Association for the Advancement of Colored People (http://naacp.org)
- National Association Black Scuba Divers (http://www.nabsdivers.org)
- National Association Market Development (http://www.namddntl.org)
- National Guide to Black Kulture and Entertainment (http://soul4U.com)
- Netnoir (http://www.netnoir.com)
- Network Journal (http:/www.tnj.com)
- NY Guide to Black Business (http://www.bigblackbooks.com)
- Right On Magazine (http://www.righton.com)

- Streetsounds (http://www.street-sounds.com)
- Today's Black Woman (http://www.tnj.com)
- Ultimatestyle Clothing (http://www.ultimatestyle.com)
- United Negro College Fund (http://uncf.org)
- Urban Calendar (http://www.urbancalendar.com)
- Urban Sports Network (http://urbansportsnetwork.com)
- USAfrica (http://www.usafricaonline.com)
- Vibe Magazine (http://www.vibe.com)
- What's the 411 (http://www.whatsthe411.com)
- World Wide Black Online (http://www.wwbol.com)
- Young Black Entrepreneurs (http://www.ybeinc.com)

SPINGARN MEDALS

List 11-9. Spingarn Medal Recipients

The National Association for the Advancement of Colored People (NAACP) created the Spingarn Medal to acknowledge the highest achievement by an American Negro. The medal was created in 1914 and named for Joel E. Spingarn, a generous donor and Chairman of the NAACP Board of Directors from 1914-1919 and from 1931-1935. The medal is issued annually and was first awarded in 1915.

Year	Recipient	Contribution
1915	Ernest Everett Just	biological research
1916	Samuel Walker McCall	service to Republic of Liberia
1917	Harry T. Burleigh	creative music
1918	William Stanley Braithwaite	literature
1919	Archibald H. Grimke	distinguished service to his race/country
1920	William E. B. Du Bois	founding of the Pan-African Congress
1921	Charles S. Gilpin	performing arts
1922	Mary Burnett Talbert	restoration of the Frederick Douglass Home
1923	George Washington Carver	agricultural chemistry
1924	Roland Hayes	music
1925	James Weldon Johnson	author, diplomat, and public servant
1926	Carter G. Woodson	publications of Negro History
1927	Anthony Overton	business acumen
1928	Charles Waddell Chessnut	novelist and literary artist
1929	Mordecai Wyatt Johnson	administration of Howard University
1930	Henry A. Hunt	devoted service to education
1931	Richard B. Harrison	dramatic reader and entertainer
1932	Robert Russa Moton	leadership in education
1933	Max Yergan	missionary as Y.M.C.A. secretary
1934	William T. B. Williams	service to Slater and Jeans Funds
1935	Mary McLeod Bethune	founder and president of Bethune-Cookman College
1936	John Hope	leader in education and civil rights
1937	Walter F. White	lobbying for Anti-Lynching Bill
1938	NO AWARD	—
1939	Marian Anderson	music and her magnificent dignity

Year	Recipient	Contribution
1940	Louis T. Wright	medicine
1941	Richard Wright	author
1942	A. Philip Randolph	leadership in field of labor relations
1943	William H. Hastie	jurist and champion for equal justice
1944	Charles Richard Drew	medical science
1945	Paul Robeson	theater
1946	Thurgood Marshall	law
1947	Percy Lavon Julian	research chemistry
1948	Channing H. Tobias	defender of American liberties
1949	Ralph Johnson Bunche	International Civil Service
1950	Charles Hamilton Houston	champion of civil rights
1951	Mable Keaton Staupers	civil rights for Negro nurses
1952	Harry T. Moore	work for democratic ideals
1953	Paul R. Williams	architecture
1954	Theodore K. Lawless	medical science
1955	Carl Murphy	publisher
1956	Jack Roosevelt Robinson	sportsmanship
1957	Martin Luther King, Jr.	dedicated fight for freedom
1958	Daisy Bates & Little Rock Nine	upholding the ideals of democracy
1959	Edward K. (Duke) Ellington	musical achievements
1960	Langston Hughes	poet, author, playwright
1961	Kenneth B. Clark	dedicated service and inspired research
1962	Robert C. Weaver	dedicated state and federal service
1963	Medgar Wiley Evers	dedicated fight for racial justice
1964	Roy Wilkins	militancy of leadership
1965	Leontyne Price	musical talent
1966	John H. Johnson	ingenuity and enterprise in publishing
1967	Edward W. Brooke III	distinguished service in public office
1968	Sammy Davis, Jr.	commitment to Judeo-Christian traditions
1969	Clarence M. Mitchell, Jr.	role in enactment of civil rights legislation
1970	Jacob Lawrence	artistic talent
1971	Leon Howard Sullivan	leadership in economic progress of a people

Year	Recipient	Contribution
1972	Gordon A. B. Parks	creative artistry in photography and film
1973	Wilson C. Riles	education
1974	Damon Keith	distinguished legal service
1975	Henry (Hank) Aaron	achievement in sports
1976	Alvin Ailey	international preeminence in dance
1977	Alexander Palmer Haley	research and literary skills
1978	Andrew Jackson Young	exquisite negotiating skills
1979	Rosa L. Parks	quiet courage and determination
1980	Rayford W. Logan	author
1981	Coleman Alexander Young	accomplishment in public office
1982	Benjamin Elijah Mays	spiritual and moral leadership
1983	Lena Horne	distinguished career in entertainment
1984	Tom Bradley	public service
1985	William H. (Bill) Cosby	humorist and educator
1986	Benjamin L. Hooks	career in law ministry and public service
1987	Percy Ellis Sutton	civil rights guardian
1988	Frederick D. Patterson	educator
1989	Jesse Louis Jackson	national leader in political arena
1990	Lawrence Douglas Wilder	extraordinary public service
1991	Colin L. Powell	career achievement in military
1992	Barbara Jordan	courageous, dedicated public servant
1993	Dorothy Irene Height	leadership for human rights
1994	Maya Angelou	international achievements in literary fields
1995	John Hope Franklin	quest for truth as historian
1996	A. Leon Higginbotham, Jr.	distinguished jurist
1997	Carl T. Rowan	journalist, public servant, trailblazer
1998	Myrlie Evers Williams	four decades of civil rights activism
1999	Earl G. Graves, Sr.	businessman, publisher, education advocate

LITTLE-KNOWN FACTS

List 11-10. Little-Known Facts

- **Lorenzo Creyton** is the owner of Billy's Casino in New Orleans, the only African American owned and operated casino.

- **Maurice Ashley,** a 33-year-old New Yorker, is the first African American chess grandmaster—the game's highest rank.

- **Martin Luther King, Jr.** was born January 15, 1929 as Michael Luther King; he was renamed Martin.

- **African soldiers** in the 1870s were dispatched to western territories to fight Native Americans.

- The winningest coach in college football history is **Eddie Robinson** (1919-) with a record of 408-165-15; led the Grambling Tigers to eight national college titles.

- Seven of the **Roots** mini-series segments (an adaptation of Alex Haley's best-selling novel) were listed among the 50 All-Time Top-Rated TV Programs in the U.S. based on data from surveys from 1961-1998.

- The youngest person to testify before Congress was 6-year-old **Richard Anderson, Jr.** He testified before the House Subcommittee on Social Security and promoting the value of saving and investing early.

- **Josh Gibson,** Negro Baseball League player, was credited with hitting 84 home-runs in the 1936 season. Gibson hit 823 homers in 22 years but was never allowed in the Major League before he died in 1947.

- **President's Panel on Race,** chaired by Dr. John Hope Franklin, completed its report in 1998 and concluded that white Americans must acknowledge the legacy of racism and accept the resulting white privileges they received before we can move forward as one nation.

- **Dr. George F. Grant,** in 1899, received United States patent number 638,920 for his invention of a golf tee.

- **M'Lis Ward,** 1999, became the first female African American captain in the history of U.S. commercial aviation.

- **Jonathan Lee Iverson,** 1998, became the first African American ringmaster of Ringling Brothers and Barnum & Bailey's, the Greatest Show on Earth.

- **Universoul Circus** is the nation's only African American owned circus, a family-oriented, acrobatic, cultural extravaganza. Website: http://www.universoulcircus.com

ORGANIZATIONS THAT HATE

List 11-11. Organizations That Hate

According to the Southern Poverty Law Center in Montgomery, Alabama, there are over 500 organized and active hate groups in the U.S. today. These groups:

- openly promote racist views
- support activities targeting African Americans, Jews, and other minority groups
- masquerade as church groups
- have shed their white hoods for suits
- have organizational structures and goals that appear legitimate
- continue to conduct acts of violence against minorities under the cover of darkness
- have increased 13 percent since 1997

Identified below are selected names of hate-based groups:

Ku Klux Klan (163 Chapters)

American Knights of the Ku Klux Klan (27)*

Knights of the Ku Klux Klan (19)

Knights of the White Kamellia (23)

Neo-Nazi (151 Chapters)

National Alliance (35)

National Socialist White People's Party (22)

World Church of the Creator (46)

Racist Skinheads (48 Chapters)

Hammerskin Nation (20)

Peckerwoods

SS BootBoys

Identity Groups (63 Chapters)

Destiny Research Foundation (3)

Restoration Bible Church Shepherd's Chapel

Wisconsin Church of Israel

Trench Coat Mafia

Black Separatists (29 Chapters)

House of David (5)

Nation of Islam (24)

Others (85 Chapters)

Council of Conservative Citizens (33)

National Association for the Advancement of White People (13)

Odin Saves Ministry

---

*Number of known chapters, branches, or divisions

NEWSPAPERS

List 11-12. African American Newspapers

National Weekly Newspapers

National Afro-American

The National Leader

New National Courier

National Newspaper Supplements

Black Monitor

Dawn Magazine

National Scene

Daily Newspapers

Atlanta Daily World

The Daily Challenge

Chicago Daily Defender

Weekly Newspapers (with a circulation over 30,000)

Birmingham Times (Alabama)

Little Rock Weekly (Arkansas)

Fresno Advocate (California)

Los Angeles Central News-Wave (California)

Los Angeles Happenings (California)

Los Angeles Sentinel (California)

Oakland Post (California)

Sacramento-Los Angeles Happenings (California)

Sacramento Observer (California)

San Francisco Metro Reporter (California)

Washington Informer (District of Columbia)

Pensacola Voice (Florida)

Tampa Sentinel-Bulletin (Florida)

Albany/Macon Times (Georgia)

Atlanta Inquirer (Georgia)

Atlanta Voice (Georgia)

Chicago Citizens Newspaper (Illinois)

Chicago Heights Tri City Journal (Illinois)

Chicago Independent Bulletin (Illinois)

Chicago New Crusader (Illinois)

Chicago Observer (Illinois)

Kansas City Globe (Kansas)

Kansas City Voice (Kansas)

Baton Rouge Community Leader (Louisiana)

Detroit Chronicle (Michigan)

St. Louis Evening Whirl (Missouri)

Omaha Star (Nebraska)

Newark/Essex Greater (New Jersey)

The Black American (New York)

Brooklyn Big Red Newspaper (New York)

New York Amsterdam (New York)

Queens Voice (New York)

Akron Reporter (Ohio)

Cleveland Metro (Ohio)

Columbus Onyx (Ohio)

Oklahoma City Eagle (Oklahoma)

Philadelphia Observer (Pennsylvania)

Memphis Tri State Defender (Tennessee)

Dallas Weekly (Texas)

Ft. Worth Times (Texas)

Norfolk Journal and Guide (Virginia)

KWANZAA

List 11-13. The Holiday of Kwanzaa

- Founded in 1966 by Maulana Karenga, Black Studies Department Chair at California State University, Long Beach

- Family holiday to honor heritage and reinforce family and community

- The holiday stresses the oneness and goodness of life

- Kwanzaa bears no ties with any particular religion or denomination

- Kwanzaa means "first fruits" in Kiswahili

- The seven-day observance is from December 26 through January 1

- The celebration begins with the lighting of a candle displayed in a kinara. Three green candles symbolize hope and the green earth; one black candle symbolizes solidarity among black people; and three red candles symbolize the blood of the African Diaspora. Each night is devoted to celebrating one of the seven principles.

- The seven principles (Nguzo Saba) are:

  —Umoja (unity)

  —Kujichangulia (self-determination)

  —Ujima (collective work and responsibility)

  —Ujamma (economic cooperation)

  —Nia (purpose)

  —Kuumba (creativity)

  —Imani (faith)

- Kwanzaa ends with a community festival called Karamu. There is music, dancing, and traditional African foods during the festival. Participants share reflections on their experiences during the year.

- Kwanzaa is an expanding tradition in America. To signal its growth, ceremonial items and Kwanzaa cards and gifts are readily available in a variety of stores.

SELECTED BIBLIOGRAPHY

Alexander, Lois. *Blacks in the History of Fashions*. New York: Harlem Institute of Fashion, 1982.

Altman, Susan. *The Encyclopedia of African-American Heritage*. New York: Facts on File, 1997.

Anyibe, James. *African American Holidays*. New York: Popular Truth, 1991.

Appiah, Kwame A. and Henry L. Gates, Jr. *Africana, The Encyclopedia of the African and African American Experience*. New York: Basic Civitas Books, 1999.

Asante, Molefi K. *African American History, A Journey of Liberation*. Maywood, NJ: The People Publishing Group, 1995.

Asante, Molefi K., and Mark T. Mattson. *Historical and Cultural Atlas of African Americans*. New York: Macmillan, 1991.

Ashe, Arthur. *A Hard Road to Glory, A History of the African-American Athlete, 1919–1945*. New York: Warner Books, 1988.

Aspinall, S. Y., "Educating Children to Cope with Death: A Preventive Model." *Psychology in the Schools,* vol. 33, no. 4, October 1966, pp. 341–349.

Bailey B. L., "Language and Communication Styles of Afro-American Children in the United States." *Florida Reporter,* Sp/Su, (1969), p. 46, p. 153.

Barrett, L. E. *The Rastafarians: Sounds of Cultural Dissonance*. (rev. ed.). Boston: Beacon Press, 1988.

Bearden, Romare, and Harry Henderson. *A History of African-American Artists, From 1792 to the Present*. New York: Pantheon Books, Random House, 1993.

Bell, Yvonne. "A Culturally Sensitive Analysis of Black Learning Style." *Journal of Black Psychology,* vol. 20, no. 1, February 1964, pp. 47–61.

Benjamin, R., and Jacqueline L. Johnson. *The Black Resource Guide* (10th edition). Washington, D.C., 1993.

Biddle, Stanton F. *The African American Yellow Pages: A Comprehensive Resource Guide and Directory*. New York: Henry Holt and Company, 1996.

Billington, M. L., and R. D. Hardaway. *African Americans on the Western Frontier*. Niwor: University Press of Colorado, 1998.

Bogle, Donald. *Toms, Coons, Mulattos, Mammies & Bucks* (3rd edition). New York: Continuum, 1995.

Boles, John B. (Ed.). *Masters & Slaves in the House of the Lord.* Lexington: University Press of Kentucky, 1988.

Boone, T. *The Negro Baptist in Pictures and History: A Negro Baptist Historical Handbook.* Detroit: Voice of Destiny, 1964.

Braithwaite, Ronald L., and S. E. Taylor (Eds.). *Health Issues in the Black Community.* San Francisco: Jossey–Bass Publishers, 1992.

Brantl, G. *Catholicism.* New York: George Braziller, 1962.

Britton, Crystal A. *African American Arts, The Long Struggle.* New York: Smithmark Publishers, 1996.

Brody, G.H., et al. "Religion's Role in Organizing Family Relationships: Family Process in Rural, Two-Parent African American Families." *Journal of Marriage and the Family,* 56 (November), 1994, pp. 878–888.

Brown, Gerry, and Michael Morrison (Eds.). *The 1999 ESPN Sports Almanac.* Boston: Information Please, LLC, 1998.

Bush, Rod. *We Are Not What We Seem, Black Nationalism and Class Struggle in the American Century.* New York: New York University Press, 1999.

Campbell, George, Jr. "Minorities in Science: The Pipeline Problem." *Science,* 258, (1992), p. 1187.

Cantor, George. *Historic Landmarks of Black America.* Detroit: Gale Research, 1991.

Casneau, A.A. *Guide for Artistic Dress Cutting.* Boston, 1895.

Christian Methodist Episcopal. *The Doctrines and Discipline of the Christian Methodist Episcopal Church.* Memphis: C.M.E. Publishing House, 1996.

Clark, E. T. *The Small Sects in America* (rev. ed.) Memphis: Abingdon Press, 1965.

Claxton, O. and P. Murrell, "Learning Styles: Implications for Improving Educational Practices." *Eric Higher Education Report #4.*

Coar, Valencia H. *A Century of Black Photographers (1840–1960).* Providence: Rhode Island School of Design, 1983.

Collier-Thomas, Bettye. *Daughters of Thunder, Black Women Preachers and Their Sermons.* San Francisco: Jossey-Bass Publishers, 1998.

Conlan, R., and J Papanek. "African American Voices of Triumph." *Leadership,* Richmond, VA: Time–Life Books, 1993.

Corbin, Raymond M. *1,999 Facts About Blacks.* Lanham, MD: Madison Books, 1997.

Costen, M.W. *African American Christian Worship.* Nashville: Abingdon Press, 1993.

Cowen, Tom, and Jack Maguire. *Timelines of African American History.* New York: Perigee Books, 1994.

Crute, Sheree (Ed.). *Health & Healing for African-Americans.* New York: Bantam Books, 1997.

DaSilva, Benjamin; Milton Finklestein; Arlene Loshin; and Jawn Sandifer. *The Afro-American in United States History.* New York: Globe Book Co., 1972.

Davis, Cyprian. *The History of Black Catholics.* New York: Crossroad Publishing Co., 1990.

Dixon, Barbara M. (with Josleen Wilson). *Good Health for African Americans.* New York: Crown Publishers, 1994.

Dunn, R., J. Beardry, and A. Klavas. "Survey of Research on Learning Styles." *Educational Leadership,* vol. 47, no. 6, (1989), pp. 50–57.

Epps, Charles H., Jr.; Davis G. Johnson; and Audrey L. Vaughan. *African American Medical Pioneers.* Rockville, MD: Betz Publishing Co., 1994.

Erickson, Hal. *Religious Radio and Television in the United States, 1921–1991.* Jefferson, NC: McFarland and Co., 1992.

Estell, K. *African American, Portrait of a People.* Detroit: Gale Research, 1994.

Ewey, Melissa. "Jonathan Lee Iverson: Ringling Bros'. First Black Ringmaster," *Ebony.* May 1999, vol. LIV, no. 7, pp. 152-156.

—— (Ed.). *Facts on File, Encyclopedia of Black Women in America, Law and Government.* New York: Facts on File, 1997.

—— (Ed.). *Facts on File, Encyclopedia of Black Women in America, Business and Professions.* New York: Facts on File, 1997.

—— (Ed.). *Facts on File, Encyclopedia of Black Women in America, Literature.* New York: Facts on File, 1997.

Findley, James F., Jr. *Church People in the Struggle.* New York: Oxford University Press, 1993.

Fitts, Leroy. *History of Black Baptists.* Nashville: Broadman Press, 1985.

Foster, Helen B. *New Raiments of Self.* New York: Berg, 1997.

Frazier, E. F. *The Negro Church in America.* New York: Schoken, 1964.

Fulop, Timothy E., and A. J. Raboteau. *African American Religion.* New York: Routledge, 1997.

Garrett, Romeo B. *Famous First Facts About Negroes.* New York: Arno Press, 1972.

Gibbs, P. G. *Black Collectibles Sold in America.* Paducah, KY: Collector Books, 1987.

Gray, Fred D. *The Tuskegee Syphilis Study.* Montgomery, AL: The Black Belt Press, 1998.

Hawley, Willis D. *Effective School Desegregation, Equity, Quality and Feasibility.* Thousand Oaks, CA: Sage Publications, 1981.

Henderson, Ashyia, and Shirelle Phelps. *Who's Who Among African Americans.* Farmington Hills, MI: Gale Group, 1999.

Hill, Levirn (Ed.). *Black American Colleges & Universities: Profiles of Two-year, Four-year and Professional Schools.* Detroit: Gale Research, Inc., 1994.

Hilliard, Asa G. (Ed.). "Testing African-American Students." *The Negro Educational Review,* vol. XXXVIII, nos. 2–3, (1987), April–July.

Hine, Darlene Clark. *Black Women in America: An Historical Encyclopedia, I and II.* Brooklyn: Carlson Publishing, 1993.

Ho, James. *Black Engineers in the United States—A Directory.* Washington, D.C.: Howard University Press, 1974.

Hodgin, June, and Caaren Wolliscroft. "Eric Learns to Read: Learning Styles at Work. *Educational Leadership,* March 1997, pp. 43–45.

Holloway, Joseph E., and Winifred K. Vass. *The African Heritage of American English.* Bloomington: Indiana University Press, 1993.

Houppert, Karen. "Nine Ways to Improve Public Schools." *Utne Reader,* no. 61 (3), January/February 1994, p. 83.

Hughes, Zondra. "M'Lis Ward, First Black Female Captain in Commercial Aviation." *Ebony,* January 2000, vol. LV, no. 3, pp. 120-124.

Irion, Paul E. "Changing Patterns of Ritual Response to Death." *OMEGA—Journal of Death and Dying,* vol. 22(3), 1991, pp. 159–172.

Jackson, Joseph H. *A Story of Christian Activism: The History of the National Baptist Convention, USA, Inc.* Nashville: Townsend Press, 1980.

Jones, Bessie, and Omax Haves. *Bess, Step it Down: Games, Plays, Songs and Stories From the Afro-American Heritage.* New York: Harper and Row, 1972.

Jones, L. N. *From Conscience to Consciousness: Blacks and the United Church of Christ.* Philadelphia: United Church of Christ Press, 1976.

Jones-Wilson, F. C.; C. A. Asbury; M. Okazana-Rey; D. K. Anderson; S. M. Jacobs; and Michael Fultz. *Dictionary of African American Education.* Westport, CT: Greenwood Press, 1966.

Katz, William L. *Black Women of the Old West.* New York: Atheneum Press, 1995.

—— *The Black West* (3rd edition). Seattle: Open Hall Publishing, 1987.

Kessler, James; J. S. Kidd; Renee Kidd; and Katherine A. Morin. *Distinguished African American Scientists of the 20th Century.* Phoenix: Oryx Press, 1966.

Kirk-Duggan, Cheryl. *African American Special Days.* Nashville: Abingdon Press, 1996.

Koger, Larry. *Black Slaveowners.* Columbia: University of South Carolina Press, 1985.

Koslow, Philip, (Ed.). *African American Desk Reference.* New York: John Wiley & Sons, 1999.

Kranz, Rachel. *The Biographical Dictionary of Black Americans.* New York: Facts on File, 1992.

Kranz, Rachel, and Philip Koslow. *The Biographical Dictionary of African-Americans.* New York: Facts on File, 1999.

Kurian, George T. *A Historical Guide to the U. S. Government.* New York: Oxford Press, 1998.

Lakey, Othal H. *The History of the C.M.E. Church.* Memphis: C.M.E. Publishing House, 1985.

LaMorte, M. W. *School Law, Cases and Concepts* (5th edition). Boston: Allyn & Bacon, 1996.

LaVeist, Thomas, and Marjorie Wigham-Desir. "Top Fifty Colleges for African Americans." *Black Enterprise,* vol. 29 (6), January 1999, pp. 71–80.

Levine, Michael L. *African Americans and Civil Rights from 1619 to the Present.* Phoenix: Oryx Press, 1996.

Lincoln, C. Eric. *The Black Muslims in America.* Boston: Beacon Press, 1961.

Lincoln, C. Eric, and Lawrence H. Mamiya. *The Black Church in the African American Experience.* Durham, NC: Duke University Press, 1990.

Lindenmeyer, Otto. *The Negro Almanac.* New York: Bellweather Publishing Co., 1967.

Low, W. A., and V. A. Clift. *Encyclopedia of Black America.* New York: McGraw-Hill, 1981.

Lowery, C., and John F. Marszalee. *Encyclopedia of African American Civil Rights.* New York: Greenwood Press, 1992.

Martin, Sandy D. *Black Baptists and African Missions, The Origin of a Movement, 1880–1915.* Macon, GA: Mercer University Press, 1989.

McKivigan, John R., and M. Snay. *Religion and the Antebellum Debate Over Slavery.* Athens: University of Georgia Press, 1998.

Mclear, Claudia T. "Learning Styles of African American Children and NSTA Goals of Instruction." *Abstract,* AERA and NARST annual meetings, San Francisco, 1995.

Metcalf, Peter, and Richard Huntington. *Celebrations of Death* (2nd edition). Oxford, England: Cambridge University Press, 1992.

Miller, M. M., and J. D. Smith (Eds.). *Dictionary of African-American Slavery.* Westport, CT: Praeger Publications, 1997.

Morris, Aldon D. *The Origins of the Civil Rights Movement, Black Communities Organizing for Change.* New York: The Free Press, 1984.

Morrow, Willie L. *Four Hundred Years Without a Comb.* New York: Cosmetology Pub., 1984.

Morton, J. O., and L. E. Morton. *A History of the African American People.* New York: Smithmark Publishers, 1995.

Murphy, L.; J. G. Melton; and G. Ward (Eds.). *Encyclopedia of African American Religions.* New York: Garland Publishing, 1993.

Neighbors, H. W., and James S. Jackson. *Mental Health in Black America.* Thousand Oaks, CA: Sage Publications, 1996.

Numan, I.M.A. *What Every American Should Know About Islam and the Muslims.* Jersey City, NJ: New Mind Productions, 1994.

The Official National Football League 1996, 1997 & 1998 Record & Fact Book. New York: Workman Publishing Co.

Orfield, Gary, and Susan E. Eaton. *Dismantling Desegregation. The Quiet Reversal of Brown v. Board of Education.* New York: The New Press, 1996.

Ornstein, N.J.; T. E. Mann; and M. Malbin. *Vital Statistics on Congress*. District of Columbia: Congressional Quarterly, 1997–1998.

Paris, Arthur E. *Black Pentecostalism*. Amherst: University of Massachusetts Press, 1982.

Payne, Wardell J. (Ed.). *Dictionary of African American Religious Bodies: A Compendium by the Howard University School of Divinity*. Washington, D.C.: Howard University Press, 1995.

Payne, Wendell. *Dictionary of African American Religious Bodies*. Washington, D.C.: Howard University Press, 1991.

Ploski, H., and J. Williams. *The Negro Almanac: A Reference Work on the Afro American*. New York: Bellwether Publishing Company, 1983.

Potter, Joan, and Constance Clayton. *African American Firsts*. Elizabethtown, NJ: Pinto Press, 1994.

Ringle, Ken. "For Black Soldiers, An Overdue Honor." *Washington Post*, January 14, 1997.

Roebuck, Julian, and Komanduri Murty. *Historically Black Colleges and Universities, Their Place in American Higher Education*. Westport, CT: Praeger, 1993.

Rosten, L. *Religions of America*. New York: Simon and Schuster, 1975.

Salzman, Jack; David L. Smith; and Cornel West. *Encyclopedia of African-American Culture and History, Vols. I–V*. New York: Simon & Schuster/Macmillan, 1996.

Sammons, Vivian O. *Blacks in Science and Medicine*. New York: Hemisphere Publishing Co., 1990.

Sanders, Cheryl J. *Saints in Exile*. New York: Oxford University Press, 1966.

Savage, Beth (Ed.). *African American Historic Places, National Register of Historic Places*. Washington, D.C.: The Preservation Press, 1994.

Shujaa, Mwalimu J. *Beyond Desegregation, The Politics of Quality in African American Schooling*. Thousand Oaks, CA: Corwin Press, 1996.

Smallwood, Arwin, with Jeffrey Elliot. *The Atlas of African-American History & Politics*. New York: McGraw-Hill, 1997.

Smith, David B. *Health Care Divided: Race and Healing a Nation*. Ann Arbor: University of Michigan Press, 1999.

Smith, Jessie Carney (Ed.). *Black Firsts: 2000 Years of Extraordinary Achievement*. Detroit: Gale Research, 1994.

—— *Black Heroes of the 20th Century*. Detroit: Gale Research, 1998.

—— *Notable Black American Women*. Detroit: Gale Research, 1992.

Smith, Jessie Carney, and Joseph M. Palmisano. *The African American Almanac*. Farmington Hills, MI: Gale Group, 2000.

Smitherman, Geneva. *Talkin and Testifyin: The Language of Black America*. Boston: Houghton Mifflin, 1977.

Snodgrass, Mary E. *Black History Month Resource Book*. Detroit: Gale Research, 1993.

Starke, B.; Lillian Holloman; and Norda Nordquist. *African American Dress and Adornment*. Dubuque, IA: Kendall Hunt, 1990.

Stewart, Jeffrey C. *1001 Things Everyone Should Know About African American History*. New York: Doubleday Dell Publishing Group, 1996.

Summers, Barbara. *Skin Deep: Inside the World of Black Fashion Models*. New York: Amistad Press, 1998.

Thein, Belinda; J. Proyer; and V. Kolb. *Contributions of African Americans to Science*. Madison: University of Wisconsin Press, 1996.

Tillery, Carolyn Q. *The African American Heritage Cookbook*. Secaucus, NJ: Carol Publishing Group, Birch Lane Press, 1996.

Van de Sande, Wendy. *Black American Information Directory* (4th edition). Washington, D.C.: Gale Research, 1995.

Walls, William J. *The AMEZ Church: Reality of the Black Church*. Charlotte, NC: AME Zion Publishing House, 1974.

Washington, Joseph R., Jr. *Black Religion: The Negro and Christianity in the United States, 1964*. Lanham, MD: University Press of America, 1984.

Weatherspoon, Floyd. *African American Males and the Law*. New York: New York University Press of America, 1998.

Williams, John B. *Race Discrimination in Public High Education*. Westport, CT: House Corner Pub., 1978.

Williams, Michael W. *African American Encyclopedia*. New York: Marshall Cavendish Corp., 1993.

Willis, M. G. "Learning Styles of African-American Children: Review." *Journal of Black Psychology,* 16(1), (1989), pp. 47–61.

Willis-Thomas, Deborah. *Black Photographers (1940–1988)*. New York: Garland Publishing, 1989.

Yount, Lisa. *Black Scientists*. New York: Facts on File, 1991.